Globalization and the Politics of Institutional Reform in Japan

Globalization and the Politics of Institutional Reform in Japan

Motoshi Suzuki

Professor, Graduate School of Law, Kyoto University, Japan

Cheltenham, UK • Northampton, MA, USA

Published by
Edward Elgar Publishing Limited
The Lypiatts
15 Lansdown Road
Cheltenham
Glos GL50 2JA
UK

Edward Elgar Publishing, Inc.
William Pratt House
9 Dewey Court
Northampton
Massachusetts 01060
USA

A catalogue record for this book
is available from the British Library

Library of Congress Control Number: 2015957854

This book is available electronically in the **Elgar**online
Social and Political Science subject collection
DOI 10.4337/9781782544784

ISBN 978 1 78254 477 7 (cased)
ISBN 978 1 78254 478 4 (eBook)

Typeset by Servis Filmsetting Ltd, Stockport, Cheshire
Printed and bound by CPI Group (UK) Ltd, Croydon, CR0 4YY

Contents

Figures

Tables

Acknowledgments

My students at Kyoto University have no first-hand experience of Japan's bubble economy in the 1980s, let alone the high growth during the period between the 1950s and the early 1970s. They are used to a deflationary society wherein throughout their lifetime they have only heard that institutional reform (e.g., third arrow of the 'Abenomics' promoted by Prime Minister Shinzo Abe) is of prime importance for combating deflation and adjusting the Japanese ways of work, education, and even life according to the global order.

When I was about their age, Japan stood between high growth and the forthcoming bubble, struggling to adjust to the flexible exchange rate regime that paved the way for the emergence of the neoliberal global order. It overcame the struggle by making a series of small-scale adjustments to hedge exchange rate risks while maintaining the existent public policy and economic institutions of the main-bank system, long-term employment, and interfirm networks. Half a century ago, my parents experienced the difficult adjustment associated with the transformation of the war command economy into a market economy to accommodate the post-World War II liberal order. The adjustment was made under the adverse war-torn social conditions through overarching institutional reforms. Three quarters of a century ago, my grandparents had survived the world depression that had worsened in Japan by the gold standard introduced to deeply integrate the emergent Asian state into the interwar international economic order as part of Cooperative Diplomacy. The fragile party government collapsed in the absence of robust political leadership, permitting the Imperial Army to take over the civilian government and push for war preparation.

This book is about how the Japanese political economy has endured adjustments to changes in the international order since the pre–World War II era. To carry out this book project, I have three points in mind: first, the prevailing international order influences the relative efficiency of economic institutions. A closed international order generates a few discernible systemic effects on the states' economic performance, allowing them to maintain their unique national rules and standards. In contrast, the neoliberal order, which has taken place with enhanced cross-border capital mobility since the 1980s, gives a liberal market economy an advantage in generating growth over a non-liberal economy. It is because the former can more vigorously attract capital than the latter through its sophisticated equity markets, property rights protection, and contractual flexibility. Aware of this asymmetry, a non-liberal state such as Japan finds it necessary to bring its national rules and standards into conformity with liberal practices through policy changes in the realms of banking, business, labor, trade, and investment. These changes generate differentiated effects on the state's sectoral interests and thus arouse acute distributive conflicts.

Second, policy decisions are made by political and bureaucratic officials with distinct concerns and professional talents. In general, politicians have distributive concerns and electoral accountability: the higher the political office, the greater distributive concern an office holder geographically has. A few years ago, when I hired a taxi in Shimonoseki, a major city in Yamaguchi Prefecture from which Prime Minister Abe was elected, the driver complained to me that Mr. Abe was less concerned about Yamaguchi than about the nation, much like his grandfather, Prime Minister Nobusuke Kishi (1958–1960), but very different from rank-and-file parliamentary members whose concerns are mainly about their districts. In contrast, unelected bureaucrats have policy expertise and information, specializing in particular policy domains with organizational loyalty. I also observed in Shimonoseki that officials from the Ministry of Agriculture, Fishery and Forestry helped to promote the exportation of blowfish, a local delicacy, by providing technical and regulatory assistance to dealers. Because blowfish has poisonous elements, dealers must show regulatory compliance with the complicated Sanitary and Phytosanitary Measures (SPS) Agreement by obtaining assistance from expert SPS ministry officials.

Third, how well a state adjusts to changes in the international order significantly depends upon the scheme of authority allocation between politicians and bureaucrats, which influences the use of their distinct professional talents and the quality of their policy adjustment decisions. At present, under the neoliberal global order, the allocation of authority has been shifting toward political leadership that is in a position to use central command and make bold decisions to coordinate policy tasks between ministries. However, in the half-century after World War II, bureaucrats became influential with delegated policy authorities and their expertise, fine tuning public policy to contribute to high growth. Increasingly, they have become unable to adjust to the emergent neoliberal order, leading to the retrenchment of bureaucratic delegation and the ascent of political command. Yet political command is not a panacea because it may be cut off from the flow of information and communication.

Here is a major structural dilemma that the state must solve, which I find fascinating but difficult to deal with as a research agenda. First, the structure of the government is hard to change in the short run. However, it will change in the long run because of changes in the Constitution, the electoral law, or the bureaucratic system, thereby determining the relative authority of politicians and bureaucrats. Thus, I have to cover a long historical period in order to observe major changes in the government structure and analyze their impact on public policy domains and economic institutions.

Second, to evaluate institutional change, an analyst has to acquire knowledge on law, politics, and economics. Luckily, in a Japanese university, my field of political science is typically part of the law faculty. Following this rule, Kyoto University, where I have been teaching for the last fourteen years, has a faculty of law that combines law with political science and is institutionally well connected to the faculty of economics. This interdisciplinary environment is suitable for thinking about and analyzing the multifaceted problem of institutional change. Personally, I was involved with the research wing of the Ministry of Education as a program officer between 2006 and 2008, which gave me the wonderful opportunity to work with top Japanese scholars in political science, law, and economics. Of course, it is difficult for a single person to specialize in multiple academic disciplines. This book is a product of my utmost, albeit imperfect, cross-disciplinary efforts.

The changes in the global order have influenced the fate of my family as well as those of many other Japanese households. I have tried not to let my personal feelings affect my analysis and sought to be as objective as possible by referring primarily to widely available evidence. Some of the chapters of this book are based on my research presentations at domestic and international academic conferences, the University of Pavia, the University of Milan, the University of California at Berkeley, and Boston University. I was brought to these outstanding institutions by my hosts and hostesses with their deep appreciation of Japanese culture and political economy. I benefited deeply from comments by Professors T.J. Pempel, Steve Vogel, and William Grimes who read the draft with care and helped me correct unsubstantiated claims. As usual, I am solely responsible for the remaining errors and omissions.

The book is published by Edward Elgar Publishing, whose managing editor, Tim Williams, visited my office at Kyoto University on an extremely cold day in January 2012 and encouraged me to turn my various papers into a book. Without his professional enthusiasm I would not have embarked on this book project. Fortunately, I have received grants from the Japan Society for the Promotion of Science, which enabled me to explore the research agenda with excellent co-researchers, Professors

Akira Okada, Kaoru Ishiguro, Keisuke Iida, Atsushi Ishida, Atsushi Tago, Yukari Iwanami, Shuhei Kurizaki, Shoko Kohama, and Yumi Nakayama who are first-rate political scientists or economists. My graduate students, Ms. Yu Keirin, Ms. Azusa Uji, and Mr. Shohei Doi, assisted my research; they worked tirelessly on collecting data and arranging the bibliography. Dee Compson, Chloe Mitchell, and Harry Fabian of Edward Elgar Publishing were extremely helpful for editing my manuscript.

Without support from all the individuals and organizations listed above, this book would not have been published. I am grateful for their advice and assistance. My final gratitude goes to my family, who have endlessly supported and encouraged me despite the boring weekends for the last two years.

Motoshi Suzuki
Kyoto under fallen autumn leaves
7 December 2015

Introduction: globalization, institutional reform, and government structure

GLOBALIZATION AND GOVERNMENT STRUCTURE

Trade, investment, information, and communication intrinsically link the Japanese and international economies. As rules and norms in the international economy change, the Japanese economy is pressured to make the appropriate institutional adjustments to remain globally competitive. The public policy reforms, which have dominated Japanese national politics from the mid-1990s to the present, are attempts to make large-scale institutional adjustments to an economic system that was becoming inefficient and less competitive under the globalizing liberal economic order.

Adjustments have meant institutional reforms in Japan's post–World War II politico-economic system, including the beliefs held by politicians, bureaucrats, and private economic agents about the role of government in the market and the resultant behavioral changes. From the reformers' perspectives, an adjustment should improve Japan's overall economic efficiency and outweigh the coordination costs, which some segments, especially inefficient sectors, would incur. With these expectations, the reformist political leaders, most notably Prime Ministers Hashimoto, Koizumi, and Abe of the Liberal Democratic Party (LDP), initiated profound public policy reforms in the financial system, labor markets, and postal services in the late 1990s and the early 2000s. However, these reform movements faced some stumbling blocks.

Several analysts have attributed limits in Japan's reforms to its fragmentary political structure, which is entrenched with special interests and numerous veto points that have hindered political leadership's policy initiatives (Calder, 1988b; Katz, 1998; Vogel, 2006). To coordinate bureaucratic tasks without the influence of bureaucratic politics and special interests, these analysts claim that an adjustment requires not just public policy reforms, but also political and administrative reforms to remove government structural impediments and to strengthen leadership's policy authority. Thus, centralization is a reaction against a decentralized government structure. That is, in a globalized world, the governing patterns need to be more coherent.

Globalization has made conventional governance virtually impossible (Ohmae, 1999). Conflicts frequently emerge between the tasks of different bureaucratic agencies as well as the interests of the governing coalition members whose solutions require coordination by central political leadership. Multiple agencies within the government and a decentralized autonomy reduce the capacity of the government to exert control over those agencies' tasks and interests (Mosley, 2003). Although political leaders are in a position to assume political responsibility for the public interest, they must have a real capacity to influence the behavior of those agencies. Globalization increases the importance of a coherent centralized government for governability and policy effectiveness (Weiss, 1998; Hirst and Thompson, [1996] 2009). This view is consistent with the international relations theory of intergovernmentalism (Keohane and Nye, 1977; Moravcsik, 1997).

In contrast, other analysts (Peters, 2001; Slaughter, 2004; Shiroyama, 2013) have claimed that the real problem of government ineffectiveness in a globalizing economy lies in an adaptation failure due to the weakening of states' bureaucratic agencies and transgovernmental networks composed of agencies and international organizations. Increasingly bereft of policy authority in a centralized government, bureaucrats are discouraged from updating information and maintaining the expertise necessary for policy adaptation to rapidly changing international rules and norms. This claim is based on the assumption that the centralized, top-down, and monopolistic nature of government is at the core of governance problems. A more decentralized government structure may be both more efficient and more democratic, and has the potential to respond more flexibly to the many challenges faced by a contemporary government.

Policy delegation to specialized bureaucratic agencies within a decentralized government, which are well connected with their foreign counterparts and international organizations via transgovernmental networks, may improve adaptation capabilities. This type of state is characterized as 'disaggregated' (Slaughter, 2004) or 'perforated' (Jessop, 2002). These institutional arrangements provide bureaucratic officials with incentives and opportunities to adapt their policy domains to changing international rules and norms by updating their information and expertise. From this viewpoint, delegation and decentralization, not command and centralization, facilitate policy adjustments. This approach to governing devalues coordinated and central responses to policy problems in favor of flexible and entrepreneurial responses that are sensitive to sectoral demands (Peters, 2001, pp. 3–4). The logic of control in the public sector has switched from hierarchy toward competition and mutuality. This position accords with the theory of transgovernmentalism (Kingsbury et al., 2005; Slaughter, 2004).

These two competing arguments imply that the question of how to set forth an appropriate government structure in the age of globalization has become a major concern in academic and policy circles. Both viewpoints hold that a state ought to adjust its policy domains to changing international policy environments by reinventing the government structure. In general, such adjustments are composed of adaptation to new international norms and rules through learning and behavioral changes as well as coordination between conflicting interests and public policy tasks. In this vein, the government structure constitutes a major instrumental variable to facilitate adjustment tasks – adaptation and coordination.

This structural controversy is intrinsically related to another controversy between globalists and comparative institutionalists. They both argue that a globalizing economy enables business firms to reinforce their bargaining power with regard to states through exit options. Firms can relocate their production or marketing facilities to foreign countries with fewer regulations and lower taxes. This generates a race to the bottom, promoting deregulation and privatization, or an adjustment to the neoliberal international order.

On the one hand, globalists (Ohmae, 1999; Takenaka, 2008) predict that globalization will benefit not only multilateral corporations, but also the nation as a whole due to the expanded employment opportunities, trickle-down effects with respect to economic growth, tax revenue increases, and so on. Notable pioneers of globalism in international political circles are Conservative Prime Minister Margaret Thatcher of Great Britain and Republican President Ronald Reagan of the United States, who were succeeded by New Labour Prime Minister Tony Blair and Democratic President Bill Clinton, respectively. Leaders in non-liberal states, including Chancellor Gerhard Schröder of Germany, President Sarkozy of France, and Prime Minister Koizumi of Japan, among others, have followed Anglo-American initiatives. Thus, the globalist hypothesis expects that governments undertake comprehensive adjustments to the neoliberal international order through not just competition, but also learning and emulation, irrespective of cultural, historical, and partisan differences (Simmons and Elkins, 2004).

In contradistinction to the globalist sweeping institutional reform, there are rival accounts for incremental change. Comparative institutionalism argues that institutional reform is necessary but depends on the path of the existing institution (Hall and Soskice, 2001). Stakeholders seek to adjust their institution to changing international order in pursuit of efficiency and competitiveness while preserving the core of the institution in pursuit of internal complementarity and social stability. Thus, the adjustment process is an incremental adaptation characterized by layering, conversion, displacement, and drift (Streeck and Thelen, 2005), which is carefully planned and executed by specialists, administrators, and regulators in a decentralized government.

PROBLEMS WITH EXISTING JAPANESE POLITICAL-ECONOMIC STUDIES

These general arguments concerning globalism and comparative institutionalism have influenced Japanese political and policy studies in significant ways. Below, the findings of the studies are summarized for the globalist and institutionalist schools, which have slightly different interpretations from analytical perspectives.

Comparative Institutionalism and Bureaucratic–Industrial Collusion

In the edited volume by Streeck and Yamamura (2003), Vogel (2003) concludes from observations of various adjustment attempts in contemporary Japan that the government has implemented selective and incremental adjustments to correct significant institutional defects without altering its foundation. This practice constitutes the Japanese way of structural adjustment but is still consistent with the general pattern of incremental change in pursuit of institutional complementarity and social stability. The comparative institutionalist hypothesis acknowledges the virtue of the existent Japanese-style coordinated market economy (CME) as well as the need for adaptation, and is sympathetic with the slightly different interpretation below.

Another analytical perspective views incremental adaptation as a consequence of political–bureaucratic–industrial collusion and a deliberate attempt to secure the vested interests under a fragmentary decentralized government (Calder, 1988b; Katz, 1998; Amyx, 2006). Even reformist leaders are barred from initiating meaningful reform by the collusion within which bureaucrats deliver policy rents to the regulated industrial sectors in exchange for post-agency employment, while rank-and-file parliamentarians pressure for lenient regulations in exchange for votes and political contributions. Accordingly, even when the leadership claims that it seeks a 'bold' adjustment via its initiative, in an attempt to persuade the opponents about the need for the adjustment, it sooner or later has to curtail the extent of the announced reform so as not to jeopardize vested interests (Vogel, 2006).

Globalist Majoritarian State and Monopolistic Leadership

The globalist perspective contends that domestic electoral and administrative reforms in the 1990s transformed the once fragmentary governing system into a coherent majoritarian system with improved political command (Berger, 2007; Rosenbluth and Thies, 2010). The new system is capable of adjusting its economic institution to the neoliberal international order through comprehensive reforms regarding banking, corporate governance, labor relations, and so on. These reforms were timed with the worsening of the deflationary economy in the aftermath of an asset bubble burst in 1991 that eroded business confidence in the CME system, which is associated with public discontent with the political–bureaucratic–industrial collusion. This perspective also overlaps with the idea of internationalization. 'Second image reversed' theory or global convergence that predicts a major transformation of a non-liberal market economy to a neoliberal order occur through a distinct path (Gourevitch, 1978).

While it suggests correctly that a coherent majoritarian system with political command, if obtainable, might solve the problems of strategic interactions between leadership and rank-and-file parliamentarians and between politicians and bureaucrats, the majoritarian hypothesis fails to notice that the post-reform political system is hardly a two-party system and that the reforms have been derived from the elitist political–bureaucratic partnership at the cabinet level, not from the voter-majority–party-cabinet link. Furthermore, because of its faith in democratic majoritarianism, the thesis fails to notice that elitist politics could engender another problem of monopolistic leadership – the central command at the top of the government hierarchy is susceptible to communication and information cutoffs. This structure discourages bureaucratic officials from acquiring the information and expertise necessary for policy adaptation. As a result, some reformist leaders and their associates may be ill informed of efficient and effective ways for adaptation, leading them to believe that the properties of CME can no longer benefit Japanese firms and to them calling for neoliberal market economy practices.

As shown above, the empirics are mixed and open to variable interpretations by the contending schools of thought, including institutionalist, globalist, political–bureaucratic–industrial collusion, and monopolistic leadership. In this book, I try to sort out these hypotheses via normative and empirical analyses. I then argue that the government structural architecture and ancillary authorities are crucial for mediating global pressure and adjustments, generating varying outcomes across public policy domains.

ANALYTICAL FRAMEWORK

Within the last century, the Japanese political economy transformed from the prewar mercantilist economy through the interwar command economy into the postwar coordinated market economy in attempts to keep pace with changing international orders. These political economic systems were essentially non-liberal, entailed close public–private relations, and employed government interference with economic transactions to high and variable extents. Thus, the non-liberal state's public policies, or national rules and standards, are qualitatively different from those of a liberal state that embraces arm's-length public–private relations based on the principle of non-interference.

The systemic transformations in Japanese political economy were associated with major political changes that were driven by war and peace. Each political change generated change in the government structure or the reallocation of policy authorities between politicians and bureaucrats through which both struggled to adjust public policies to an emergent international order. However, each systemic transformation was not a complete abandonment of the past. A new system maintained several institutional arrangements of an old one, keeping the legacy of non-liberalism, primarily because political, bureaucratic, and private actors had incentives to maintain existing arrangements. In recent times, the Japanese political economy is faced with yet another major turning point, at which it is urged to effect a systemic transformation one more time in order to keep pace with a new order – that is, the global neoliberal order. This has evoked the quintessential problems of authority reallocation and policy change.

To analyze the contemporary and historic systemic transformations, I use a framework that links policy authority allocation (either bureaucratic delegation or political command) to adjustment mechanisms (either adaptation or coordination) for international orders. My analysis regards authority allocation as an important intervening variable due to the fact that significant public policy changes emerged despite the rare occurrence of partisan shifts in national politics. Likewise, existing scholarly analysis of policy change in postwar Japan has focused predominantly on the location of policy authority and the relationship between politicians and bureaucrats (Muramatsu and Krauss, 1984; Inoguchi, 1993; Pempel, 1998). This authority-centric analysis is in sharp contrast with comparative public policy studies in North America and Europe (Alt, 1985; Garrett, 1998), which often use partisanship as a primary explanatory variable to account for changes in policy regimes and institutions. In these states, governing parties almost always have robust central commands within their respective democratic governments to initiate policy changes. However, in the Japanese case, political command with substantive policy authority is not readily available, and must be created via appropriate authority reallocation and skillful political strategies, which therefore have to be my major analytical concern.

Thus, the analytical framework of this book is as follows:

- To construct and maintain efficient economic institutions, the government needs to adjust its public policy domains. Without appropriate policy changes, economic institutions will lose competitiveness, reducing the public well-being and even undermining the governing party's electoral prospect.
- Economic institutions consist of private arrangements underpinned by public policy domains and are characterized by 'institutional bundling'.
- An institutional reform means 'institutional rebundling', which is a change in private arrangements induced by policy reforms in public domains. Institutional rebundling is often difficult because agents are bound rationally and are unable to reach an efficient solution under informational uncertainty or high transaction costs. Alternatively, agents have the malicious intent of preserving existing institutions in pursuit of their self-interest.
- The nature of discrepancy between the prevailing international economic order and a state's economic institutions should determine the mechanism of adjustment. That is, in simple binary terms, the government is tasked with *adaptation* (policy reform in one or more domains to keep pace with changing international order with complementary cross-domain effects) and *coordination* (policy reform in multiple domains to keep pace with changing international order with substitutive cross-domain effects).[1]
- Adaptation and coordination can be performed efficiently via distinct 'policy authority allocation' schemes over policy domains using 'bureaucratic delegation' and a 'central political command', respectively.
- Even if a desired change in one policy domain is *complementary* to that in another domain, the change may be hindered by informational uncertainty. That is, agents (private actors and bureaucratic officials) in one policy domain are uninformed of agents' behavioral choices in a different domain, inhibiting an efficient solution. This scenario mimics a stag hunt or assurance game in which hunters fail to capture a stag jointly because they individually pursue hares.
- Change can be facilitated by efficient 'information transmission' between bureaucratic officials who manage the two different policy

domains. Using their technical information and expertise, they can discern a relatively efficient equilibrium via learning and an inter-ministerial communication channel.

- Political leadership can promote policy adaptation via bureaucratic delegation that encourages bureaucratic officials to further their specialization, learning, and inter-ministerial communication.
- If a suggested change (say, foreign exchange liberalization) in one policy domain is *substitutive* for a corresponding change in another domain (say, interest rate control for private banks), the change may be hindered by a distributive conflict. That is, agents in the latter domain (banks) will suffer a loss from the change in the former policy domain, and thus veto the change. This mimics a battle of the sexes or coordination game in which a couple of friends fail to choose the same dating spot due to divergent preferences.
- The solution to the coordination problem may be achieved by *compensating* the sufferers for the losses, by *persuading* them to accept the change, or by *coercing* them to acquiesce to the change. However, success is constrained by the high transaction costs associated with compensation, persuasion or coercion, under decentralized arrangements. In this case, the solution should be facilitated by powerful central command capable of performing either one or more of the three.
- In theory, the nature of the discrepancy between the state's economic institutions and the international order should determine the appropriate adjustment mechanism and policy authority allocation. Accordingly, the extent and process of policy change (dependent variables) are determined by change in the international order (independent variable) and policy authority allocation and related political strategies (intervening variables). Different authority allocation schemes siphon the leadership's policy goals, the governing coalition's sectoral interests, and bureaucracies' organizational interests into policy domains with different extents. Change in authority allocation reconfigures the distribution of goals and interests, inducing public policy domain changes and affecting institutional reforms.

OUTLINE

The above analytical framework has both normative and positive elements that will be discussed in greater detail in Part I, Chapter 1. However, the normative and positive hypotheses are often met with empirical defiance. In practice though, the authority allocation schemes are influenced by the politics of bureaucracy and the governing party's coalition as well as by leadership's strategies to untangle them. In the real world, authority allocation may fail to produce desirable policy outcomes for two reasons. First, it suffers from a *structural dilemma* as an authority allocation scheme to achieve both efficient adaptation and coordination concurrently is hard to come by. The central command may be strong in coordination, but weak in adaptation, while the opposite is true for a bureaucratic delegation. Second, agents may deliberately engage in *structural manipulation* or choose an authority allocation scheme that differs from what the normative theory recommends due to an electoral or a political reason.

In the absence of a robust central command, deconcentrated bureaucracies fail to execute coordination and stifle policy adjustment. For example, suppose that coordination is concerned with comprehensive trade liberalization that encompasses industrial and agricultural products. Due to fears of relative inefficiency and loss, the farming community wishes to prevent comprehensive liberalization altogether and receive protectionist rents from the closed trade regime. Bureaucratic delegation may provide the agricultural ministry with veto power to defend the vested interests at the expense of national consumerists' interests. This type of government is referred to as a *degenerate* decentralized government and is the critical focus of many empirical studies of contemporary Japanese political economy.

Another case of inappropriate authority allocation is that, even if adaptation is needed, leadership may choose a central command in order to fulfill its policy goals without proper parliamentary and bureaucratic consultation, proclaiming that the goals are in the 'public interest' regardless if this is true. Via the central command, the leadership may be able to make a bold policy change, but the change may be inappropriate because the top leadership in the government hierarchy is ill informed and not helped properly by disillusioned bureaucrats with poor information and expertise. The result is a policy domain divergent from public interest or international order. This type of government is referred to as a 'monopolistic' government and is largely ignored by contemporary scholarship.

In Chapter 2 of this book, I will extrapolate four empirical models on the Japanese government and its performance from the existing scholarly literature. Two of the four models are consistent with the aforementioned theory, while the other two are degenerate versions. All four models are useful for conducting historical and contemporary analyses in the following chapters. Each empirical analysis will intend to test the models, rather than provide comprehensive descriptions or explanation of institutional reform at hand.

In Chapter 3, a historical analysis will focus on the pre–World War II

Japanese political economy. It will show how the Meiji oligarchs presided over institutional reform from feudalism to modern industrialism under the forced free trade regime without tariff autonomy imposed upon Meiji Japan as part of the treaty port system by Western powers until the early twentieth century.

On the other hand, during the post-oligarchic party politics in the Taisho era (1912–26), the Japanese political system became a quasi-parliamentary democracy with two rival political parties vying for power under the Meiji Imperial Constitution. However, despite embryonic liberalism at home, the party governments had difficulties conforming to the interwar liberal international order. The collapse of party government was followed by bureaucratic, constitutional-dictatorial, and grand coalition government. The major question here is why the Taisho democracy collapsed and centralization took place, with the disastrous consequence of total national mobilization and warfare.

The empirical analysis in Chapter 4 will focus on the four decades after World War II when the Japanese-style market economy, known as a coordinated market economy (CME), thrived and produced phenomenal growth under the international order of embedded liberalism. It is widely known that the Japanese-style CME emerged as a stable equilibrium institution underpinned by the relevant public policy domains. I will show how the Japanese-style CME evolved from the interwar planned economy via occupation reforms, creating a bundle of private arrangements, including the main bank system, manager-centric contingent corporate governance, long-term employment, and integrated industrial networks. From the mid-1950s through the early 1990s, the Liberal Democratic Party (LDP), a product of the merger of two conservative parties, maintained the bureaucratic-cabinet system, delegating policy authority to bureaucracies and protecting the CME via public policies. In the meantime, the cross-sectoral governing coalition, composed of bankers, business managers, skilled regular employees, and farmers, remained remarkably unchanged. How could this be possible, given phenomenal economic growth, shifting comparative advantages, and the associated social change?

In Part II of this book, I will conduct contemporary analyses with an emphasis on the process of altering the authority allocation scheme through political and administrative reforms in the 1990s. The reforms were made in part to adjust the ailing CME to the change in the global order toward neoliberalism. To overview the crucial reforms, in Chapter 5 I will examine the electoral and administrative reforms that are said to produce a majoritarian-consumerist tendency, centralize the government structure, and strengthen political leadership appropriate for neoliberal policy change. My analysis will show how the mixed electoral system with the resurrection rule has generated an imperfect two-party system with a weak majoritarian-consumerist tendency and resilient sectoral representation. Likewise, the administrative reforms still have allowed bureaucratic decentralization particularly in the policy domains with strong demands for expertise and balancing social interests. Given the possibility of structural dilemma and manipulation, policy change must emanate from political leadership's initiative, central command, as well as its creative political strategy. From this perspective, I will analyze several policy domains that have recently undergone variable adjustments to a neoliberal international order, including corporate governance and labor relations (Chapter 6), international trade (Chapter 7), and banking (Chapter 8).

In Chapter 6, the ongoing reforms on corporate governance and labor relations will be analyzed. Both reforms are highly technical and are often referred to deliberative councils sponsored by bureaucratic ministries for detailed scrutiny. I will show that the LDP-led government has used not only conventional referral to deliberative councils, but also strategic referral to an advisory council in the Cabinet Office for radical change. The leadership employed the different referral strategies for policy change and maintenance, depending on who would be affected. The distinct referral patterns constitute the politics of counseling that is swayed by the governing coalition with some corrective influences from opposition parties.

In Chapter 7, I will turn to international trade. Trade is the linchpin of Japanese economic growth because it provides resources and markets for a resource-poor island state, also bringing international competition to the shore as a stimulus for efficiency improvement. Globally, because of the multilateral negotiation deadlock, the World Trade Organization (WTO) regime has permitted contracting states to conclude bilateral or regional free trade agreements (FTAs). In response, the Japanese government initially took to bureaucratic delegation – the four-ministry co-chair system – to adapt to the FTA movement under the devolved global trade order. By taking advantage of bureaucratic expertise, the system has concluded a number of technically sophisticated and mutually beneficial agreements with small economies, while satisfying the interests of efficient and inefficient industrial sectors at home. However, the bureaucratic system has been confronted with limits and the resulting unfavorable trade position. The Abe LDP Cabinet has shifted to central command to reach 'welfare-improving' FTAs with large economies, which are believed to stimulate economic growth but will generate a major distributive problem. I will show how the conservative cabinet used issue-dimensional politics with an emphasis on the national security imperative in relation to the US rebalancing strategy under changing security orders in East Asia, while struggling to keep political support from the governing coalition via policy ideas borrowed from opposition parties.

Chapter 8 will shift analysis to banking and the politics of crisis. Banking, the key financing component of the Japanese-style CME, was faced with a new global financial order, defined by the Basel minimum capital requirements for commercial banks. Again, the LDP government initially used bureaucratic delegation to enforce the Basel requirements, based on the expectation that regulatory compliance with the requirements would help modernize the Japanese banking system and adapt it to the global order with a minimal influence on lending. However, an acute non-performing loan crisis shattered expectations, making coordination between compliance and lending intractable to the bureaucracy-led policy domain. I will show how crisis politics drew transnational financial networks and a major opposition party into the policy domain and led to eventual compliance by establishing a central command mechanism capable of implementing strict supervision and public fund injection to bail out banks.

Throughout Parts I and II, I will explain that the historical and contemporary Japanese political economies are both affected by the quintessential problem of adjusting public policy domains and economic institutions to shifting international orders through authority allocation schemes and political strategies. The mechanism and process of policy and institutional reform are not policy rational, but politically contentious and variable across time and policy domains. In the concluding chapter of this volume, Chapter 9, I will discuss the nature of political leadership for a non-liberal state faced with the neoliberal global order. I will discuss the political implications of a structural tendency toward central command and the impacts of transnational networks and opposition parties on policy and institutional reform.

NOTE

1. Adaptation and coordination approximate what Pempel (1998) calls the first-order change and second-order change, respectively, to characterize a regime change.

PART I

Theory and history

1. Theory of institutional reform and government structure

1.1 INTRODUCTION

As noted in the Introduction, globalization entails a controversy over the appropriate policy authority allocation between bureaucratic delegation for adaptation and political command for coordination. The controversy has resonated in the terrains of Japanese politics and political science. Because Japan is a state with limited natural resources, it is highly dependent on international commerce for its economic prosperity. Consequently, Japan is extremely sensitive to the problem of adjustment to the international order that regulates cross-border economic transactions. Due to its non-liberal legacy, adjustment to a liberal international order has been and continues to be a major policy and political problem for Japan.

Until recently, many studies on the Japanese political economy (Patrick and Rosovsky, 1976; Aoki, 1983; Aoki and Dore, 1994) analyzed institutional stability and maintenance by focusing primarily on cooperation among relevant economic actors in supporting the existing economic institution, which is known as the Japanese-style coordinated market economy (CME). It is widely acknowledged that the Japanese-style CME generated remarkable economic growth with stable employment during the post–World War II period from the early 1950s through the late 1980s. However, since the early 1990s, it has not fared well under the neoliberal global economic order where the keys to prosperity are competition, openness, and innovation as opposed to cooperation, control, and fine-tuning.

More recently, believing that institutional maintenance is no longer appropriate, reformist political and bureaucratic officials have tried to change the CME institution, the public policy domains, and even the authority allocation scheme. The scope of the changes is immense with regard to the beliefs and behaviors of politicians, bureaucrats, business managers, workers, and citizens about the role of government in the market as well as the institutions that encompass the relationships between government and markets, between banks and firms, and between managers and workers. Accordingly, institutional reform entails conflicts and compromises, and is highly contentious and deeply politicized.

The sources of conflict are informational and distributive, contained in the games of assurance and coordination, respectively. Accordingly, solving these problems requires adaptation and coordination mechanisms, which are facilitated by bureaucratic delegation and political command, respectively.

In this chapter, I develop a normative analysis that sets the stage for the positive and empirical analysis in the subsequent chapters. Specifically, I try to address the following questions: What is an institution? Why is it difficult to change an institution? How can an institution be changed? What are the roles of government in facilitating institutional reform? Why does policy authority allocation matter?

This chapter is structured as follows. Section 1.2 looks at two problems of institutional reform: institutions and institutional bundling, and globalization and institutional rebundling; Section 1.3 examines two mechanisms of adjustment: adaptation through information transmission, and coordination through Coasian bargaining; Section 1.4 develops an analytical framework that relates the appropriate authority allocation to the relationship between agencies' tasks; Section 1.5 concludes.

1.2 TWO PROBLEMS OF INSTITUTIONAL REFORM

1.2.1 Institutions and Institutional Bundling

According to Greif (2006, p. 39), institutions are 'a system of interrelated rules, beliefs, norms, and organizations'. Rules specify normative behavior and provide a shared cognitive system, coordination, and information, whereas beliefs and norms provide the motivation to follow them. For North (1990, p. 3), 'institutions define the incentive structure of a society'. The institutional rules determine the kinds of economic activities that will be profitable and viable as well as shape the adaptive efficiency of firms and other organizations via rules that regulate entry, governance structures, and the flexibility of organizations. In particular, rules to encourage the development and utilization of tacit knowledge, and therefore creative entrepreneurial talent, are important.

For instance, Japan's institutions in the post–World War II period entail a bundle of private arrangements (Aoki, 2001; Whittaker and Deakin, 2009). These are outlined as follows:

- *Main bank system*, through which commercial banks provide their client firms with long-term loans (also known as 'patient capital') and external oversight for investment and managerial efficiency.

- *Manager-centric or contingent corporate governance*, in which firm managers are recruited from firms' rank-and-file workforces and execute long-term business plans by which they provide their fellow workers with long-term employment.
- *Long-term employment practices and limited mid-career job markets* incentivize workers to acquire firm-specific loyalty and skills suitable for fine-tuning and product differentiation, and are the source of Japanese firms' competitive advantage.
- *Integrated industrial networks and cross-stockholding* are arrangements of reciprocal stockholding between firms that create horizontal and vertical industrial networks, reducing risks of hostile takeover and maintaining manager-centric corporate governance with limited stockholders' influence.

All of these arrangements constitute the Japanese-style market economy, referred to as 'stakeholder capitalism' or a 'coordinated market economy' (CME). CME embraces the interests of stakeholders, including the main bank officials, corporate managers, regular employees, suppliers, and other affiliated firms, rather than those of stockholders in the sense of Dore (2000). In addition, CME relies upon organizations, rather than markets, for nurturing specific human assets in the sense of Williamson (1985). Thus, it differs from 'stockholder capitalism' or a 'liberal market economy' (LME) with market-consistent arrangements, including (1) stock issuance; (2) committee system with independent external directors; (3) flexible labor markets; and (4) flexible corporate structures via organizational splits, mergers and acquisitions.

An institution rarely stands alone for two reasons. First, an institution is internally coherent. Private arrangements in one domain are related closely to those in others, constituting 'institutional bundling' or 'complementarity'. In the case of Japanese CME, the main bank system and cross-stockholding are closely related to manager-centric corporate governance and long-term employment.

Second, an institution is embedded within the linkage between private arrangements and public policy domains. A policy domain is defined as a set of public policy programs for a specific industrial sector or function that incentivize related private agents to improve the efficiency of their economic production or transaction, in the sense of Shonfield (1965). A state's economy includes a multitude of policy domains, each of which needs to be consistent with other domains to make the state's economic institutions coherent, efficient, and compatible with the prevailing international order. Each policy domain is administered by a bureaucratic organization of competence that:

> ha[s] three interrelated roles, to produce and disseminate rules, perpetuate beliefs and norms, and to influence the set of feasible behavioral beliefs. . . Institutions generate behavior, rules correspond to the beliefs and norms that motivate it, while organizations contribute to this outcome in the manner mentioned previously. (Greif, 2006, p. 37)

Specifically, public policy domains pertaining to the present analysis of the Japanese-style CME include bank law, the Commercial Code (Shoho), antimonopoly law, labor law, the pension system, trade law, foreign exchange law, and so forth. The following bureaucracies are assigned to administer the related public policy domains with the specified roles:

- *The Ministry of Finance* (MOF) provides commercial banks with low interest-rate environments, segmented competition, and informal bailout guarantees with which the banks secure regulatory rents and offer patient capital to firms.
- *The Ministry of International Trade and Industry* (MITI, currently the Ministry of Economy, Trade and Industry [METI]) controls the Commercial Code and antimonopoly laws to permit an executive-dominant board of directors, limit minority stockholder protection, and cross-stockholding for the formation of manager-centric corporate governance and industrial interfirm networks.
- *The Ministry of Labour* ([sic] – currently the Ministry of Health, Labour [sic] and Welfare – MHLW) implements the irrational dismissal principle to help maintain long-term employment practices.
- *The Ministry of Health and Welfare* (currently the MHLW) administers the multilayered pension system, composed of national, sector-specific, and firm-specific entities, to aid in the consolidation of firm loyalty among workers.

Institutions are hard to change for at least two reasons. The first hinges on the built-in stability derived from institutional bundling and the public–private linkages mentioned above. If one tries to change part of an institution, the other parts of the institution constrain the change. Likewise, if public officials try to change private arrangements by altering public policy, private agents may resist the change, and vice versa, in order to maintain complementarity. The second reason is closely related to the first: institutions involve vested interests. If public officials try to change public policy in an attempt to induce change in private arrangements, holders of vested interests, who believe it will hurt those interests, will veto the policy change.

Core members of the governing coalition, who provide stable support for the party constantly in power, often hold vested interests. A governing coalition may be class or sector based. Rogowski (1989) assumes that the governing coalition is class based and is composed of groups and individuals who hold abundant production factors (capital, labor, or land) within the state. These factors may move across industrial sectors as the sectors wax and wane in the wake of their shifting comparative advantages. Due to their mobility, abundant factors govern the national economy and form a dominant class. In the scholarship of political economy, such class-based coalitions are consistent with Marxism and the Heckscher-Ohlin theory of international trade.

In contrast, a sectoral coalition emerges as technological sophistication reduces the cross-sector factor mobility. At a high stage of technological development, expertise and know-how appropriate for one sector may not be useful for another, discouraging factor-holders from moving across sectors and compelling holders of different factors to cooperate with one another within separate sectors (Hiscox, 2002). This type of economic coalition accords with the Ricardo-Viner theory of international trade.

In the early Meiji era (1868–1880s), because the Japanese economy was still agrarian, land was the dominant factor of production, while landlords were the principal members of the governing coalition for the oligarchic government that financed its coffers primarily through land taxes. As mercantilist capitalism burgeoned in the 1890s under the competitive international order, capital owners became increasingly influential and colluded with landlords. As a result, the capital–land coalition reigned from the late nineteenth century through the end of World War II. In the postwar occupation period, the capital–land coalition collapsed because of the Supreme Commander for Allied Powers (SCAP)-led *zaibatsu*[1] liquidation and agrarian reform. These reforms improved the socio-political status of labor with an uninvited effect of emboldening militant workers and stoking class conflict. However, the conservatives banded together and restrained labor, leading to a class compromise in which regular employees of large firms with managerial prospects joined the capital–land coalition, tipping the socio-political balance in favor of the conservatives (Gordon, 1988).

Under the order of embedded liberalism that regulated postwar international commerce, the Japanese industrial economy experienced diversification and technological sophistication along with the institutionalization of the CME. For many reasons, the governing coalition became cross-sectoral, composed of bankers, business managers, skilled workers, and farmers, providing stable support for the LDP, which remained in power continuously between 1955 and 1993.

Both in general and in the specific case of Japan, institutions gain staying power and legitimacy. Thus, the concept of path dependence is useful for explaining the resilience of institutions. However, as indicated above, institutions change over long periods with coalitional changes despite their presumed stability. In this book, the concept of path dependence is reinterpreted as the logic of a punctuated equilibrium in which an institutional reform is precipitated by change in international order. The mechanism of change is conditioned and constrained by the politics of the governing coalition, which influence policy authority allocation and the governing party's motive.

1.2.2 Globalization and Institutional Rebundling

Institutions are pressured to change due to exogenous forces, endogenous forces, or both. Either public or private agents, depending upon the specific policy domains, may drive an institutional reform, which means a reciprocal change between public policy domains and private arrangements. It can be stated with a high level of confidence that the pressure for institutional reform in contemporary Japan is derived largely from an exogenous force – globalization, which thrives under the neoliberal order.

Globalization is defined as 'a process of removing officially imposed restrictions on movements of resources between countries in order to form an "open" and "borderless" world economy' (Scholte, 2005, p. 56). Economically, liberalization means market-driven and market-accommodating changes in institutions, releasing the market economy from political public control and turning it over to private contracts. Processes and outcomes of liberalization in advanced democratic states take different forms and proceed at different rates due to the effects of various institutional arrangements interacting with exogenous events and endogenous challenges. Liberalization is often associated with an arrangement to inform related agents of policy benefit, to mitigate its negative effect on a particular sector, or both, depending on the nature of the policy change.

Economic organizations are more sensitive to globalization than governments, because they are unable to survive once they fail to adapt to the changing global rules and practices. However, renegotiations over existing institutions or institutional rebundling in the wake of globalization are often difficult mainly due to the rigidities associated with themselves and vested interests within political organizations, as discussed earlier. Under institutional bundling with multiple policy domains, public officials who seek to change institutions through public policy change need to employ a novel technology, depending on the nature of the relationship between policy domains.

There are two classes of cross-domain relationships. One is that an increased payoff in one policy domain may be enhanced by a simultaneous increase in another policy domain. This type is *complementary*. The second is if an increased payoff in one policy domain may be reduced by a simultaneous increase in another policy domain. This type is *substitutive*. If unrelated, they are said to be *independent*. In this book, independence is considered part of complementarity without a loss of logical consistency. The appropriate adjustment mechanism depends on whether a policy change involves a complementary or substitutive relationship between policy domains. A more detailed exposition is offered in the next section.

1.3 TWO MECHANISMS OF ADJUSTMENT

1.3.1 Promoting Adaptation through Information Transmission

A complementary relationship seems relatively easy to manage; rational bureaucratic officials in different policy domains can achieve desirable policy changes through reciprocity. However, they cannot do so single-handedly, if the officials are bound rationally in that they have imperfect information on others' policy domains and are unable to conduct efficient communication and learning. In the absence of efficient cross-domain communication, boundedly rational officials would be unaware of policy changes in other domains. Even if a policy change did occur, they would be hesitant to pursue a policy change in their own domain for fear of being excluded (i.e., uncertainty about a complementary effect from another domain). For North (1990), this type of policy (institutional) change is an informational problem of belief selection under uncertainty. Due to their limited information-processing ability, boundedly rational officials have to rely on an innovative communication method to determine what and how to change.

Table 1.1 shows a game of stag hunt or assurance that analyzes the above informational problem. Suppose that a proposed institutional reform in the wake of globalization is derived from policy changes in Domains 1 and 2 from the protection equilibrium (1, 1) in the lower right cell to the liberalization one (2, 2) in the upper left cell. Let us assume that both agents can jointly avoid asymmetric responses in the upper right and the lower left cells since neither cell is a Nash equilibrium. Each response means the collapse of institutional bundling and thus, can be avoided even by boundedly rational agents.

In the game, there are still two Nash equilibria in the upper left and lower right cell, meaning that Agents 1 and 2 might achieve either one of the equilibria. Even though they recognize that they would be better off by choosing liberalization jointly, they might remain in the inefficient

Table 1.1 Policy change, informational uncertainty, and adaptation

		Agent 2	
	Domain 1/Domain 2	Liberalization	Protection
Agent 1	Liberalization	2, 2	0, 0
	Protection	0, 0	1, 1

protection equilibrium due to uncertainty about a policy change in other domains. For instance, even if Agent 1 chooses liberalization, Agent 2 without such information may be hesitant to pursue the corresponding policy change in his or her own domain for fear of being excluded in an asymmetric outcome. For joint policy changes, each agent needs to convince the other of not just the desirability of the joint changes, but his or her willingness to make a policy change in his or her own domain.

One prominent mechanism to achieve an efficient equilibrium in a stag-hunt game is 'cheap talk' in the sense of Crawford and Sobel (1982),[2] which is defined as a sender's (say, Agent 1) costless message to a receiver (Agent 2) about the sender's intended action to induce an analogous cooperative action from the receiver. The solution to the multiple equilibria is primarily informational in that the sender can eliminate the receiver's uncertainty, providing that receiving precise information prompts him or her to undertake a policy change. This informational effort helps the expectations of two agents converge, facilitating joint policy changes. In this case, a policy change is viewed as a process in which agents adapt their beliefs and behavior to a new equilibrium. In this book, the mechanism of such a policy change is viewed as *adaptation*.

According to Aoki (2000, pp. 24–5), this type of adaptation process ensues if, and only if, a system of predictive and/or normative beliefs helps guide agents' learning, realizing a new pattern of play, which becomes collectively recognized as how the game is now being played. From this perspective, cheap talk is a mechanism to assist such collective recognition. For North (1990, pp. 80–81), information facilitation promotes the adaptive efficiency concerned with 'the willingness of a society to acquire knowledge and learning, to induce innovation, to undertake risk and creative activity of all sorts, as well as to resolve problems and bottlenecks of the society through time'. The adaptive efficiency can be improved through 'the development of decentralized decision-making processes that will allow societies to explore many alternative ways to solve problems'. The decentralized decision-making approach stressed by North is viewed as being equivalent to bureaucratic delegation, which is discussed in the next section.

The postwar Japanese political economy is replete with instances of inter-ministerial cooperation that can be considered as adaptation. For instance, although initially reluctant, the MOF approved a shift in the foreign exchange regime from an adjustable peg to floating in February 1973 (Nakamura, 2012, pp. 747–52). This quickly led to private expectations for the eventual appreciation of the Japanese yen in relation to the US dollar and other major currencies. To reduce foreign exchange risks, Japanese export firms felt it necessary to invest abroad. But, to do so, they needed extra capital, some of which needed to be denominated with foreign currencies. The MITI proposed an amendment to the Commercial Code that would permit Japanese firms with high financial credentials to issue convertible corporate bonds, facilitating their risk diversification. In this case, bond market liberalization complemented foreign exchange liberalization as a result of inter-ministerial communication between the MOF and the MITI.

1.3.2 Promoting Coordination through Coasian Bargaining

In a second case, the inter-domain relationship is substitutive in that bureaucratic officials in separate policy domains have divergent interests. Hence, the more specialized the officials are in their policy tasks, the more they invest resources to pursue their own tasks, increasing the likelihood of reducing others' payoffs. The inevitable effect is an increase in the negative externality costs. Although specialization may increase adaptive efficiency gains, it may also create a condition for coordination failure.

This problem of coordination with divergent interests is modeled as a battle of the sexes game, as depicted in Table 1.2. In the game, a shift from the protection equilibrium (1, 2) in the lower right cell to the liberalization equilibrium (a, 1) in the upper left generates a distributive conflict between the two agents ($a \geq 3$). Agent 2, who incurs a loss, opposes the shift. On the contrary, Agent 1 does the same for the opposite shift from the upper left to the lower right cell.

A prominent solution to a coordination problem with divergent interests is to ask for consent and offer compensation to the agent who is expected to lose from a proposed change. According to Aoki (2000, pp. 24–5), this coordination process can converge if, and only if, agents' new action choices based on such expectations generate satisfactory payoffs for both. Satisfactory payoffs for the liberalization shift can be achieved when Agent 1 offers compensation c ($a - 1 > c > 1$) to Agent 2. This compensatory solution is equivalent to Coasian bargaining in the sense of Coase (1960)

Table 1.2 Policy change, distributive conflict, and coordination

		Agent 2	
	Domain 1/Domain 2	Liberalization	Protection
Agent 1	Liberalization	a, 1	0, 0
	Protection	0, 0	1, 2

Note: a ≥ 3.

whereby agents coordinate their choices through arbitration by a third party.

In the real world, a compensatory program often fails due to the lack of credibility or high transaction costs. In order to be effective, both agents must view a compensatory solution as a credible and efficient transaction. This requires a central command that coordinates the agents' behaviors. The central command's role is one or both of the following. For one, it punishes an agent for failing to fulfill the compensatory obligation necessary to secure credibility. For another, it helps reduce transaction costs to induce a voluntary transaction between agents. In both cases, the central command takes on a hierarchy capable of monitoring agents' behavior and realigning their incentives with joint actions. Both agents may submit to this authority because they realize that, in the long run, they will be better off in a system with the authority to impose coordination on them. Conversely, a central command is likely to exist due to the inability of agents to coordinate their actions by their own efforts.

In 1993, GATT signatories were about to reach a historic agreement to conclude the Uruguay Round that would launch sweeping trade liberalization over commodities, agriculture, and services, and would newly initiate trade-related property rights protection. A major snag was the dissent from Japanese agriculture, which was expected to lose because of its relative productive inefficiency. In contrast, internationally competitive Japanese industries were expected to gain greatly from the set of proposed measures, indicating a large interest divergence and distributive conflict between the two sectors within Japanese society. To achieve an efficient solution for its own and the world economy, the Japanese government decided to offer a large-scale compensatory package of up to 6 trillion yen (presumably paid from the industrial earnings) to the agricultural sector in order to obtain its consent and avoid the humiliation of subverting a monumental international agreement. This *quid pro quo* deal is archetypal Coasian bargaining supported by a central political authority.

1.4 POLICY AUTHORITY ALLOCATION AS A STRATEGIC VARIABLE FOR INSTITUTIONAL REFORM: NORMATIVE ANALYSIS

The previous section discussed the mechanisms of adaptation and coordination to solve informational and distributive problems concerning a policy change. Solutions to the two problems require different techniques and the human talents of public officials – bureaucrats and politicians. In general, bureaucrats have greater policy and administrative expertise in collecting and analyzing information, while politicians are more sensitive to a distributive problem and can take a commanding position to direct compensation or coercion to solve the problem.

To promote policy change through the mechanisms defined above, the government needs to build effective 'authority allocation schemes' that take advantage of the distinct human talents and incentives that are defined in greater detail in the next section. In other words, the authority allocation scheme determines the division of roles between political leadership and bureaucracy, thus influencing their incentives and behaviors. One scheme, referred to as *political command*, prioritizes the leader's policy authority over bureaucracy. Political command enables leadership to initiate new policy programs, change old ones, and guide bureaucracy's behavior accordingly. Another scheme, referred to as *bureaucratic delegation*, means that leadership delegates policy authority to the bureaucratic agency with formal jurisdiction over a particular policy domain. It incentivizes the agency to acquire further information and expertise to make professional decisions (Table 1.3).

An authority allocation scheme is a major facet of the government structural architecture. The structural approach to a policy change has international connections since an institutional reform means the adjustment of the state's economic institutions to the international order. There are at least two international relations theories that account for a change in national economic institutions. These theories place varying emphases on the informational and the distributive problems discussed earlier and

Table 1.3 Policy change, adjustment mechanism, and authority

	Type 1	Type 2
Policy Task	Complementary	Substitutive
Problem	Informational	Distributive
Adjustment mechanism	Adaptation	Coordination
Authority allocation	Bureaucratic delegation	Political command

propose distinct international solution approaches with the corresponding national authority allocation schemes.

One prominent theory, known as 'transgovernmentalism' (Raustiala, 2002; Slaughter, 2004), views the policy adjustment problem essentially as informational and finds that decentralization is appropriate. The theory holds that globalization is driven by a set of highly technical international rules that are accessible only to specialized bureaucratic officials. It assumes that public-spirited bureaucratic officials can learn and build 'best practices' in competitive settings through transgovernmental networks and then take advantage of the fruits of globalization by adapting the state's policy domains to the international rules. For efficient policy adaptation, the government needs to delegate policy authority to the specialists for policy adaptation.

The other theory of international cooperation, known as 'intergovernmentalism' (Keohane and Nye, 1977), views an adjustment problem as distributive and finds centralization appropriate. Globalization and the related institutional reforms necessitate the aggregation of diverse domestic interests into well-ordered preferences, the negotiation with foreign counterparts, and creation of formal international agreements for policy cooperation, all of which can effectively be promoted by coherent political leadership through international commitment and formal legal processes.

In sum, the decentralized structure suggested by transgovernmentalism provides bureaucracies with policy autonomy and incentives for furthering their specialization and information useful for adaptation. In contrast, the centralized structure suggested by intergovernmentalism strengthens the authority of the political leadership and empowers its ability to coordinate bureaucracies' behavior. In both theories, the government structural architecture is important, especially for a non-liberal state, such as Japan, which stresses the role of public policy in economic growth and the distribution of the fruits of growth across society. In the remainder of this section, I will discuss individual incentives and organizational foundations of the two structural approaches and their international connections.

1.4.1 Decentralization and Bureaucratic Delegation

Individual incentives

As argued thus far, primary actors in a decentralized government are bureaucratic officials who are provided with specific policy tasks in predetermined areas of competence. According to Wilson (1989), bureaucratic officials are interested in their professional reputation in the eyes of their peers by showing their administrative and policy competence. They are also interested in personal career promotion within their bureaucratic ministries by contributing to the organizational goals. They have long-term employment contracts and are rewarded with promotions for their contributions to the organizational goals, which are often measured on a reputational basis. These arrangements encourage bureaucratic officials to nurture long-term policy perspectives, making their personal career goals largely consistent with the organizational goals.

If given the task of adjusting their policy domain to international norms and rules, bureaucrats employ incremental adaptation because under institutional bundling a radical policy change in their domain might cause irreparable damage to social trust and related private arrangements and thus to their personal and organizational reputation. Thus, cautious bureaucrats are averse to such a radical policy change, and instead seek gradual adaptation of the existing policy domain, securing policy consistency and institutional complementarity. This line of argument accords with the incrementalist policy-making thesis embraced by Lindblom. According to Lindblom (1979, p. 523):

> [D]espite the absence or weakness of central coordination of the participants, their mutual adjustments of many kinds (of which bargaining is only one) will to some degree coordinate them as policy makers. In many circumstances their mutual adjustments will achieve a coordination superior to an attempt at central coordination, which is often so complex as to lie beyond any coordinator's competence.

Bureaucratic organizations

In general, bureaucratic independence and a decentralized structure ensure informational and policy incentives. Heterogeneity in government promotes intellectual diversity, nurturing the ability of learning for policy adaptation. Particularly, in a changing international environment, bureaucracies must be able to adapt to new policy arrangements, which means that individual ministries' and agencies' tasks must be continuously redefined and enhanced for efficiency. In the age of globalization, the need for information and expertise is particularly strong. Furthermore, because globalization is promoted and regulated by a multitude of highly technical international rules, government is urged to engage in global rule-making and adapt public policy domains skillfully to these international rules. Bureaucrats rather than elected officials have the information and expertise necessary for such rule-making and policy adaptation, but bureaucrats must be incentivized to improve information-processing and policy-adaptation capabilities by being delegated policy authority and stimulated in their careers.

Rigidity of a centralized government

The decentralization thesis is based on the assumption that the centralized, top-down and monopolistic nature of government is at the core of governance problems. The associated assumption is that a more decentralized and deconcentrated government can be both more efficient and more flexible to policy adaptations faced by a contemporary government. This approach to governing devalues coordinated and central responses to policy problems in favor of a flexible and entrepreneurial response that also may be sensitive to particular demands (Peters et al., 2000). The decentralization thesis is supported by both theory and practice as follows.

Theoretically, Hayek criticized the faith in centralized decision-making: 'Knowledge which we use never exists in a concentrated or integrated form but solely as dispersed bits of incomplete and frequently contradictory knowledge, which all the separate individuals possess' (Hayek, 1945, p. 517). He continued:

> If we can agree that the economic problem of society is mainly one of rapid adaptation to changes in the particular circumstances of time and place, it would seem to follow that the ultimate decisions must be left to the people who are familiar with these circumstances, who know direct of the relevant changes and of the resources immediately available to meet them. (Ibid., p. 524)

Weber (2009) followed by arguing that expertise becomes a power base: 'Every bureaucracy seeks to increase the superiority of the professionally informed by keeping their knowledge and intentions secret' (p. 233). Thus, government necessarily entails dual authority – a formal hierarchical authority and the authority of expertise. The appropriate authority allocation scheme lays out the two types for maximal effectiveness. Nonetheless, it seems that Hayek and Weber would agree that bureaucratic experts are in a position to direct policy adaptation in a knowledge-based society.

Lindblom (1979) argues in the context of Weberian rational-bureaucratic authority that, in a pluralistic decentralized government, no single monolithic elite controls government and society, but multiple elites compete and bargain or muddle through for control and state interests. Lindblom's rational evolutionary perspective accords with polyarchy or pluralist democracy advanced by Dahl (2006). Peters et al. (2000), who observed administrative changes in many advanced industrial countries during the past several decades, have concluded that despite a number of different trajectories and various foundations, one dominant pattern has emerged from those changes in pursuit of political and administrative controls away from the political center of government. Reforms tend to decentralize power among the levels of government, and consequently, diminishing power at the political and administrative centers. Thus, the logic of control in the public sector has switched from a hierarchy and toward competition and mutuality (see Hood et al., 2004).

Transgovernmental networks

In the age of globalization, the decentralization thesis has recently been integrated into the international relations theory of transgovernmentalism (Slaughter, 2004; Kingsbury et al., 2005). The theory postulates that bureaucratic officials engage in domestic and international processes of muddling through with their foreign counterparts in order to reduce the gaps between legal and national jurisdictions, leading to the creation of transgovernmental networks. According to Slaughter (2004, pp. 3–4), such networks have several common functions across various issue areas: among other things (1) to 'expand the regulatory reach' that help governments close the gaps between their jurisdictions; (2) to 'build trust and establish relationships' among their participants, which are 'conditions essential for long-term cooperation'; and (3) to facilitate regular information exchanges and develop 'databases of best practices'. Essential to policy adaptation in a globalizing world are shared expert knowledge, comity, and mutual trust among domestic and international bureaucratic officials.

The structural foundation of transgovernmental networks is a 'disaggregated state', or a sophisticated administrative state with the separation of powers and specialized bureaucratic agencies. In such a disaggregated state, legislative, bureaucratic, and judicial actors already have the legal power and authority delegated by the state's political leadership – as well as the initiative and capability – to enter into such relationships with foreign counterparts. From this perspective, globalization is a derivative of transgovernmental networks. Accordingly, specialized agencies are the ones that adapt the states' policy domains to international rules and practices.

1.4.2 Centralization and Political Command

Individual incentives

The thesis of centralization is in direct contrast to that of decentralization with respect to the theory of governance and globalization. There are two perspectives on the incentive of political leadership. One is an elitist perspective in which leadership is in a position to define the 'national interest' and pursue it as their career objective in the form of a policy platform (Schumpeter, 1976). In popular democracy, it is the electorate, who presumably support their policy platform, that choose their political leaders. To implement the platform, political leaders have the constitutional power to (1) initiate policy programs by directing bureaucratic officials to take certain actions; (2) exact obedience; (3) monitor bureaucratic behavior; and (4) reward good and punish bad behavior.

The other is a pluralistic perspective in which a state's preference and policy are aggregated from individual and group preferences through democratic processes, but the policy outcomes depend crucially on which individuals and groups are represented through formal and informal political processes (Dahl, 2006). With pluralistic public preferences, interest aggregation is a crucial governing function to generate sensible public policy. Policy behavior is determined by the relationship between individuals and groups, which is arbitrated by public officials through the state's legislative, administrative, and adjudicative institutions.

The elitist and pluralist perspectives are in frequent conflict but can be made compatible in the following sense. Suppose that leaders initiate a policy change as part of their platform. However, the change produces shocks to the policy domains that were predetermined by interest aggregation, generating losses for certain groups of individuals and gains to others. Sensitive to the distributive effect, leaders take the appropriate response to reduce losses and maintain gains, in order to re-establish the balance of interests and policy consistency. The extent of compensation is determined through political bargaining, and such a compensatory act constitutes coordination that helps the relevant actors' expectations converge, making policy change acceptable to them. Such a balanced response requires sensitivity, coherence in government, and a central command.

Central organization

A centralized political authority has an advantage over decentralized bureaucracies – it has a superior ability to make bureaucracies' policy behaviors mutually consistent. Centralization can reduce coordination failures, permitting a single leader to command the actions of all bureaucracies in the government. In other words, the central leadership coordinates different bureaucracies to resolve frequently occurring conflicts between tasks.

However, centralization comes at the price of costly communication and reduced agency discretion and initiative, which lower the benefits of specialization that accrues in a decentralized government. Centralization means higher costs of communication than in decentralization. With the reduced agency initiatives and specialization, a government becomes unable to adapt its policy domains and the economic institution to changing international rules. In general, a large policy change demands coordination, and thus centralization. A drawback of centralization may be an adaptation failure.

Globalization and the virtue of centralization

As globalization deepens the extent of policy adjustment shocks (frequency and scale), governments must improve their coherence and central command. From the intergovernmentalist perspective, legal formalism and political accountability are at the core of a policy change (Keohane and Nye, 1977). To promote a change at the international level, a treaty should be negotiated and agreed upon by political leaders accountable to the public with the help of professional diplomats and regulators. The agreed-upon treaty needs to be ratified and enacted by the legislature into a body of law that gives the government's regulatory agency the legal mandate to enforce it under executive and legislative supervision. Deviation from the treaty needs to be adjudicated by the judiciary to secure treaty compliance.

In this view, transgovernmental regulatory networks alone are insufficient to generate legitimacy, adjustment, and compliance. The political theory behind a policy change is *not* that the state is disaggregated and bureaucrats have the intrinsic power to coordinate with their foreign counterparts, but rather that the cabinet or executive branch, to which the bureaucrats are subservient, has the ability to set, *on behalf of the state*, the terms on which bureaucrats deal with their counterparts (Anderson, 2005, p. 1285). 'Much of [network] activity arises under the shadow of an intricate web of obligations arising from obligations assumed under treaties and international organizations' (Alvarez, 2001, p. 211). Informality associated with regulatory agreements detaches these state bureaucracies from the process of enforcing international regulatory standards. To secure adjustment and compliance, political leadership ought to take central control and lead policy coordination. Formal international treaties provide leadership with authority and legitimacy in meeting treaty obligations, which means adjustment to the international order including treaties. At the same time, treaties serve as *commitment* devices that prompt leadership to comply with treaty obligations; non-compliance creates external and internal audience costs that hurt the leadership's credibility and political support. In turn, leadership seeks to negotiate and conclude international treaties strategically in order to pursue a policy change, defeating opposition from special interests and bureaucratic politics.

1.5 CONCLUSION: STRUCTURAL DILEMMA, MANIPULATION, AND FLEXIBLE AUTHORITY ALLOCATION

The political leadership highlighted here is the one imbued with democratic governance in which the public chooses the officials of political organizations via competitive elections. These officials are in a position to envision the 'national interest', configure the government structure, and define the division of roles between political and bureaucratic officials in order to facilitate the appropriate mechanism of adjustment, either adaptation or coordination, in pursuit of the national interest. Normatively, democratic governance with either a decentralized or centralized structure restricts the oligarchic or rent-seeking behavior of public officials in pursuit of their own policy goals or patronage for their clients.

The analysis in this chapter implies that the government structural architecture involves a dilemma. On the one hand, the political command associated with a centralized structure is appropriate for control and coordination, but is likely to stifle policy adaptation because its central authority discourages bureaucratic officials from pursuing specialization and personal or organizational initiatives. On the other hand, the bureaucratic delegation associated with a decentralized structure is appropriate to promote the information and expertise necessary for communication and adaptation, but is unable to compel reluctant agencies to undertake costly coordination due to the leadership's reduced capacity to punish, reward or persuade them. Hence, an optimal architecture that can effectively deal with all types of institutional reforms is difficult to obtain.

In addition to the structural dilemma, self-centric public and private actors often hinder the choice of an appropriate structure. That is, influential groups in and out of government can manipulate the government structure to promote their own and their clients' interests. These groups seek to design a structure to ensure that their interests are well protected and carried out over time. That is, they seek to embed their particularistic interests into the structure (Moe, 2005; Aoki, 2010, p. 234).

In the age of globalization, policy authority allocation should be made strategically and flexibly based on an expansive set. In summary, this chapter shows that policy authority allocation is a frequent target of political contestation. The next chapter analyzes the government structural architectures empirically in the context of Japanese politics.

NOTES

1. A large Japanese business conglomerate.
2. Schelling (1960, pp. 57–9) argued that a focal-point effect can promote cognitive adjustment to an efficient equilibrium, but did not specify how to produce such an effect.

2. Empirical models of government structures and international adjustments

2.1 INTRODUCTION

In this chapter, the generalized normative analysis in the previous chapter meets related empirical models of Japanese politics. Recall that normative analysis suggests that neither a decentralized nor a centralized government can provide an optimal structural architecture for all conceivable cases. That is, there is an irrevocable dilemma between the two structural architectures. Thus, leadership needs to choose the appropriate authority allocation scheme according to the prevailing international order to define the problem of policy adjustment in relation to the state's institution.

In contemporary Japan, the government centralization thesis has gained favor. Many elected officials, analysts, and pundits invariably argue that Japan should centralize the existing decentralized structure and establish strong political leadership capable of performing at least three roles:[1] (1) readjustment of public policy domains to the emerging global order; (2) inter-ministerial task coordination for comprehensive liberalization and regulatory reform; and (3) the elimination of rent-seeking politics. The reformists argue that failure to fulfill these three roles has contributed to the underperformance of the Japanese economy for the last two decades. This normative argument has been put into practice since the early 1990s when Japan undertook political and administrative reforms to reinforce the leadership's policy authority in attempts to promote policy readaptation, inter-ministerial coordination, and rent elimination.

This centralization effort is not limited to contemporary Japan, but is also observed in the pre– and immediate post–World War II eras on at least three accounts. First, the Meiji oligarchs built a highly hierarchical government to protect the state's sovereignty and independence against colonial threats through the rapid transformation of feudalism into industrial capitalism and militarism. However, in conjunction with the promulgation of the Meiji Constitution, the government structure became decentralized and even fragmented to maintain the premodern institution of imperial sovereignty within the modern constitutional government, while bureaucracies were defined as servants of the emperor and counterweights to the parliament, with the cabinet as a mediator. Second, in the 1930s, as international competition intensified and imperialistic order emerged, Japan monopolized the government again to pursue political and economic unification for total national mobilization and war preparation. Third, the postwar government took advantage of the monopolistic authority inherited from the Supreme Commander for the Allied Powers (SCAP) in an attempt to rebuild the war-torn society and renovate industrial capacities. Once these imminent national objectives were achieved, the government regained a decentralized structure to facilitate continuous policy adaptation to changes in the international order through bureaucratic initiatives.

The contemporary and historical experiences summarized above embody the continuous struggles to establish the appropriate authority allocation schemes to seek imminent political values under changing international order. Different from the normative analysis, the empirical world entails cases in which the government structure is exploited by political actors as a choice to pursue not only the state's interest, but also their own or their clientele's sectoral interests. As a result, *degenerate* versions of a decentralized and centralized government emerge.

The following sections review the existing analytical models on the Japanese government structures in the pre- and postwar periods. The models can be divided into four basic types: (1) bureaucratic-adaptive or bureaucratic-cabinet; (2) central command; (3) bureau-pluralistic; and (4) monopolistic government. Each model describes the structural features, rationales, and pitfalls. The first two models roughly accord with the normative analysis in that the government structures are well adapted to perform immediate adjustment tasks. In contrast, the last two offer degenerate versions in which the government structures are ill suited to the adjustment needs and produce inefficient outcomes. Below, rearranging the order of presentation, I will show empirical models extrapolated from the existing scholarly literature on Japanese politics and discuss these models from organizational and rational perspectives. I will indicate that the existing studies are conscious of government structures and their impacts on policy behavior and outcomes; they often attribute policy ineffectiveness to inappropriate structures.

2.2 MODELS OF A DECENTRALIZED GOVERNMENT

2.2.1 Bureaucratic-cabinet Government

The decentralized bureaucratic-cabinet system (Iio, 2007, p. 49) has continuously been the defining feature of historical and contemporary Japanese politics despite the recent political and administrative reforms that have arguably centralized the government structure. From the bureaucratic-cabinet system's perspective, wherever efficient policy adaptation occurs, highly specialized bureaucrats and not commanding politicians have the ability to learn complex international rules, reflect rule changes in governmental policies, and implement these changes (Drucker, 1998). The bureaucratic-cabinet government hypothesis implicitly assumes the public interest theory of regulation and takes a benevolent view of bureaucratic organizations in which these organizations are rational, trustworthy, and public-spirited experts who produce and implement rules to ensure general economic efficiency and welfare for society. Equally important, Japanese bureaucratic organizations have been increasingly connected with transgovernmental policy networks and actively involved in negotiations for global rules and regulations with their foreign counterparts and international organizations (Shiroyama, 2013). These transgovernmental connections help improve bureaucrats' information and expertise, allowing them to adapt their policy domains appropriately to the changing international order. The existing literature accounts for the efficiency and legitimacy of a bureaucratic government from organizational and rational perspectives.

Organizational theory

Tsuji (1995) provided a prominent organizational analysis of the post–World War II Japanese bureaucratic system. He perceived the system as a continuous institution that evolved from the prewar constitutional monarchy. The democratic Constitution ensures that Weberian rational-legal authority is enshrined at the core of modern Japanese bureaucracy. Bureaucratic organizations are given well-defined missions and jurisdictions, which are functionally differentiated. Limited political appointments and a weak central command ensure the policy autonomy and political independence of bureaucracies. Similarly at the ministerial level, each ministry is composed of sub-units or bureaus with discrete policy domains that are only weakly linked. The policy autonomy of the bureaus and the bottom-up decision processes motivate bureau officials to acquire information and expertise for policy innovation. In addition, the practices of ministry-based recruitment and promotion embrace meritocracy, developing organizational norms of elitism and sectionalism. Yet, Tsuji noticed that the structural features of elitism, sectionalism, and the bottom-up decision-making process might also yield bureaucratic degeneration, if applied inappropriately.

Iio (2007, p. 49) characterized the postwar Japanese government as the 'bureaucratic-cabinet system' (*kanryo naikaku sei*) or the 'United Ministries of Japan'. He argued that bureaucratic initiatives are secured within the decentralized governing structure by Article 3(1) of the Cabinet Law, which stipulates that 'the Ministers shall divide among themselves administrative affairs and be in charge of their respective share thereof as the competent Minister, as provided for by other law'. Thus, once appointed by the prime minister, ministers are accountable for their ministries rather than for the cabinet, and they are advocates of their ministries' positions in cabinet meetings where unanimity is the decision norm. This means that a single minister's objection can bring the cabinet to a halt; that is, each ministry effectively has veto power. These institutional arrangements protect the ministries' political independence, but weaken the ability of the cabinet as the government's primary decision-making body to coordinate the ministries' policy actions.

The bureaucratic-cabinet system was the core of the 1955 political regime that was characterized as a 'bureaucracy-inclusive democracy' (Inoguchi, 1993) or 'patterned pluralism' (Muramatsu and Krauss, 1984). Both concepts imply that bureaucracies play prominent roles not just in policy-making and implementation, but also in interest aggregation and arbitration within their jurisdictional policy domains through collaboration with social groups and elected officials. In this sense, Makihara (2009, pp. 179–249) goes further and argues that the bureaucracies can complement the cabinet in policy coordination. He pointed out two peak bureaucratic organizations – the Ministry of Finance (MOF) and the Cabinet Legislation Bureau (CLB) – that perform the functions of arbitrating inter-ministerial disputes on budgetary and legal issues, respectively.

Even for issues unrelated to budget or law, two other inter-ministerial coordination mechanisms exist – vice-ministers' (top administrators of ministries and agencies) conference and consultation between ministers' bureaus (*daijin kanbo*). These mechanisms rely on the norms of equality and comity, consensual decision-making, and administrative memorandums for comprehensive coordination (*sogo-chosei*) at the inter-ministerial level. Even if a coordination problem occurs between ministries' tasks, the decentralized government still can resolve it through horizontal inter-ministerial negotiations. Conversely, the absence of a robust central command within the Japanese government can be ascribed to the efficiency of horizontal coordination at the bureaucratic level.

However, existing evidence and empirical analyses in the rest of this book suggest that inter-ministerial coordination is moderate at best. Particularly when ministries' policy tasks are substitutive, which can be represented as negative coordination in a battle of sexes (see Table 1.2 in Chapter 1), the two ministries with equivalent authorities can hardly resolve the coordination problem because neither is in a position to compel the other to alter its policy task against its organizational interest. Hence, inter-ministerial coordination as suggested by Makihara (2009) can be understood as adaptation with complementary policy tasks or positive coordination (Table 1.1 in Chapter 1), rather than negative coordination with substitutive policy tasks.

Rational theory

Under a democratic constitution, such as the postwar Japanese Constitution, which stipulates political supremacy over bureaucracy, a decentralized government can be viewed as a result of the political leadership's deliberate delegation of policy authority to bureaucratic officials. It is generally known from the principal–agent theory that bureaucratic delegation ensues when any one of the following four conditions is met: (1) preference symmetry between politicians and bureaucrats; (2) informational uncertainty that compels risk-avoidant politicians to avert policy responsibility; (3) ex post monitoring of bureaucratic policy performance; and (4) politicians' long tenure (Huber and Shipan, 2008).

In the Japanese case, during the long tenure of the Liberal Democratic Party (LDP) government, at least three conditions were met for bureaucratic delegation. First, preference symmetry was secured through substantial political recruitment from the elite bureaucratic circles – during the heyday of the 1955 system, about 30 percent of LDP parliamentary members were ex-bureaucrats who provided the party with policy information, bureaucratic connections, and even ministries' policy positions. Second, if a policy environment was uncertain or complex, politicians turned to bureaucratic delegation in order to encourage bureaucrats to improve their information and expertise in pursuit of policy improvement. Third, a principal (political leader) could monitor and control an agency's (bureaucrat's) behavior with the appropriate mechanisms of oversight and incentive. Indeed, the governing LDP had Policy Affairs Research Committees (PARCs) overseeing bureaucracies' performance as a 'fire alarm'.[2] PARCs have strong connections with interest groups that provide PARC officials with independent information on bureaucratic policy performance. The groups also offered post-agency employment, which PARC officials could use as an incentive to improve bureaucratic performance to the groups' advantage.

Because the party had a stable coalition of supporters and was expected to maintain government control for the foreseeable future, LDP members had long-term reputation-based relations with bureaucrats. Therefore, bureaucrats seldom initiated policy programs that might undermine the LDP's political and electoral foundation; if they had done so, PARC officials would have noticed it and urged the party leaders to curtail next year's budget or post-agency employment opportunities allocated to their ministry. This implicit contractual relationship made it possible for the LDP leadership to safely delegate policy authority to bureaucrats without worrying about moral hazard.[3]

2.2.2 Bureau-pluralistic Government

Despite the positive appraisal with postwar high economic growth, the bureaucratic-cabinet system has increasingly been met with criticism, as bureaucratic performance appears to have dwindled over growth stagnation and scandals. Critics often point to ministries' organizational inefficiency, inability to coordinate their policy actions, and single-minded pursuit of ministries' or even bureaus' organizational interests, rather than the public well-being.

Organizational theory

Imamura (2006) ascribes a degenerate bureaucratic system largely to the norm of 'sectionalism' derived from the fragmentary structural and personnel arrangements as well as ministry-based recruitment and promotion. Imamura suggests that sectionalism undermines the decentralized coordination mechanisms, frequently generating inter-bureau conflicts within a ministry and inter-ministerial conflicts within the government. In the absence of a robust central command, these conflicts make rational policy-making and implementation extremely difficult. The rigorous jurisdictional arrangements over segmented policy domains provide bureaus and ministries with the power to veto policy proposals that cut across jurisdictional lines and undermine their organizational interests. Emboldened with the veto power, bureau and ministry officials conduct inter-bureau and inter-ministerial negotiations, in which their bargaining power rather than policy rationality is the key to decision outcomes.

Pertinent to this book's topic, for a non-liberal state like Japan, a degenerate bureaucratic government would disallow adjustment to a liberal international order because its national rules and standards differ significantly from the order and because the ministries as custodians of the rules and standards object to the adjustment due to their own organizational interests.

Rational theory

Despite policy irrationality, a degenerate decentralized government can be explained from the perspective of individual and organizational rationality that dismisses the public interest approach assumed by the bureaucratic-adaptive model as politically naive and empirically wrong (Wilson, 1989). It takes the view that far from being public minded, bureaucrats are narrowly self-interested and are persistent in their bureaucratic missions even at the expense of rival ministries. This individual rationality perspective is entailed in Aoki's (2000, p. 156) model of 'bureau-pluralism', which accounts for the reduced efficiency of a decentralized government particularly at the time of changing international order to which it has to adjust national rules and standards.[4]

Within this model, pluralistic interests are represented and arbitrated on the basis of collusion between an industrial association, parliamentarians, and a relevant administrative bureau controlling that industry. Industrial interests are represented by elected officials (known as single-issue 'tribal [*zoku*] parliamentarians')[5] of the ruling party and are submitted to a relevant bureau in its jurisdiction, while bureaus in turn represent and promote jurisdictional interests that are compatible with their own interests in the administrative processes. Interest groups provide bureaucrats with not just policy information, but also post-agency employment in exchange for regulatory rents. The bureau-pluralistic network is resistant to change because it is an internal equilibrium underpinned by the individual, bureaucratic, and industrial interests.

The bureau-pluralistic argument can be reframed as an agency problem in the parlance of the principal–agent theory. The theory holds that a principal (political leader) cannot easily monitor or even control an agency's (bureaucrats') behavior, due to informational asymmetry, inappropriate incentive schemes, or both. Oversight and incentive measures are often ineffective if bureaucrats collude with industrialists and tribal parliamentarians to cheat on the political leadership to provide lax regulations or excessive subsidies for private rents. Tribal parliamentarians have incentives to cater to narrowly defined sectoral interests primarily because of the electoral system of the 1955 regime.

Under the electoral system, which still has a lingering effect on contemporary Japanese politics, members of the House of Representatives were elected through single non-transferable votes (SNTVs) for which three to five members were chosen in each of 130 districts across the nation (510 seats in total with some variation over time). The winning vote threshold in each district was typically well below 50 percent and could be achieved by obtaining support from a major industrial sector in a district (e.g., agriculture, construction, manufacturing, etc.) and its stakeholders (employees, managers, suppliers, their families, etc.). Moreover, because a major party needed to win at least two seats in each district, the party had to run multiple candidates who were compelled to vie against one another for district votes. Thus, intra-party conflict ensued, weakening its president, who would be a prime minister candidate. Thus, under weak political leadership and strong sector–candidate ties, parliamentarians colluded easily with bureau officials in order to protect the sector's interest for its continuous electoral support at the cost of national well-being. This is also the reason why tribal parliamentarians who might be in a position to arbitrate inter-ministerial policy conflicts would actually do so for rents in the bureau-pluralistic manner (Inoguchi and Iwai, 1987).

Although admitting that intimate party–bureau–industrial connections are a contributing factor to postwar Japanese economic success, advocates of the bureau-pluralistic model argue that these connections have lost utility because they are increasingly ill-fitted to a globalizing economy and because worsening of bureau-pluralism yields a feeling of unfairness and substantial economic losses. Calder argued that '(d)ecentralization of administrative and political power is also increasing, leading to more complex and pluralistic Japanese decision-making processes that make it simultaneously easier both for competitive firms to escapc from government constraints and for non-competitive firms to co-opt them' (1995, p. 209). The consequence will be disastrous, costing the nation dearly due to income and employment losses.

2.3 MODELS OF A CENTRALIZED GOVERNMENT

2.3.1 Central-command Government

For a non-liberal state, adjustment to a liberal international order generates a direct, major impact on its existing institutions and policies through displacement (i.e., the wholesale replacement of traditional rules and institutions with new ones). Such new programs require creative policy engineering to avoid resistance. Institutions are redirected toward new goals, functions, or purposes, which may be derived through changes in power relations, such as the empowerment of actors who were not involved in the existing design of an institution or the emergence of strong political leaders at the top of the centralized government structure capable of resolving the contestation to promote institutional reform. To adjust its economic system to a liberal international order, a non-liberal state has to undergo a major reallocation of the policy authority for the central command. As shown in the next section, many observers find that considerable centralization and leadership empowerment have occurred in contemporary Japanese politics.

Organizational theory

Strong leadership is often attributed to an individual's competence and characteristics. Insofar as strong leadership is observed ubiquitously across multiple cabinets, as in recent Japan, one has to invoke a structural theory that ascribes the dominance of political leadership to the organization of government. There are at least three sources for a strong prime minister. First, as suggested by Kitaoka (2008), the prominent source of leadership is provided by the Constitution of Japan promulgated in 1947. Under the democratic Constitution, the prime minister is chosen by the Diet (Article 67) and thus basically enjoys parliamentary support during his or her tenure. Even if the lower house passes a motion of non-confidence that he or she fails to counter, he or she can still dissolve the House of Representatives and call for a snap election to become resurrected as the new prime minister (Article 69).[6] The Constitution acknowledges the cabinet as the state's executive body (Article 65), giving the prime minister the powers and duties to represent the cabinet, submit bills, report national affairs and foreign relations to the Diet, and exercise control and supervision over various administrative branches (Article 72). Last, the prime minister has the power to appoint and fire cabinet ministers (Article 68). These powers granted to the prime minister by the postwar Constitution are far greater than those granted to the prewar prime minister by the Meiji Imperial Constitution (see Section 2.3.2 under Core-executive model).

Second, Harukata Takenaka (2006) and Machidori (2012) argued that recent prime ministers have expanded their policy authority by changing the executive organizations and the procedure for cabinet-sponsored legislative bills. For the former, Prime Minister Hashimoto improved the policy-making and inter-ministerial coordination capabilities of the Prime Minister's Office (the Cabinet Office since 2001) by recruiting elite bureaucratic officials from ministries and agencies. For the latter, Prime Minister Koizumi reduced the long-standing practice of prior consultation on cabinet-sponsored bills with the governing party officials, in an attempt to enhance his law-making initiative. Although such consultation was used to obtain the majority party's support for the cabinet-sponsored bills within parliamentary deliberations over which the cabinet had limited control, it had a negative side-effect of providing rank-and-file party members with opportunities to taint cabinet-sponsored bills with special interests and constrain the prime minister's legislative initiative.[7] The abolition of prior consultation practices would enhance the prime minister's law-making power in an uncompromising fashion.

Third, the prime minister's control over bureaucratic and rank-and-file party officials has improved via the following reforms. In June 2014, the Abe Cabinet created the Cabinet Bureau of Personnel Affairs within the Cabinet Office, which evaluates senior bureaucratic officials' job performance and controls appointments for top administrative positions across all ministries and agencies.[8] In addition, electoral reform for the House of Representatives has given party chiefs the power to nominate party candidates (to be explained in greater detail in Chapter 5). In sum, these reforms have altered the previous practices and improved the Japanese prime minister's executive, legislative, and appointment powers, generating strong centralizing effects on the government structure and party organizations.

Rational theory

Contemporary prime ministers use their constitutional powers and organizational mechanisms to exert their own policy initiatives rather than delegate policy authority to bureaucracies. The general logic of the central political command is just the opposite of that of bureaucratic delegation discussed earlier. In general, it can be predicted that central command ensues for (1) a large preference asymmetry between politicians and bureaucrats; (2) informational certainty that enables politicians to take policy initiatives and engage directly in policy-making; (3) the absence of ex post monitoring of bureaucratic policy performance; and (4) politicians' short tenure (Huber and Shipan, 2008). In contemporary Japan, at least two rational reasons have occurred for politicians cutting back on bureaucratic delegation.

As for (1), political recruitments have decreased from the elite bureaucratic corps, with corresponding increases in recruitment from business and in the hereditary succession of parliamentary seats from incumbent LDP members to their siblings.[9] The reduced bureaucratic recruitment has enlarged the preference asymmetry between politicians and bureaucrats, eroding the reputational foundation that underpinned the bureaucratic-cabinet system. Furthermore, the Democratic Party of Japan (DPJ), which assumed power for the first time between 2009 and 2012, had a strong incentive to reduce bureaucratic delegation and implement its own policy platform because DPJ officials perceived that bureaucracies were programmed to defend the interests of the governing coalition of the LDP, which had been in power for more than half a century. For both major parties, the preference asymmetry increased between politicians and bureaucrats.

As for (2), it has become increasingly difficult to obtain correct policy information and analysis due to the multiplicity and complexity of international rules and recurring exogenous shocks under the global order. For the same reason, it has become difficult to evaluate bureaucratic performance with respect to (3). The former (2) should heighten the need for specialization and bureaucratic delegation, while the latter (3) should reduce it. Under the compounded policy environments, contemporary Japanese political leaders have turned to the Cabinet Office through which they can coalesce with top bureaucratic officials to improve inter-ministerial policy coordination as well as information and analysis, because they perceive an increasing preference asymmetry between them and rank-and-file bureaucratic officials, as noted in (1).[10] This type of political–bureaucratic collaboration at the pinnacle of the government hierarchy is referred to as the core-executive model explained in the next subsection.

As for (4), the replacement of the SNTV system with a mixed electoral system for the House of Representatives has made government turnovers possible. In fact, the LDP lost the 2009 general election to the DPJ, which proceeded to control the government from 2009 to 2012. Increased electoral competition has augmented both parties' willingness to appear competent in running the government by taking direct policy initiatives before the public eye. Due to the strong electoral and political incentives for policy control, political leadership has centralized the government structure.

In sum, scholars have observed that contemporary Japanese political leadership is increasingly robust and is built upon the above organizational and rational foundations. Yet they apply slightly different analytical models, including the Westminster, core-executive, and presidential models, to characterize Japanese political leadership differently with varying views on a prime minister's relationships with voters, party members, cabinet ministers, and bureaucratic officials as well as the relevant institutional arrangements.

2.3.2 Three Types of Centralized Government

Westminster model

According to Estévez-Abe (2006) and Ohyama (2003), the Japanese parliamentary system has been transforming into a Westminster system in the sense that it is (1) majoritarian with (2) a competitive two-party system, (3) internally coherent parties, and (4) a prime minister and cabinet firmly supported by a majority party. The system also entails the nearly complete fusion of the executive and legislative powers. In other words, the party with a majority in Diet forms the executive, defined by key positions (that is, prime minister and cabinet). The cabinet is collectively responsible for its decisions, and its members (or ministers) are individually responsible to the Diet for the work of their ministries and agencies. The majoritarian system is favorable to a liberal market economy that embraces consumer rather than sectoral interests because only a political party committed to pursuing majoritarian interests can win an election and control the government. This is a major change from the pre-reform system, which was characterized as (a) one-party predominant with (b) a multi-party system, (c) internally divided parties, and (d) a prime minister plagued with intra-party factional conflicts. Institutional reforms have corrected at least three of the four defects.

Since the mid-1990s, the power of the prime minister has improved markedly through electoral and administrative reforms. The old electoral system, the SNTV for the House of Representatives, was replaced with a mixed system that combines the first-past-the-post (FPTP) votes with the proportional representation (PR) votes. Among the 475 seats of the lower house, 295 are chosen through FPTP votes in single-member districts (SMDs), whereas the remaining 180 seats are chosen through PR votes in nine regional blocks (with the use of non-binding party lists). According to Duverger's Law, FPTP votes will produce a two-party system in which two parties compete for power and either one can capture a majority of seats in a parliamentary house; minor parties will become ineffective because of strategic voting or rational candidate withdrawal (Cox, 1997).[11]

In FPTP elections without primaries, a single candidate must be chosen by a party to run for each SMD to avoid vote fragmentation and to win a seat. This electoral arrangement shifts candidate nomination authority from factional to party leadership. Similarly, PR elections give party leaders opportunities to rank party candidates on a party list. Both electoral schemes compel rank-and-file party members to be subservient to their party leadership in pursuit of the nomination. A case in point is the 2005 general election, in which President Koizumi of the LDP refused to give party nominations to members who opposed his postal privatization bill. Instead he gave party nominations to hand-picked candidates who pledged to endorse the bill.[12] As a result, the mixed system has diminished factional politics and provided an institutional basis for a strong political leadership by empowering its nominating authority (Cox et al., 1999).

Important for the theme of this book is that the FPTP-centric electoral system has a transformative effect on the state's economic policy toward market liberalism. Rival parties need to appeal to the interest of a majority in the electorate or consumerist interest in order to obtain a sufficient number of votes and win office. Having assumed power, the victorious party leads a majoritarian government to cater to consumerist interests by improving market efficiency through regulatory policy, including competition law, property rights protection law, free trade policy, and so on. This is in direct contrast to the distributive policy that is earmarked for a narrowly defined sector of society and is often pursued by parties under a consensual democratic system based on proportional representation (including SNTV, which is a kind of PR with candidate votes). The PR produces a multiple party system in which small parties vie for seats by representing sectoral interests of business, labor, agriculture, and so forth, and the government has to be formed by a coalition of parties and maintained through coordination of sectoral interests that are represented by the parties in the coalition (Rogowski and Kayser, 2002; Persson and Tabellini, 2004).

In sum, the promotion of a liberal market economy inheres in a majoritarian political system whose party leadership has a strong electoral incentive to facilitate market efficiency through property rights protection and regulatory policy. Therefore, a liberal market economy co-evolves with a majoritarian political system. It is argued that the Japanese political system has become increasingly majoritarian under the FPTP-centric electoral system and, consequently, favorable for a liberal market economy (Rosenbluth and Thies, 2010).[13]

Core-executive model

As for the theory of core executive, Mitsutoshi Ito (2007) argued that the improvement in the prime minister's policy authority is primarily due to a major amendment to the National Government Organization Act (Kokka Gyosei Soshikiho) in 1998 that reorganized government bureaucracies and created a powerful Cabinet Office on top of the government hierarchy.[14] This amendment provides the prime minister with the power to initiate, legitimatize, and implement his or her policy projects (Harukata Takenaka, 2006; Iio, 2007). With the new administrative power and capable supporting staff, the prime minister can mimic a chief executive officer of a major business firm and run the government as a principal in control of bureaucracies as agents.

The use of core executive is not new to Japanese political history. During the Meiji Restoration, there existed the oligarchic government that could be characterized as the first coordinating core executive in Japan (Holliday and Shinoda, 2002, p. 94). Even before the cabinet system was formally introduced in 1885, a Cabinet Research Bureau was created in 1867, a Cabinet Legal Office in 1873, and a Cabinet Secretariat with five officers in 1879. From 1885 to 1889, the Japanese prime minister headed the cabinet with direct authority to instruct each ministry and preserve discipline with respect to cabinet decisions. The use of core executive for the Meiji Restoration could be justified by the imperative for rapid adaptation to the competitive international order of the late nineteenth century that threatened the sovereignty and independence of the embryonic modern state. Likewise, it may be viewed as legitimate for the contemporary Japanese leadership again faced with the similar, albeit less precarious, pressure to adapt to the global order of the early twenty-first century under which its economy has struggled to maintain competitiveness. What follows summarizes the prime minister's instruments and motives for playing a core-executive role.

Instrumentally, the prime minister can rely on the Cabinet Office staffed with the best and brightest drawn from ministries to initiate specific policy projects and to conduct comprehensive coordination across ministries and agencies from the pinnacle of the government hierarchy. For broad policy ideas, he or she can consult with the Committee on Fiscal and Economic Policy in the Cabinet Office, which is composed of top officials from the Bank of Japan, the Financial Services Agency, and business communities. The committee can give the prime minister a set of advice, legitimization, and even publicity pertinent to his or her policy agenda, which differs qualitatively from those of the deliberative councils set forth by bureaucratic ministries that legitimize the existent policies in their policy domains. In addition, political appointment has expanded beyond the positions of ministerships and parliamentary vice-ministerships to encompass a newly created position of senior vice-ministership, thereby increasing the prime minister's ability to oversee bureaucratic performance. This central control of bureaucratic appointment is unprecedented in postwar Japanese political history in which elected officials desisted from interfering with bureaucracies' personnel affairs for bureaucracies' autonomy and political independence based on the prewar experiences of policy distortions derived from such interference (see Chapter 3). Thus, the prime minister's expanded appointment power has evoked concerns about excessive political interference and policy monopoly.

As for motives, Japanese political leaders, similar to leaders in other countries, are pressured to make swift policy decisions to deal with global problems. They participate in international meetings sponsored by G7, G20, WTO, IMF, APEC, and so on, and are asked to fulfill Japan's responsibility as a major state. They are irritated by slow bureaucratic deliberations and sectoral concerns. In a nutshell, prime ministers have increasingly perceived bureaucratic organizations as antithetical to their policy agenda and have sought to internalize the policy authority within close elite circles at the Cabinet Office and to control bureaucratic organizations as agents.

Presidential model

As observed by Krauss and Nyblade (2005) and Musashi (2008), contemporary prime ministers are seen to behave like presidents, with the capacities of the major campaign manager for his or her party and the chief policy-maker in government. Even though indirectly chosen, the prime minister can appeal directly to the public using modern public relations techniques in order to gain popularity and public support for their policy agenda. While disclaiming parliamentary and intra-party procedures, the prime minister can exploit public support to legitimize his or her policy agenda in democratic terms and to obtain consent from his or her party colleagues, coalition partners, and even opposition members. There is positive correlation between a prime minister's popularity and the passage of government bills in the Diet, which in turn reinforces his or her incentive to be presidential.

According to Poguntke and Webb (2007), this phenomenon of presidentialism has appeared across parliamentary systems in Europe as well as in Canada and Australia. Poguntke and Webb attributed this in part to the internationalization of political economy in which swift and coherent decisions are demanded. Surrounded by similar political and policy environments, the Japanese prime minister is no exception to the international trend for presidentialism.

A caveat is in order. Within the context of presidentialization, popular selection of prime minister was debated formally by the Prime Minister's Office in the 1990s and was rejected for the reasons of (1) the risk of populism; (2) incongruity with Article 1 stipulating the emperor as 'the symbol of the State' and Article 6 stipulating that 'the Emperor shall appoint the prime minister as designated by the Diet'; and (3) disconnecting the governing party from the prime minister and the cabinet to the detriment of parliamentary democracy.[15] Despite the formal rejection of presidentialism, an informal variant may appear in practice, depending on the time of office – the tenure of Prime Minister Junichiro Koizumi is often selected as the closet match.

2.3.3 Monopolistic Government

Because of its commanding position, a centralized government may not be suited to information collection and analysis, which are crucial to rational policy-making and implementation. A centralized government will degenerate into a monopolistic one if its structure is highly hierarchical and if its coercive power undermines individual rights and initiatives excessively. A monopolistic government stifles the flow of communication between bureaucratic units and political leadership, which prevents proper analyses and results in irrational policy decisions.

One prominent example is the prewar cabinet of Prime Minister Fumimaro Konoe, who Tsutsui (2009) characterized as a populist leader. With his charismatic personality and noble background, Prime Minister Konoe tried to exert his leadership to prevent the increasingly assertive Imperial Army from taking over the government but committed disastrous economic and diplomatic policy blunders (see Chapter 3). In attempts to appease the army, he acquiesced to Foreign Minister Yosuke Matsuoka's dismissal of diplomats with liberal orientations and admitted the conclusion of the tripartite pact, the adoption of the East Asia Co-prosperity Sphere (Dai-to-a Kyoeiken), and refused to negotiate peace with Chiang Kai-shek without legitimate diplomatic information sources. Although Japanese war aggression was attributed to the subsequent military government, Konoe was not immune to the criticism that his cabinet laid the groundwork.

It is alleged that a sign of monopolistic government has re-emerged under recent economic stagnation; populist leaders have taken advantage of public discontent and sought to promote radical policy shifts in pursuit of a quick economic recovery and electoral gain (Ohtake, 2003). Their strategies have been to enhance government centralization and circumvent bureaucratic and parliamentary deliberations by reinforcing the prime minister's commanding authority. In an extreme case, centralization might create another monopolistic government and discourage bureaucracies from pursuing information and expertise for sensible policy adaptation to changing the international order.

Organizational theory

The organizational and legal arrangements discussed already for leadership empowerment can be exploited by the prime minister to act as a monopolistic leader. Empowerment and monopolization are two sides of the same coin. For instance, a threat of parliamentary dissolution may silence meaningful opposition, whereas the abusive use of bureaucratic appointment power may create subservient officials with biased information and twisted expertise just to please their superiors. Thus, a centralized authority is untenable due to its failure to generate sufficient diversity or problem-solving strategies (Miller, 1992, p. 94). Without the appropriate delegation, a centralized government would suffer from high communication costs, reduced agency initiatives, and failure to adapt appropriately to changing international order.

Rational theory

It seems collectively irrational for leadership to seek monopolistic power. However, from the perspective of individual rationality, there are at least two explanations for monopolistic leadership. According to Ohtake (2003), political monopoly is an outcome of intense electoral competition, which compels incumbent leaders to take central command and demonstrate their policy competence to the voters in attempts to stay in power. Another explanation hinges on human nature and attributes monopolistic leadership to the Machiavellian pursuit of power and glory (Samuels, 2005). Although a competent leader may have the benevolent intent of serving the public interest with the maximal use of his or her constitutional power, it is difficult to ascertain the leader's human nature objectively. What is certain is that the more commanding their position, the less constrained the egoistic pursuit of power and glory may be. It is known within the scholarship of constitutional law that a decentralized arrangement is an effective structural counterweight to monopolistic human behavior (Takahashi, 2006). If the counterweight is reduced for leadership empowerment, the prospect of a monopolistic government looms large.

2.4 STRUCTURAL DEFECTS AND ANCILLARY AUTHORITIES

As hypothesized in the previous chapter and evidenced in the preceding sections of this chapter, government structural architecture has an irrevocable dilemma. On one hand, a centralized government is strong for coordination but is ineffective in adaptation by stifling bureaucratic innovation. On the other, a decentralized government is useful for bureaucratic innovation but is ineffective in inter-ministerial coordination due to the absence of a central command or manipulation by rank-and-file bureaucrats and party officials for regulatory rents. Practitioners notice these structural defects of dilemma and manipulation, and often use ancillary authorities to reduce them, broadening the conventional wisdom on policy authority.

2.4.1 External Pressure as an Ancillary Coordination Authority

As noted earlier, bureau-pluralistic practices may be an internal equilibrium under a decentralized government. Policy reformers who are scattered across the governing party, bureaucracies, and the public may be unable to coordinate their actions out of individual rationality and gather a sufficient political momentum to centralize the government structure and eliminate inefficient practices in the absence of a robust central command. Under these circumstances, the only force for policy change may be found outside the state.

Schoppa (1997) observed that, to break the domestic impasse and effect coordination for policy change, Japanese reformers coalesced strategically with external forces, such as the United States, which is the largest importer of Japanese products and the national security guarantor. The United States took part in the 'transnational alliance' and pressure for an institutional reform in Japan if it viewed the change was in its own interest to expand market shares. Thus, successful reform ensued if interests overlapped sufficiently to form a powerful transnational alliance that approximated a quasi-central authority to exert coordination pressure upon a decentralized government. Hence, the external pressure or *gaiatsu* effectively constitutes an 'external ancillary authority' that reformers in Japan exploit to promote coordination for policy change.

In the age of globalization, external ancillary authorities are more than just the United States. Multilateral and regional institutions of which Japan is a contracting party can be used as agents to promote policy change at home. By definition, these institutions entail rules, norms, and principles that a contracting state has accepted as international obligations to pursue public interest (Keohane et al., 2009). If a protectionist force or regulatory capture emerge that hinder the implementation of the obligations to protect sectoral interests at the expense of public interests, the international institutions are used to exert pressure for compliance.

2.4.2 Political Opposition as an Ancillary Information Provider

Particularly within a centralized government, political leadership at the pinnacle of the organizational hierarchy may easily be cut off from communication, while bureaucratic officials are discouraged from acquiring specialization and supplying appropriate information to leadership.[16] Instead, under a competitive party system, an opposition party may provide the rival governing party with useful policy information to overcome an impending policy adaptation problem. It may do so because of its own political interest in appealing to the electorate, especially when it has a high policy qualification for running government better than the incumbent party in power. The more competitive the party system, the more willing an opposition party is to be a provider of policy information. Indeed, the creation of such a competitive party system was the official goal of the 1994 electoral reform that replaced the SNTV with a mixed electoral system for the House of Representatives.

However, in the delegated system where bureaucratic officials are well incentivized to acquire information and expertise, the informational utility of a competitive party system may be relatively low. This was the reason why parliamentary deliberations were often infertile under the LDP-led predominant party system (mid-1960s to mid-1970s), whereas the bureaucracies to which the governing party delegated policy authority were immersed with specialization and were ardent information providers and policy innovators. Incidentally, during the period of competitive party system between the early 1970s and the mid-1980s, opposition parties successfully raised the problems of social welfare minimalism, environmental degradation, urban decay, and so on, that were not well addressed by the bureaucracies or the LDP but were major public concerns. Despite intense inter-party competition, the governing LDP could manage to stay in power, while consenting partially to the opposition parties' policy ideas to mend these problems (Steiner et al., 1980). In effect, the opposition parties supplanted the informational role that was unfulfilled by the bureaucracies under the system of delegation with jurisdictional rigidity.[17]

Since the electoral reform in the 1990s, the utility of a competitive party system again has increased in the wake of government centralization, which has had a negative effect on bureaucratic incentives for specialization. This is vindicated by the fact that, only five years after the electoral change in 1999, the Law to Activate Deliberation in the Diet was enacted with the consent of all political parties in order to promote the exchange of opinions between parliamentary members, hold regular debates between the prime minister and opposition party chiefs, and reduce bureaucratic officials' roles in parliamentary deliberations (Ito, 2001). (The exception to this law is members' requests to respond to their questions.)[18] This suggests that because globalization increases the need for policy coordination and government centralization, vigorous parliamentary deliberations might be viewed as an important ancillary source of policy information to complement the declining bureaucratic information capability.[19]

2.5 CONCLUSION

Having reviewed the models on government structures, I am agnostic about the relative descriptive and explanatory utilities of the models because they might depend on the time and policy domains. In the remaining parts of this book, I will analyze contemporary and historical Japanese politics in reference to adjustments due to the changing international order by utilizing the models. In Chapter 3, I will examine the relationship between international order, government structures, and policy outcomes from the Meiji Restoration through the interwar period with an emphasis on the issue regarding the fall of party governments and the rise of militarism as a major policy adjustment failure.

NOTES

1. Among numerous writings on the subject, some representative ones include Ozawa (1994) as a politician, Takenaka (2008) as a scholar, and Furukawa (2011) as a bureaucrat.
2. This argument was originally developed by McCubbins et al. (1989) and applied by Ramseyer and Rosenbluth (1997, Chap. 7) to Japanese politics.
3. The government of the Democratic Party of Japan (DPJ) that was formed in the 2009–12 period did not have these properties and openly challenged the existent policy practices by refusing to delegate to the bureaucracies. However, as the bureaucratic government thesis predicts, the DPJ government failed to implement its new policy proposals without appropriate bureaucratic cooperation.
4. Similar models are advanced by Inoguchi and Iwai (1987) and Saito (2011).
5. See Inoguchi and Iwai (1987) for an extensive analysis of tribal parliamentarians.
6. Article 69 is said to provide the prime minister with *defensive* dissolution power. In contrast, Article 7 is said to provide *offensive* dissolution power. It states that 'the Emperor, with the advice and approval of the cabinet, shall perform the following acts in matters of state on behalf of the people: Promulgation of amendments of the constitution, laws, cabinet orders and treaties; Convocation of the Diet; Dissolution of the House of Representatives; and Proclamation of general election of members of the Diet'.
7. Since the end of Prime Minister Koizumi's tenure, the prior consultation practice has been resurrected to a limited extent.
8. The establishment of the Cabinet Bureau of Personnel Affairs was outlined by the Basic Act for Reforming Personnel Affairs on Government Officials (Kokka Komuin Seido Kaikaku Kihon-ho) in 2008. Previously, personnel affairs were divided and managed separately by three ministries with the following arrangements: the Personnel Affairs Agency handed out appointments while the Ministry of Finance made personnel budgets in accordance with the staff size and organization outlined by the Ministry of Home Affairs. These practices helped individual ministries maintain their autonomous personnel management.
9. For instance, recent Prime Ministers Hashimoto, Obuchi, Mori, Koizumi, Abe, Fukuda, Aso, and Hatoyama are either second- or third-generation parliamentarians.
10. In effect the Cabinet Office is given the twin tasks of adaptation and coordination. The empirical analyses in Part II of this book discuss how the Cabinet Office has executed the twin tasks for policy adjustments to the neoliberal order.
11. However, because it is not a genuine FPTP election, the mixed system has only produced an imperfect two-party system. The two leading parties obtained approximately 80 percent of the seats on average in the general elections for the House of Representatives held under the mixed system between 1996 and 2012. See Chapter 5 for the detailed analysis.
12. More precisely, Prime Minister Koizumi combined the power to dissolve the lower house with the power to nominate party candidates in an attempt to enact postal privatization. An interesting caveat is that the parliamentary house that had voted down the privatization bill was the upper house, not the lower house. In effect, by reconvening a new lower house with many pro-privatization members as a sign of popular approval, Prime Minister Koizumi successfully compelled the upper house to endorse the bill.
13. See Chapter 5 for more discussion on the relationship between a majoritarian political system and liberal market economy.
14. The idea of core executive is derived from the scholarly analyses of British political leadership by Rhodes (2007), Rhodes and Dunleavy (1995), and Smith (1999).
15. See the final report on popular selection of prime minister in Japanese at the website of the Prime Minister's Office http://www.kantei.go.jp/jp/singi/kousen/kettei/020807houkoku.html [in Japanese]; last accessed on 16 March 2015.
16. METI official Shigeaki Koga stated that bureaucratic officials sabotaged against the DPJ Cabinet that pursued political predominance in policy-making. This kind of

statement is extremely rare for an incumbent bureaucratic official. See *PHP Biz Online Shuchi*, 20 June 2011, at http://shuchi.php.co.jp/article/263/ [in Japanese]; last accessed 15 June 2014.

17. Having experienced the shrinking votes, the LDP expanded the roles of government to cover the overlooked policy domains. The Environmental Protection Agency and the National Land Agency were created in 1971. The ratio of the annual social welfare expenditure to national income doubled between 1970 and 1980.
18. Before the enactment of the Law to Activate Deliberation in the Diet, bureaucratic officials frequently made statements in the parliament as government officials (*seifu i'in*) to defend their ministries' legislative bills and policy positions.
19. A few caveats are in order. The governing party may not use information provided by the opposition if its quality is subpar, or if it hurts the governing coalition's interest. For the same reason, opposition parties cannot be a catalyst for coordination when they represent social interests that diametrically oppose the interests represented by the governing party. All they can do is provide information rather than coordination facilitation.

3. Adjustment struggles under pre–World War II international order

3.1 INTRODUCTION

The Meiji Restoration period (1868–90) highlighted the struggles to establish the appropriate government structure to meet the immense external challenges facing a fragile backward state. One major struggle was the task of transforming the premodern feudal state into a modern industrial state under the highly competitive international order of the late nineteenth century. The domain-clique government (*baku-han seifu*) headed by oligarchs (*genro*) was the first attempt, which was built upon the Great Council of State (Dajokan Sei), which had constituted the bureaucratic division of the Imperial Court system for centuries. The domain-clique government was the first coordinating core executive in Japanese history (Holliday and Shinoda, 2002, p. 94). Even before the cabinet system was formally introduced in 1885, a Cabinet Research Bureau was created in 1867, a Cabinet Legal Office in 1873, and a Cabinet Secretariat with five officers in 1879 (Naikaku-Seido Hyakunen-shi Hensan Iinkai, 1985, p. 30). From 1885 to 1889, the prime minister headed the cabinet with direct authority to instruct each ministry and preserve discipline with respect to cabinet decisions.

Despite the lack of elaborate constitutional structure, the domain-clique government was widely viewed as legitimate due to its commitment to protect the state's vital independence and sovereignty from colonial threats, unlike the preceding feudal Edo regime. However, its twin objectives of a rich nation and strong army (*fukoku kyohei*)[1] were mutually incompatible. Both required a substantial amount of capital, which early Meiji Japan lacked due to the limited national income and tax bases. To achieve the objectives, Marquis Hirobumi Ito proposed minimal mercantilism and restrained militarism due to the precariousness of the Japanese state with a shortage of capital and technology and a non-autonomous tariff regime under the competitive international order.[2] Through intense bargaining with his fellow oligarchs, Ito's proposal was adopted as the policy platform followed by the Meiji government for the next 20 years.

Within the constraint of minimal mercantilism, the government employed the schemes of small government and state–society collaboration, rather than big government and absolute state control, in order to achieve the industrial transformation of the agrarian economy.[3] In 1872, it launched an industrial development program (known as Shokusan Kogyo – Promotion of Industry) for coal, mining, silk, and shipbuilding inherited from the feudal lords. Until it regained partial tariff autonomy in 1907, the Meiji government had been compelled to work with the non-autonomous tariff regime that the Edo feudal regime had accepted under duress from Western powers as part of their treaty port systems. Since trade protection measures could not be taken, Japanese firms were exposed to direct international competition with the West and thus were pressed to improve efficiency through the exploitation of comparative advantage. Because the non-autonomous tariff regime revealed its relative abundance in labor and relative scarcity in capital, the Japanese economy specialized in light industries that turned out to be internationally competitive, contributing to economic growth in the early Meiji era. The domain-clique governments sought to modernize the embryonic industries with the help of imported Western technologies under state ownership and administrative control by the newly established Ministry of Industry (Kobu-sho). Having obtained technological and entrepreneurial know-how, all state-owned enterprises, except for military ones, were privatized and sold at low prices over the next five to 20 years to affluent merchants, who later became industrial capitalists or *zaibatsu* (conglomerate) families.

In 1889, the Meiji Imperial Constitution was promulgated to establish a modern government of constitutional monarchy, generating profound changes in the Japanese political economy. The Constitution replaced the centralized domain-clique government with a decentralized one that was led by a political party in the Imperial Diet. Yet its political centrality was deceptive – a party government was chosen by oligarchs with some reference to electoral outcomes and needed the moral support of the Imperial Court as well as the administrative support of bureaucracies. In addition, state expenditures were limited and financed primarily through the newly introduced land tax. Because the land tax rate exceeded the feudal rent, small farm owners had to sell their land to large landowners who became enfranchised under the Meiji Imperial Constitution. Together landowners and industrial capitalists participated in the governing coalition as vested interests, complicating national governance even further.

My analysis in the rest of this chapter focuses on a puzzle regarding the eventual collapse of party governments and the subsequent rise of militarism. As noted above, the Japanese political system became a quasi-parliamentary democracy within the framework of the Meiji Imperial

Constitution and followed Ito's minimal mercantilism and restrained militarism under the competitive international order of the nineteenth and early twentieth century. However, the party governments eventually collapsed in 1932, having tried to implement 'Cooperative Diplomacy' (*Kyocho Gaiko*) in attempts to adjust to the interwar liberal international order, known as the Versailles-Washington system. The puzzle is why party governments collapsed despite apparent harmony between parliamentary democracy at home and the interwar liberal order abroad. The demise of party democracy was followed by bureaucratic, constitutional-dictatorial, and grand coalition government, with intensifying militarism, total national mobilization, and warfare.

The puzzle has been debated intensely by scholars of Japanese political history. For instance, Mitani (2010) evaluates the formation of party government as an attempt to adjust to the interwar liberal international order but attributes its demise to the institutional defects of the Meiji Imperial Constitution. Mitani argues that the Constitution embraced the notions of imperial sovereignty and bureaucratic consultation and generated a decentralized fragmentary government with weak central control that was incapable of coordinating bureaucratic ministries and the associated vested interests. Second, Banno (2014) claims that inter-party competition, intensified by suffrage expansion and eventual universal male suffrage, yielded political corruption and distributive rents for the vested interests, reducing the party governments' political legitimacy and benefiting the military as the last and ultimate guardian of national governance. Third, Sakai (2007) argues that intense international conflict elevated the influence of the military at the expense of the civilian government, which fueled Japanese militarism and then amplified international conflict. This synergic effect derived from international and domestic politics paved the way for the collapse of party government and the destruction of the Japanese state.

In the rest of this chapter, I apply the empirical models on government structure discussed in the previous chapter to analyze the relationships between international order, government structure, and policy outcomes from the Meiji Restoration through the interwar period. The analysis intends to reconcile the domestic analyses of Mitani and Banno with an international analysis such as Sakai's on how the party government could adjust to the interwar liberal international order.

3.2 DECENTRALIZED GOVERNMENT UNDER THE COMPETITIVE INTERNATIONAL ORDER

3.2.1 Meiji Imperial Constitution and Fragmentary Government

A modern government of constitutional monarchy set forth by the Meiji Imperial Constitution entailed a decentralized structure with the following characteristics.

Article 4 stated that, in principle, the emperor held sovereign authority over the legislative, executive, and judicial powers. In practice, actual governance functions were distributed across the Imperial Diet, the Ministers of State, the Judicature, and the Privy Councilors. In this vein, the Meiji Constitution had no specific provision for an executive branch, other than Article 55 that stipulated that '(1) (t)he respective Ministers of State shall give their advice to the Emperor, and be responsible for it. (2) All Laws, Imperial Ordinances, and Imperial Rescripts of whatever kind, that relate to the affairs of the state, require the countersignature of a Minister of State'.

The cabinet and the prime ministership therefore had to be established by a separate statute, the Cabinet Ordinance (Naikaku Kansei). The prime minister was defined as *primus inter pares*, or the first among equals, with a duty to maintain unity among the administrative ministries (Article 2 of the Cabinet Ordinance). A problem of the Meiji Constitution was that the power to appoint and fire ministers was granted to the Council of Elders and not the prime minister. An influential constitutional lawyer, Professor Kenkichi Uesugi, interpreted this as a provision to allow ministers to fulfill their advisory roles (*hohitsu*) for the emperor without fear of being terminated (quoted in Takahashi, 2006, p. 110).

The major objective of functional delegation was to maintain imperial sovereignty and protect the monarchy from policy responsibility.[4] This advisory role as well as functional delegation accords with the theory of bureaucratic government discussed in the previous chapter; a decentralized structure might not be suited to promoting a non-liberal state's policy adjustment to the liberal international order. Under a decentralized government, administrative independence gave bureaucracies a monopoly on decision-making within their jurisdictional terrains, reducing the prime minister's coordination ability and making government policies incoherent (Beasley, 1993, p. 36). However, despite the functional fragmentation, the post–domain-clique government under the Meiji Constitution was still effective in pursuing wealth and power under the competitive international order of the late nineteenth and the early twentieth century. How could it adjust to the order?

3.2.2 Adaptation to the Pre–World War I Competitive International Order

The constitutional fragmentation described above did not produce a negative effect – the post–domain-clique governments were still capable of pursuing the joint tasks of state-led industrialization and military expansion. Internationally, moderate militarism and mercantilism were both legitimate under the competitive international order of the late nineteenth and the early twentieth centuries and thus constituted strategic counterparts that were manageable even by a decentralized government with limited coordination capabilities. The preceding laissez-faire international order eroded because of the Long Recession (1880–1914) that coincided with the decline of a liberal Britain and the ascent of a mercantilist Austria-Germany. The United States was still unwilling to pursue 'Open Door' diplomacy in Northeast Asia as a result of its cost–benefit analysis (Beasley, 1993, p. 100).

Mercantilism

Under the competitive order, Japanese mercantilism accelerated with the restoration of full tariff autonomy in 1910, generating a profound change in its economic institutions. The cabinet led by Prime Minister Taro Katsura began a policy of high import tariffs to further industrial development and concentrate capital and labor in the coal, steel, and machinery industries.[5] To facilitate state-led industrial finance, the Katsura Cabinet approved the establishment of the Development Bank of Japan (Nihon Kokyo Ginko) in 1902, which provided long-term loans based on bond issuance. Furthermore, it refurbished private commercial banks, which had been weakened from 1880 through 1902 in order to prioritize stock markets. In effect, the interventionist trade and investment policies produced a ('cheap talk') effect of attracting bank lending to key industries as well as a positive effect of expanding loan markets at the expense of stock markets (Table 3.1).

In the wake of state-led finance, block-stockholding practices at the firm level grew even further after a modern commercial code based on the German civil law was enacted in 1899, altering ownership diffusion under the existing embryonic stockholder capitalism.[6] Earlier in 1872, commercial banks had been established across the state under the National Bank Law, but their roles had been limited to bank note issuance rather than lending due to the lack of banking expertise and lending risks. Hence, the privatized firms had to rely on stock issuance; the first stock market was opened in Tokyo in 1878 and several regional markets in other major cities followed in subsequent years. To hedge risks, investors created holding

Table 3.1 Sources of industrial finance for all sectors

	(1) Stocks	(2) Reserves	(3) Bonds	(4) Loans	(5) Others	(4) + (5)/(1)
1902–05	66.2	16.7	9.0	2.5	5.6	0.12
1906–10	63.8	17.9	8.5	3.0	6.8	0.15
1911–13	62.1	17.8	10.7	3.3	6.0	0.15
1914–15	56.7	16.3	12.2	6.3	8.6	0.26
1916–20	55.7	22.9	11.7	2.6	7.1	0.17
1921–25	55.9	19.1	13.4	4.5	7.1	0.21
1926–27	51.6	13.2	21.8	6.1	7.4	0.26
1928–30	51.0	11.2	20.9	6.9	10.1	0.33
1931–35	52.4	11.1	21.6	7.0	8.0	0.28
1936–40	53.8	14.1	15.8	7.0	9.0	0.30

Note: Numbers are averages (percentages) for the respective periods. The data are obtained from Teranishi (2006, p. 17).

companies (later they became *zaibatsu* headquarters) to control a group of subsidiary firms whose stocks they held. To extract their utmost performance, the holding companies remunerated the subsidiary firms' managers based on profits (Okazaki, 1994). In this sense, Ohkawa and Rosovsky (1973, p. 39) appropriately characterized the Meiji Restoration as a dual structure of a pre-modern political oligarchy and a modern industrial society.

The microfoundations of improved bank lending and block-stockholding led to industrial concentration and helped *zaibatsu* to dominate the national economy in the absence of antimonopoly laws.[7] The concentration facilitated the shift from the labor-intensive light industry to capital-intensive heavy chemical and machinery industries that were non-competitive internationally (Table 3.2). Because of their inferior quality, the products of heavy and machinery industries had to be marketed only within the Japanese mainland and the occupied Korean Peninsula and 'Man-Mo' region (Manchuria and Inner Mongolia). As productive capacities grew via state-led finance, the economic incentive for territorial expansion would intensify to absorb the products. The state-led industrialization transformed the trade structure, shifting the main export items from raw materials to finished goods, and import items from finished goods to raw materials (Table 3.3). As a result, Japanese state-led industrialization amplified economic competition with the industrialized Western powers.

Table 3.2 Change in the industrial structure

Year	1885	1900	1920	1940	1960	1970	1980	1998
Agriculture and fisheries	45.2	39.4	30.2	18.8	12.8	5.9	3.6	1.7
Industry	14.7	21.2	29.1	47.4	40.8	43.1	37.8	31.7
Mineral	0.8	1.8	3.4	2.7	1.5	0.8	0.5	0.2
Manufacturing	10.7	15.0	20.6	37.0	33.8	34.9	28.2	22.6
Construction	3.2	4.5	5.0	7.7	5.5	7.5	9.0	8.9
Services	40.2	39.4	40.7	33.8	46.4	50.9	58.7	66.7
Wholesale and retail	–	–	–	–	11.4	13.9	14.8	11.3
Finance and insurance	–	–	–	–	3.5	4.1	5.0	4.7
Real estate	–	–	–	–	7.4	7.8	9.1	13.5
Transport and communication	2.5	3.7	6.5	4.9	7.3	6.7	5.9	6.3
Hotels, restaurants	–	–	–	–	7.4	9.3	11.3	17.5
Public services	3.5	3.1	2.9	3.4	6.2	6.1	8.2	8.0
Others	–	–	–	–	3.3	0.0	4.4	5.3
Total	100.0	100.0	100.0	100.0	100.0	100.0	100.0	100.0

Note: The figures are percentages of nominal added values of respective industries.

Source: The data are obtained from the Economic Planning Agency (2000).

Militarism

Militarism augmented under post–domain-clique governments saddled with a weak fiscal discipline and an increasingly competitive international order. Unlike the Meiji oligarchs, these governments based on either political parties or transcendental arrangements could not count on automatic parliamentary and bureaucratic support.[8] They had to assemble political support from party members as well as the military and bureaucratic officials. To do so, they were compelled to acquiesce to spending requests for electoral and organizational purposes.

The Imperial Army and Navy sought to exploit the government's weak fiscal discipline and the competitive international order to justify their arms build up and growing expenditure (Figure 3.1). As the Concert of Europe[9] eroded, controlled warfare became a legitimate foreign policy instrument for major powers. Accordingly, the Japanese limited wars against the Chinese and Russian empires in 1894–95 and 1904–05 were

Table 3.3 Trade structure by product

	Food	Raw Materials	Intermediate Products	Finished Products	Others	Total
Export						
1885	11.8	3.8	16.5	3.3	1.7	37.1
	(31.8)	(10.2)	(44.5)	(8.9)	(4.6)	
1886–90	15.6	6.9	26.5	7.7	2.2	58.8
	(26.5)	(11.7)	(45.0)	(13.0)	(3.7)	
1891–95	18.9	10.0	45.5	23.9	3.6	101.9
	(18.5)	(9.8)	(44.7)	(23.5)	(3.6)	
1896–1900	22.5	20.2	80.7	44.5	5.3	173.2
	(13.0)	(11.7)	(46.6)	(25.7)	(3.0)	
1901–05	35.2	27.0	132.8	85.4	7.7	288.2
	(12.2)	(9.4)	(46.1)	(29.6)	(2.7)	
1906–10	47.3	39.2	196.5	131.6	6.5	421.2
	(11.2)	(9.3)	(46.7)	(31.3)	(1.5)	
1913	62.1	51.3	328.1	184.9	6.0	632.5
	(9.8)	(8.1)	(51.9)	(29.2)	(0.9)	
Import						
1885	6.4	1.6	7.0	13.9	0.5	29.4
	(21.8)	(5.4)	(23.8)	(47.3)	(1.7)	
1886–90	11.4	4.3	16.6	24.5	1.1	58.0
	(19.7)	(7.5)	(28.6)	(42.3)	(1.9)	
1891–95	20.4	19.6	18.9	32.7	2.4	93.9
	(21.7)	(20.8)	(20.1)	(34.9)	(2.5)	
1896–1900	54.8	62.9	41.6	72.8	3.2	235.2
	(23.3)	(26.7)	(17.7)	(30.9)	(1.4)	
1901–05	84.4	112.3	53.0	86.2	5.0	340.9
	(24.8)	(32.0)	(15.5)	(25.3)	(1.5)	
1906–10	64.5	175.4	81.8	116.3	3.7	441.6
	(14.6)	(39.7)	(18.5)	(26.3)	(0.8)	
1913	120.6	353.5	126.9	124.0	4.4	729.4
	(16.5)	(48.5)	(17.4)	(17.0)	(0.6)	

Sources: The data are obtained from the 'Main Economic Indicators after Meiji', Bank of Japan (1966, p. 280) and from Oku (1990, p. 162).

still in conformity with the order.[10] To enhance its fighting capability even further, the Imperial Army requested the creation of two divisions in 1912. Having been rejected by Prime Minister Saionji for reasons of fiscal integrity, the army took advantage of the cabinet rule stipulating military ministers as active-duty officers, refused to nominate a new army minister

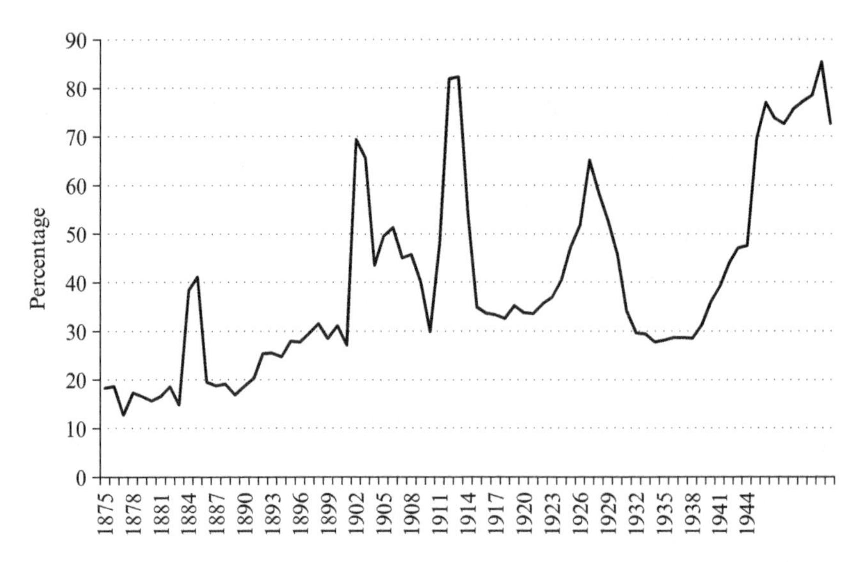

Source: The figure is constructed from the statistical archives of Teikoku Shoin Co. Ltd., Tokyo.

Figure 3.1 Percentage of military spending in government expenditure

and brought down his cabinet, successfully obtaining two divisions from the succeeding cabinet.[11]

From the vantage point of the Western powers, Japan's mercantilist-militarist assertiveness appeared well coordinated and coherent; mercantilism and militarism were strategic complements under the pre–World War I international order. However, both accelerated independently in Japan through the manipulation of a decentralized Meiji constitutional government with fragile political support and a weak fiscal discipline.

3.3 DEGENERATION OF PARTY GOVERNMENT UNDER THE INTERWAR LIBERAL ORDER

3.3.1 Party Government and the Versailles-Washington System

Interwar liberal international order

After the end of World War I, the complementary relationship between mercantilism and militarism evaporated in the course of a change in the international order. The Treaty of Versailles sought to transform the prewar mercantilist order into a liberal one. Based on the Wilsonian principle that international peace and prosperity would inhere in a liberal order, states were urged to pursue open trade and disarmament. The League of Nations was created as the key international organization to promote the Versailles system and alter the pre–World War I norms. In addition, in the region of Northeast Asia, the United States sought to reinvigorate Open Door Diplomacy and establish a liberal trade order in pursuit of its commercial opportunities.

Ascendance of party government and Cooperative Diplomacy

Between 1920 and 1932, cabinets were formed by majority parties in the House of Representatives based on the dictum of 'constitutional democracy' (*kensei no jodo*). This shift to party democracy was a consequence of parliamentary practice as well as principle. In practice, the Meiji Constitution stipulated that a parliamentary majority was needed for legislative bills to be enacted by the Imperial Diet. In principle, the ascendance of party government was Japan's political response to the interwar liberal international order in conjunction with the internal development of civil society via modernization, urbanization, and mass education. The period when party cabinets reigned was referred to as the 'Taisho Democracy', which relied on a parliamentary system at home and the Versailles-Washington system abroad.

In addition, in order be a responsible and often 'silent partner' in the new international order, Japan, led by party cabinets, took on the principle of 'Cooperative Diplomacy' with the West and tried to act as a status quo state, upholding the Versailles-Washington system. Cooperative Diplomacy was officially adopted by Foreign Minister Kijuro Shidehara under the Kenseikai Cabinet led by Prime Minister Taka'aki Kono (1924–26) and another Kenseikai Cabinet led by Prime Minister Osachi Hamaguchi (1929–31), yet, embryonic Cooperative Diplomacy had already emerged with the abolition of the Ishii-Lansing Agreement concluded with the United States in 1917 that had given Japan a special privilege in trade with China for honoring the Nine-Power Treaty[12] reached in 1922 based on the spirit of Open Door Diplomacy. This was followed by Hara Seiyukai Cabinet's ceasing interventionist policy in northeast China and participating in the Four-Power Loan Consortium to China.

Between 1922 and 1932, Cooperative Diplomacy was followed more or less by two rival parties – the Kenseikai (later Minseito) and the Seiyukai, which alternated in government. For both parties, Cooperative Diplomacy was a means to balance Japanese and Western interests and pursue growth and strength within an international framework to which Japan was willing to conform. Because of their democratic nature, the party governments seemed to be suited to pursuing Cooperative Diplomacy and facilitating policy adjustment to the liberal international order.

Nonetheless, Cooperative Diplomacy involved the irrevocable contradiction that a liberal outlook was weighted against an authoritarian constitutional framework and mercantilist vested interests. And weighing Cooperative Diplomacy against aggressive mercantilism, the party government was aware of the international imperative to pursue the former, but was unable to achieve necessary domestic coordination because of intense inter-party competition and inter-ministerial disagreements under a series of post–World War I economic recessions. As the rival parties vied against each other for power, their governments became increasingly acquiescent to greater military spending, like their post–domain-clique predecessors, in order to obtain a wide range of constituent and bureaucratic support (see Figure 3.1). Prime Minister Takashi Hara, who led the first party-centric cabinet, launched four major expansion programs for arms, industry, railways, and higher education. Subsequent party governments followed a similar path, reverting gradually to the policy of aggressive mercantilism (Okazaki, 2004). Two additional factors were behind the policy change.

First, because of the earlier economic success, the policy of aggressive mercantilism was entrenched deeply within the vested interests represented in the decentralized government, including *zaibatsu* monopolists, urban bourgeoisie, and military officials.[13] The wars against China and Russia had given Japan a dominant commercial position in the Man-Mo region. In view of the past mercantilist success, these groups became increasingly assertive in claiming Japanese privilege in the region for further industrial expansion. More precisely, each of the groups had internal disagreements that made them acquiescent to Cooperative Diplomacy at the initial stage, however, a radical faction gradually gained a dominant position over a moderate one within each group, as the domestic economy stagnated in the aftermath of the war boom and the Republic of China intensified its sovereign claim in the region.

Second, the Imperial Army skillfully manipulated industrial interests for territorial expansion in the Man-Mo region (Yanagisawa, 2002). State-led industrial production defied the market principle and continuously needed state help in locating resources and markets, which remained scarce because Western powers were reluctant to liberalize their colonies. The army was instrumental in exploiting this industrial weakness by making available the resources and markets in an expanded territory in the region for industrial use.[14] In particular, new *zaibatsu* led by Nihon Sankyo, Nihon Chisso, Showa Denko, and Rikagaku Kenkyujo, were eager to embark on collaboration with the radical army officials and the new bureaucrats (to be discussed below) by building major industrial networks in the region.[15]

The military–industrial marriage of convenience was made possible by the fragmentary government within which political leadership had limited control over the bureaucracies.[16] The continuation of aggressive mercantilism was an outcome of failed internal coordination and was a means to maintain the military–industrial coalition that sustained the fragile governments.

3.3.2 Coordination Deadlock

The policy of aggressive mercantilism was increasingly inappropriate for the interwar liberal order. The League of Nations outlawed war via the Kellogg-Briand Pact and called for naval disarmament at the London Conference. It also urged the restoration of the most favored nation (MFN) network through world economic conferences, although contracting states were slow to respond to the call by maintaining the prewar high tariffs and quantitative restrictions (Irwin, 1993, pp. 103–5). In addition, Western states began to adopt the gold standard to preserve monetary credibility and prevent beggar-thy-neighbor competitive currency devaluation. Furthermore, to reduce international tensions and preserve the status quo, Western states attempted to negotiate for spheres of influence agreements and naval disarmament treaties. More specifically, their legal approach included (1) the Four-Power Treaty (1921), which secured mutual respect and peaceful conflict resolution in the Pacific among Japan, the United States, the United Kingdom, and France, (2) the Nine-Power Treaty (1922), which secured the Open Door, guaranteeing equal access in China, and (3) a naval disarmament treaty that constrained naval build up based on weighted ratios consistent with existent naval powers.

These international agreements were supposed to guide Japan's Cooperative Diplomacy and facilitate its adjustment to the liberal order as an external ancillary authority. However, Japan's decentralized government was internally divided on compliance with the treaties. Some found the 'liberal' shift unfair to Japanese industries, which they thought still held inferior technological and foreign-reserve positions and could not compete well in international markets without tariff protection and a devalued currency.[17] Others found that the status quo–preserving sphere of influence agreement was unfavorable to Japan with limited colonies (have nots), compared to the Western powers with many (haves).[18]

The difficult tasks of coordination had to be performed between competing vested interests of the governing coalition. Specifically, the Nine-Power Treaty needed coordination between the diplomatic interest in cooperation with the West and the military–industrial interest in controlling Manchuria. The London Naval Treaty on disarmament needed coordination between the diplomatic interest in securing peace with the West and military–industrial interest in expanding Japan's naval fleets. The adoption of the gold standard needed coordination between the financial interest to maintain a credible currency (wealthy *zaibatsu* stockholders and bankers)[19] and social interest in rescuing the recessionary economy (peasants, workers, and small business owners).

The coordination problems posed a serious challenge to the fragmentary party government with limited policy control.[20] Comparing the two rival parties, the Minseito was generally a bit more willing to pursue Cooperative Diplomacy than the Seiyukai. The distinct partisan positions could be attributed to their distinct political support structures. Useful for understanding the support structure is the Heckscher-Ohlin trade theorem that focuses on factors of production. The theorem predicts that, given interindustry factor mobility, individuals and groups endowed with abundant factors will support open trade because they are expected to gain rises in income from it. In contrast, those endowed with scarce factors will oppose open trade because their income is expected to decline. It can be said from the theorem that the Minseito received support from the internationalist urban bourgeoisie who were expected to gain from open trade and thus supported Cooperative Diplomacy with open trade. In contrast, the Seiyukai was supported by the conservative landlords and the *zaibatsu* capitalists who were expected to lose due to their scarce production factors.[21] As a result, Cooperative Diplomacy became a target of partisan contest.

The partisan difference was evident between the Giichi Tanaka Seiyukai Cabinet (1927–29) and the following Hamaguchi Minseito Cabinet (1929–31). The former sought to revamp Cooperative Diplomacy through the expansion rather than the maintenance of the Japanese special privilege in the Man-Mo region, while the latter tried to reinvigorate Cooperative Diplomacy by complying with the Nine-Power Treaty that acknowledged the *existing* Japanese special privilege.

For the above reasons, the Hamaguchi Cabinet was determined to continue Cooperative Diplomacy. With an electoral victory in the 1931 general election, the Hamaguchi Cabinet decided on (1) the reinstatement of the gold standard; (2) the conclusion of the London Naval Treaty on disarmament; and (3) diplomatic rapprochement with China through non-expansion in the Man-Mo region and the restoration of China's tariff autonomy based on the spirit of the Nine-Power Treaty. In making these bold decisions, the Hamaguchi Cabinet used extraordinary means, including an optimistic economic forecast for (1), imperial consent for (2), and cabinet coherence for (3) (all of which will be explained in the next section). However, Cooperative Diplomacy was rapidly losing favor as the three conditions eroded.

3.4 CENTRALIZATION AND THE CONSEQUENCES

3.4.1 Demise of Party Government and Rise of State-dependent Economy and Confrontational Diplomacy

Among the above-mentioned conditions, condition (1), of an optimistic economic forecast, declined sharply when the gold standard worsened the depression-hit economy after a brief recovery, producing a strong deflationary pressure with substantial social dislocations. Condition (2), of imperial consent for the conclusion of the London Naval Treaty, weakened when the adoption of the London Naval Treaty on disarmament in 1930 and the non-expansionist Man-Mo policy were nullified by hardliners within the navy and the army, respectively. The restraining positions for the two services were linked to each other. Because of the linkage, the hardliners in the two services embarked on natural collaboration in claiming that the cabinet's policies were in violation of the emperor's war powers (Article 11 of the Meiji Constitution) in the midst of increasing international tensions between Japan and the West as well as between Japan and China.

Finally, condition (3), of cabinet coherence for diplomatic rapprochement with China, deteriorated when the Minseito Cabinet suffered an internal disagreement over rapprochement with China and the Nine-Power Treaty. Under pressure from hardline naval officials, Navy Minister Takeshi Takarabe reversed his earlier position on the disarmament treaty, and resigned from the post in protest. Furthermore, the Kwantung Army Command conspired in the mysterious Mukden Incident[22] in 1931, against the Army Headquarters' restraining order. The Kwantung Command exploited the incident to conquer much of Manchuria in retaliation against the Kuomintang Zhang Xueliang's division bombing of the Japanese southern Manchuria railway. The Command established the 'Manchukuo' with the throne of the Ch'ing Dynasty's last emperor to justify its military action.

The succeeding Seiyukai Cabinet led by Prime Minister Tsuyoshi Inukai (1931–32) reversed a large part of Cooperative Diplomacy the Hamaguchi Cabinet had tried to create. The Inukai Cabinet under the leadership of Finance Minister Korekiyo Takahashi terminated the gold standard to reflate the economy. The reflationary policy was associated with monetary ease, currency devaluation and fiscal expansion via government bond issuance for arms build up and further state-led industrialization.[23] The recession and reflation produced significant political economic effects – it orchestrated a quick economic recovery but created a state-dependent economy that became subject to manipulation for a command economy (this point will be discussed in the next section). The policy of moderation over the Man-Mo region was reversed towards expansion for territorial and commercial purposes. This would effectively reduce the policy gap between the Japanese central government and the Kwantung Army command.

However, the subsequent fiscal retrenchment reduced military spending, frustrating radical navy officials. In an aborted coup attempt by its young navy officers, which became known as the 5.15 Incident, Prime Minister Inukai was assassinated, ending the nascent parliamentary democracy in 1932. The party cabinet was replaced with a grand coalition cabinet (*kyokoku ichi naikaku*) headed by Prime Minister Makoto Saito (1932–34) with support from the two rival parties and bureaucracies under the auspices of the last Meiji elder, Prince Kinmochi Saionji.[24] The grand coalition was based on a two-party system and was an attempt to resist the fascist movement emerging in depression-torn Japan, similar to the one in Italy under Mussolini. According to Banno (2014) and Yukio Ito (2007, p. 279), the Saito Cabinet essentially inherited the internationalist approach from the party cabinets with the objectives of preventing Japan's diplomatic isolation and reducing the influence of the Imperial Army, which was increasing rapidly after the Mukden Incident in 1931.

However, bit by bit, Japan was being drawn into expansionist policy as radical elements encroached into the central government. Because of its coalitional weakness, the bureaucratic cabinet was unable to solve the pending coordination problems. In an attempt to make coherent foreign and military policies, the Saito Cabinet established a council of five key ministers (*goso kaigi*), including the prime minister along with the finance, foreign, army and navy ministers, to execute the urgent task of inter-ministerial coordination. However, because the ministers were still allowed to advocate for their respective organizations' positions, the prime minister was unable to sort out inter-ministerial differences. The coordination failures were fundamentally structural; the grand coalition was merely a facade, with state interests being effectively superseded by ministerial interests.

An increasingly incoherent diplomacy was also seen in Japan's reactions to the League of Nations. Despite its initial cooperative position, the Saito Cabinet was pressured by the military to take recalcitrant positions. Against US and European opposition, the Saito Cabinet extended unilateral diplomatic recognition to a puppet regime, the 'Manchukuo', asserting that it was the 'linchpin of Japan'.[25] The cabinet went even further in the League's special session in March 1933, rejecting the Lytton Report that denounced Japan's Manchurian policy for violating the principle of the Open Door to guarantee equal access to commercial opportunities in northern China (or the Nine-Power Treaty).[26] The report acknowledged

Japan's treaty interest in the area, while pressuring Japan for compliance with the Open Door principle, recognition of self-governance in Manchuria, and reconciliation with China.

The Saito Cabinet chose to withdraw Japan's membership from the League by consenting to the Foreign Ministry's recommendation. Having observed that the Imperial Army invaded northern China to prevent the Republic of China's infiltration into the Manchukuo, the Foreign Ministry predicted that the League would view the army's invasion as a violation of China's sovereignty and would impose international sanctions based on Articles 15 and 16 of the Covenant. The ministry's recommendation for withdrawal was intended to avoid the forthcoming sanctions based on the belief that even after withdrawing, Japan still could amend its relationship with the West by remaining in multilateral forums, including the World Economic Conference and the London Naval Disarmament Conference (Inoue, 2011). In the meantime, the navy was concerned that the withdrawal would strip Japan of the right to maintain its mandate system in the Pacific Islands, which the navy believed acted as a navigational buffer against the United States' Pacific Fleet. The navy's concern was assuaged by the Foreign Ministry's legal claim that Japan, albeit being out of the League, could still be granted with a system of mandate in the Pacific because the United States, a non-member state, had been requested by the League to establish a system of mandate in Armenia.

Behind the increasingly inept cabinet, bureaucratic officials in the army, navy, and foreign affairs effectively ran the government. This was an outcome of a fragmentary government where bureaucracies pursued their policy actions separately in the absence of a robust central command. To the detriment of the Japanese state, their conspiratorial behavior hindered coordination for the liberal order and further disconnected Japan from the international community.

3.4.2 Constitutional Dictatorship, Command Economy and East Asian Co-prosperity

With another bureaucratic government failure, Japan finally sought centralization via a grand coalition government in 1938. Because the bureaucratic government was innately fragmentary, Prime Minister Keisuke Okada (1934–36) of the minority government transformed the government into a constitutional-dictatorial (*rikken dokusai*) cabinet in pursuit of coherence and control by establishing extra-legal units – the Cabinet Council and the Cabinet Research Bureau (later the Planning Bureau).

The oxymoronic concept of a constitutional dictatorship was invented by Professor Masamichi Ryoyama to create an authoritative central body capable of processing information from bureaucracies and making rational decisions that were acceptable to the public in case of emergency. It was similar to the roundtable of top organizations (*entaku kyotou kaigi*) advocated by Professor Tatsukichi Minobe without labor representatives. Both concepts rejected military dictatorship and were intended to defend constitutionalism against rising fascism. Specifically, the Cabinet Council assembled ministers, party officials, business leaders, and civil society representatives to advise the prime minister. The Cabinet Research Bureau assembled senior bureaucrats and academics to supply the council with policy information and analysis.

However, the council was inept at solving inter-ministerial conflicts. It simply recommended ministerial-level conferences and was unable to impose cabinet-level central coordination upon bureaucracies in most cases (Makihara, 2009, pp. 140–47). The constitutional-dictatorial cabinet stifled the flow of communication and had to acknowledge the policy recommendations by the Administrative Research Council that was dominated by 'new bureaucrats' (*shin kanryo*). These radical officials believed in command economy and economic planning and formed an informal network across ministries, including interior, finance, commerce and industry, telecommunication, foreign affairs, and army. They successfully put their ideas into practice. For example, they enacted the electric power control law, which nationalized electric power companies for state control of supply and distribution, passed a foreign exchange control law in 1933, and approved a series of industry control laws to establish bureaucratic command and control over industrial production, price, credit, distribution, import and export concerning oil, coal, steel, and textiles. The economy was already rejuvenated through a reflationary monetary policy and the abolition of the gold standard under the leadership of Finance Minister Takahashi (1932–34). These state-control measures could be justified only as an ideological drive for a Soviet-type command economy, but not as anti-recession measures. However, with the forceful state interventions, the national economy was disconnected from markets, making industrial interests more reliant on state power.

Unable to coordinate, the Okada Cabinet conceded to bureaucracies' unilateral policy actions even further. Most embarrassing was its consent to the Manchukuo annexation demanded by the Imperial Army for territorial expansion and self-sufficiency, by the Ministry of Commerce for industrial recovery and by the Ministry of Interior for emigration of the expanding rural population in Japan. Furthermore, Foreign Minister Hirota endorsed a radical Foreign Ministry official's call for an East Asian version of the outdated Monroe Doctrine (known as the Amou Doctrine) to legitimize the anti-Open Door policy to shut out the West from

Manchukuo. This shattered the prospects for international cooperation. Having failed to coordinate a liberal international order, the bureaucratic government effectively settled on an imperialistic order in pursuit of a co-prosperity sphere in East Asia. That is, the pursuit of an imperialistic order was the outcome of miscoordination of the liberal order by the fragmentary government that permitted ministerial interests to supersede state interest in the absence of a central command.

3.4.3 Monopolistic Government and Command Economy

Fragmentation was finally met with coercive unification. In 1938, Prime Minister Konoe (1937–39, 1940–41) combined the Cabinet Research Bureau (Naikaku Chosa Kyoku) with the Cabinet Resource Bureau (Naikaku Shigen Kyoku) to create a powerful Cabinet Planning Bureau (CPB, Kikaku-in). Furthermore, the prime minister abolished the existing political parties to establish a pro-government grand party (Taisei Yokusan-kai – the Imperial Rule Assistance Association). His aim was to reduce partisanship associated with the competitive party system as well as sectionalism associated with deconcentrated bureaucracies (Tsutsui, 2009, p. 170).[27] Both reforms were meant to unify politics and bureaucracy.[28]

Unification (*tou-itsu*) meant a central command or even coercive political control. However, it had a serious drawback. Unification stifled the flow of communication and precise information analysis. With limited information flow, Prime Minister Konoe, advised by the ultra-nationalistic bureaucratic officials known as renovation bureaucrats (*kakushin kanryo*) in the CPB, enacted the National Mobilization Law (*Kokka Sodoin Ho*), the Japanese version of Nazi Germany's Enabling Law, to legitimize the government fiat that could supersede bureaucratic scrutiny and parliamentary deliberation. The law was meant to focus the human and material resources of public and private domains on the central government to prepare for the eventual war against China and beyond. The law undermined individual liberty and the system of separation of powers weakly guaranteed by the Meiji Constitution. Consequently, it created the ultimate coercive mechanism to coordinate divisive domestic interests in pursuit of imperial expansion.

As for banking, the Temporary Capital Distribution Law (Rinji Shikin Chosei Ho) in 1937 prohibited firms from raising capital for new business ventures, mergers, and acquisitions unless in the three designated industrial categories (military and related industries) without government approval. This law was solidified via the Financial Operation Law (Shikin Unyo Ho) in 1940, the Financial Control Mechanism (Kinyu Tosei Kai) in 1942, and the Designated Financial Institution Mechanism (Shitei Kinyu Kikan

Seido) in 1944. These measures, designed by renovation bureaucrats in the CPB, were imposed upon the banks who found state-led lending unprofitable and risky. Despite the unprofitability of bank loans, the coercive measures of a command economy had long-lasting effects as it concentrated business information on the banks at the expense of stock markets.

As for corporate governance, the CPB-led social national reforms completely transformed stockholder-centric management. The reforms set forth dividend control through the Business Accounting Control Law of 1942 (Kaisha Keiri Tosei Rei) and the Industrial Patriotic Society (Sangyo Hokoku Kai) or cooperative body that sought to integrate the tasks of managers and white- and blue-collar workers. The goal was to establish public-spirited firms free from stockholders' control to expand production rather than maximize profit (Okazaki, 1994, p. 74). These interwar economic reforms arguably produced a reverberating effect on the postwar economic system (see the next chapter for the details).

Furthermore, the Konoe Cabinet falsely believed, with the recommendation by Foreign Minister Yosuke Matsuoka, that the conclusion of the anti-communist treaty with the Axis powers (Germany, Italy and Japan) would improve the relationship with the United States, ignoring the fact that Nazi Germany was confronting Great Britain, an ally of the United States (Tsutsui, 2009, p. 229). The cabinet once again falsely believed without logical reason that adopting the East Asian Community (Toa Kyodotai) for a regional free trade zone, independent of the international trade regime dominated by Europe and North America, would be acceptable to East Asian countries and the West. This notion was developed into a more imperialistic Greater East Asia Co-prosperity Sphere (Daitoa Kyoei Ken) by renovation bureaucrats and generals, who conspired for industrial and territorial expansion.

To confront such radicalism, liberal Foreign Ministry officials appealed that Japan shared interests not with the Axis powers, but with the United States and Great Britain, and made diplomatic efforts to maintain communication channels with the liberal states until the cabinet signed the treaty with the Axis powers (Inoue, 2011). These messages did not reach the prime minister at the pinnacle of the highly hierarchical government structure. In addition, Prince Konoe did not take seriously the opportunities to negotiate with the Republic of China, which were led by Chiang Kai-shek who sought peace with Japan under intense pressure from the communist insurgency led by Mao Zedong.

Instead of an olive branch for international peace, China's behavior was interpreted as an external threat, which the fragile Konoe Cabinet used in pursuit of domestic political control. Additionally, Prince Konoe used imperial expansion as a means to re-coordinate the competing interests of agriculture, industry, and the military, by building farms and industrial networks in the vast northern China through territorial monopolization. The monopolistic government provided a coercive central command with limited information-processing capabilities – the worst combination, which put Japan's national security at peril.

3.5 CONCLUSION

In this chapter, I have shown that from the Meiji Restoration to the eve of the Pacific War, government structural architecture was a quintessential political problem for Japan. Political leaders struggled to find the appropriate government structure for wealth and power under a continually changing international order. They tried a plethora of structural arrangements, including oligarchic, decentralized democratic, decentralized bureaucratic, and monopolistic. From a purely normative viewpoint, the appropriate structure was set out, consistent with the nature of the major policy problem at hand, in order to promote state interests.

The normative theory of structural architecture discussed in the previous chapter takes this structural dilemma into account and urges political leadership to invent measures to ameliorate the dilemma under a prevailing international order. The historical analysis in this chapter has shown that the Meiji oligarchic government adapted to the competitive international order of the late nineteenth century through minimal mercantilism and restrained militarism. Both strategies were legitimate under the order and were implementable by the oligarchic government with core-executive elements because of central control and strategic complementarity.

However, the post–oligarchic party governments under the Meiji Imperial Constitution were unable to adjust to the interwar liberal international order, the Versailles-Washington system, in spite of the liberal democratic movements at home. One might attribute the collapse of party governments to excessive inter-party competition and international conflict. However, the subsequent non-partisan constitutional-dictatorial government also failed. Political competition had been part of national politics from the Meiji oligarchic period and was not limited to the party governments. Likewise, international conflict had already been intense even before the party governments came to power and was fueled in part by Japan's aggressive mercantilism.

An alternative culprit for the demise of party governments might be governmental fragmentation as argued by Mitani (2010) and the inability to make appropriate domestic coordination for the interwar liberal order. The constitutional arrangement of *primus inter pares* was kept to protect imperial sovereignty and vested interests at the expense of the prime minister's leadership. Moreover, coalitional members took advantage of the decentralized structure in pursuit of particularistic interests – monopolized markets and territorial expansion in Manchuria as well as the enlargement of the sphere of influence in the Pacific. Self-centered actors resisted any structural change that might threaten their interests and policy authorities, by capitalizing on ministerial resignation and political violence against the party governments. Even as the international order shifted toward a liberal direction, the government policies grew increasingly out of sync with the emergent order. The liberal elements within the modern industrial society were barred from keeping the policy manipulation in check because state-led industrial growth made them dependent on state power for resources and markets. The result was a massive coordination failure and the continuous expansion of militaristic mercantilism.

To regain policy control, political leaders sought to improve inter-ministerial coordination via the strategies of authority reallocation, including a grand coalition, constitutional dictatorship, and unification. The strategies for central command generated a serious repercussion, stifling the flow of communication to the leadership. Furthermore, it disconnected bureaucracies from international networks, politicized them, and compelled them to provide biased information and analysis for the leaders' liking. Externally, the abrogation of international connections made adaptation and coordination meaningless. Internally, it destroyed the commitment devices weakly provided by the Meiji Imperial Constitution with which political leadership could restrain itself from monopolistic governance. Because the hierarchical government was informationally inefficient, politically unchecked, and internationally disconnected, the leadership sought to coordinate divergent social interests for the equilibrium of imperialism.

In retrospect, for a non-liberal state, the interwar liberal international order was more difficult to deal with, in comparison with the prior mercantilist order, because domestic coordination in the former was more involved and inimical to vested interests, particularly under a decentralized government in which members of the governing coalition could veto the leadership's coordination attempts. Centralization after the coordination failures worsened the situation. In the next chapter, I will analyze how postwar democratic Japan fared under the international order of embedded liberalism.

NOTES

1. The notion of *fukoku kyohei* was older than the Meiji Restoration and was invented in the late Edo era. It was inherited and practiced by the Meiji oligarchic and constitutional governments.
2. The Meiji oligarchs were divided on their preferences over the impending issues of state governance and economic modernization (Ikai, 2005; Banno, 2014). Ito's proposal of constitutional authoritarianism and minimal mercantilism triumphed as the least evil for a burgeoning state as a result of repeated interpersonal bargaining. Ito believed that parliamentary democracy would dilute political authority and weaken state power, while maximal mercantilism and assertive militarism would exhaust Japan's inadequate economic resources. Moreover, a market economy would diffuse the resources thinly across industries, failing to make them internationally competitive.
3. The Meiji government was financially strained with the issuance of public bonds and was under the threat of hyperinflation. Thus, the choice of small government was inevitable.
4. The principle of imperial sovereignty with its bureaucratic advisory role was the core of the theory of imperial institution advocated by Professor Tatsukichi Minobe. The Meiji government adopted the principle as its official doctrine between 1890 and 1935 to justify administrative leadership by the cabinet that executed daily government business.
5. Officially, a major tariff revision in 1910 was implemented to secure tax revenues. However, Yamazawa (1984) claimed that the real objective was to protect domestic industries.
6. Contrary to Gourevitch and Shinn (2007), there is no apparent correlation between the embryonic stockholder capitalism and the first-past-the-post (FPTP) electoral system that was used for the House of Representatives between 1890 and 1900. As noted in the text, stockholder capitalism preceded the introduction of FPTP votes. And, surprisingly, the FPTP system coincided with a multi-party system, not a two-party system, because of the emergence of numerous localized parties (Kawato, 1992, pp. 148–63). More importantly, the Imperial Diet had a limited policy influence under the Meiji oligarchic government. I attribute the development of stockholder capitalism in Meiji Japan to the non-autonomous tariff regime, as argued by Rajan and Zingales (2003).
7. This shift to block-stockholding accords broadly with La Porta et al.'s (2000) hypothesis postulating that countries with civil law traditions have a block-stockholding model, while common law countries have a diffusion model. But, again, I argue that the adoption of the German commercial code was motivated by the mercantilist intent and attribute the emergence of block-stockholding and industrial concentration to the competitive international order, to which the Meiji government sought to adjust.
8. A transcendental cabinet was either a domain-clique cabinet led by a Meiji oligarch or a bureaucratic cabinet. Both types rejected direct partisan affiliation but obtained a party's support. After the retirement of Prime Minister Katsura in 1913, the oligarchs reduced their direct political influence by retreating from cabinet ministers towards king-makers who nominated future prime ministers to the emperor. The non-oligarchic transcendental cabinets were those led by Prime Ministers Gonbei Yamamoto (1913–14, 1923–24), Masatake Terauchi (1916–18), and Keigo Kiyoura (1924).
9. A group of countries in Europe that formed a decision-making alliance between 1814 and 1914. The members were the United Kingdom, Austria, the Russian empire, Prussia, and later, France.
10. The Meiji government had promoted industrial development mainly through tax and subsidy incentives until it regained full tariff autonomy in 1910.
11. The cabinet rule was created in 1900 by Prime Minister Aritomo Yamagata, who had strong ties to the Imperial Army, in order to maintain the influence of the military within government to vie with emergent political parties.
12. A 1922 treaty affirming the sovereignty and territorial integrity of China.

13. There was a negligible difference between the two parties over the expansionist policy in Manchuria because the policy more or less benefited both parties' clients.
14. The mercantilist import substitution policy for heavy and chemical industries was not backed up by appropriate technological infrastructures. The products were sold mainly in domestic markets and Manchuria where exports were preferentially financed by government loans (Teranishi, 2005, p. 133).
15. In comparison, the old *zaibatsu*, including Mitsui, Sumitomo, and Mitsubishi, were well connected with the major political parties and the civilian bureaucracies.
16. The military root of Japanese imperialism is well documented by Crowley (1966), Tsunoda (1967), and Kitaoka (1978).
17. Prince Fumimaro Konoe, who became prime minister in 1938, was a strong believer of this position.
18. This position was supported by Ichita Kobashi, Vice-Minister of the Interior Ministry under the Seiyukai Cabinet led by Prime Minister Hara.
19. Another reason for the reintroduction of the gold standard was fiscal reconstruction through issuance of government bonds in overseas markets (Teranishi, 2005, p. 156).
20. The party cabinets sought to strengthen their positions with regard to bureaucracies. The Minseito Cabinets placed party officials within bureaucratic ministries as ministers and political vice-ministers in deference to the political independence of bureaucracies, while the Seiyukai Cabinets internalized bureaucrats within its party organization through political recruitment (Shimizu, 2013). Both parties tried to signal to the members of the governing coalition that they could run an effective government by sharing policy authority with the administratively competent bureaucrats.
21. Rogowski (1989) advanced a similar argument for the United States and other industrial countries.
22. Also known as the Manchurian Incident, this was a staged event engineered by rogue Japanese military personnel as a pretext for the Japanese invasion of Manchuria in 1931. A small quantity of dynamite was detonated near Mukden in Japan. The Imperial Japanese Army accused Chinese dissidents of the act and responded with a full invasion that led to the occupation of Manchuria.
23. The reflationary policy evoked resentment in the West by depreciating the Japanese currency and generating 'social dumping'.
24. Initially, the prince had been reluctant to admit a grand coalition cabinet because of his belief in a two-party system. He rejected the Minseito's request for the formation of a grand coalition to deal with the Mukden Incident before he picked the Inukai Seiyukai Cabinet to succeed the Wakatsuki Minseito Cabinet.
25. The expression was used against the Wakatsuki Minseito Cabinet by the Seiyukai parliamentarian, Yosuke Matsuoka, who later became foreign minister of the second Konoe Cabinet.
26. The Minseito Wakatsuki Cabinet consented to the League of Nations investigation into the Mukden Incident, led by Sir Joseph Lytton, as part of Cooperative Diplomacy.
27. The Minseito officials were attracted to the principle of socioeconomic equality enshrined in social nationalism. Concerned about being left out, the Seiyukai officials were drawn to the movement. Both parties eventually accepted the unification.
28. Tsutsui (2009) views the Konoe Cabinet as a victim of monopolistic populism.

4. Postwar bureaucratic-cabinet system and sectoral adjustments to the international order of embedded liberalism

4.1 INTRODUCTION

In the previous chapter, I illuminated the pre- and interwar struggles of the government structural architecture and their consequences. I demonstrated numerous structural arrangements, including transcendental, party, bureaucratic coalition, constitutional dictatorship, and monopolism. Each structure attempted to solve the immediate policy problems between Japan and the prevailing international order. The most serious problem hinged on coordination between the twin state objectives of industrialism and militarism. While the objectives were largely complementary under the pre–World War I competitive international order, they became substitutive under the interwar liberal international order, posing a major policy challenge for the fragmentary government set forth by the Meiji Imperial Constitution, which was originally meant to protect imperial sovereignty but was increasingly used to cater to the vested interests.

In this chapter, I turn to the relationship between the government structural architecture and the international order in the post–World War II period, where Japan achieved rapid economic growth. The average yearly growth rate of the gross domestic product (GDP) between 1950 and 1970 exceeded 10 percent, lifting GDP per capita from 100th position to fifth in the world. In the realm of security and foreign policy, Japan allowed the defense strategy to link to the US grand strategy and made part of its territorial assets available to US forces in order to enable them to extend their deterrent capabilities in the region and provide security guarantees to Japan (Samuels, 2007, pp. 38–59). Because of the alliance arrangement, Japan was released from the task of building a large-scale military that otherwise might have been needed under the Cold War environment. Thus, Japan could maintain the notion of 'defensive defense' that constituted the security policy goal of the Yoshida Doctrine. The doctrine, initiated by Prime Minister Shigeru Yoshida in the 1950s, served as Japan's postwar grand strategy to promote security and prosperity within the constraints of the war-renouncing Constitution and the prevailing economic conditions of the time. Based on the doctrine, the succeeding government led by the Liberal Democratic Party (LDP) pursued a non-aggressive, low-cost security policy.[1] Instrumentally, the LDP government set out non-legal rules, including the three non-nuclear principles,[2] the defense budget ceiling,[3] the restrictive defense perimeter, and defensive armament. These rules worked as signals to domestic pacifists and foreign skeptics that Japan would not revive pre-1945 militarism. As a consequence, Japan was able to comply with the spirit of the pacifist Constitution and prevent a costly arms race between the lightly armed Japan and the neighboring states that had suffered from its past militarism and were concerned about its resurgence.

Thus, the most significant adjustment problem for Japan in the postwar period was an economic one – how to adjust the Japanese-style capitalist economy to the postwar liberal international order.[4] Pertinent to the theme of this book, the democratic government was again decentralized with bureaucratic policy delegation, similar to that under the Meiji Imperial Constitution, even though the postwar Constitution provided the prime minister with substantial policy and political authority. Given these empirical observations, a prominent question is how the decentralized government in a non-liberal state could achieve rapid economic growth – a successful policy adjustment – under the liberal international order. Another related question is why the LDP cabinets delegated the policy authority to bureaucracies under the new democratic Constitution that provided them with substantive powers. Bureaucratic delegation entails risks of agency slack because there is no perfect ex ante or ex post oversight. Using the constitutional power, they could set policy directly without worrying about agency slack.

These questions are theoretically significant in that the underlying facts are antithetical to the well-received Gerschenkron hypothesis on economic growth for a 'late developer' like Japan. According to Gerschenkron (1962), a late-developing state has to have a centralized political-economic structure in order to compete against developed states with superior financial and technological positions. For a late developer to play a successful catch-up game, a centralized government with strong leadership and coherent bureaucracies is more appropriate than a decentralized one to focus limited human and material resources on oligopolistic banks and selected growth industries. Hence, despite its relative backwardness, a late developer can grow quickly by importing modern technologies from abroad, exploiting economies of scale, and learning from other states' experiences with virulent ideologies.

Based on a similar assumption of an activist government, Johnson (1982) attributed the postwar Japanese economic success to the policy prowess of the Ministry of International Trade and Industry (MITI) with a strong legacy of an interwar command economy. Johnson's 'developmental state' is similar to Gerschenkron's late developer in several ways. First, the state is an internally coherent one in which the governing party shares the developmental ideology with the bureaucratic organizations and delegates policy authority to them. With this mandate, economic bureaucrats design and implement mercantilist export-oriented strategies, which are known as industrial policy. They extensively use non-legal administrative guidance and fiscal investment and loan programs (FILPs) to supersede rigid, time-consuming parliamentary processes. In postwar Japan, administrative guidance was issued by the industrial bureaus of MITI on a discretionary basis with respect to entry control, recession cartels, industrial restructuring, and even mergers and acquisitions in order to funnel limited resources to growth sectors. Similarly, the FILPs were programs in the special budgetary account administered by the Financial Bureau of the Ministry of Finance (MOF) to lend funds accruing from postal savings and insurance fees to targeted industries through public financial institutions. In Johnson's view, the developmental state is committed to dynamic resource reallocation not through markets ('market rationality'), but through regulatory and financial mediums controlled by the economic bureaucracies ('plan rationality').[5]

Both Johnson's developmental state and Gerschenkron's late developer presume that government is strategic, internally coherent, and centralized. Their assertions contradict the observed decentralized government in postwar Japan. Suppose that the Japanese government was decentralized as it really was. Under the decentralized structure of a non-liberal state, execution of substantive coordination concerning resource allocation between sectors seems difficult given the facts that the sectors underwent shifting comparative advantages and were regulated by the ministerial bureaus committed to protecting their own sectoral interests. Without robust market mechanisms, the non-liberal state had to rely on the ministries' coordination efforts for swift reallocation of resources from inefficient to efficient sectors.

However, as argued in Chapter 1 of this book, in the absence of central command, a decentralized government should suffer from coordination failures, stifling dynamic resource reallocation. The larger the cross-sector comparative-advantage shift, the more frequent the coordination failure, and the greater the economic loss. Thus, neither the late developer nor the developmental state hypothesis is able to explain the growth outcomes with cross-sector comparative-advantage shifts that Japan experienced over a 40-year high-growth period.

In contradistinction to these strategic state hypotheses, institutional economists (Okazaki and Okuno-Fujiwara, 1999; Teranishi, 2005; Aoki, 2010) have argued that the Japanese postwar economic growth is largely attributed to an efficient economic system based on viable private organizations and complementary public policy domains. In this book, the postwar Japanese economic system is referred to as a coordinated market economy (CME) in the sense of Hall and Soskice (2001).[6] In the Japanese-style CME, private agents deal with economic contracts and transactions through organizations rather than markets by developing unique institutional arrangements, including the main bank system, management-centric contingent corporate governance, interfirm networks, and long-term employment. These arrangements contribute to human capital improvement, steady research and development, and positive externalities of knowledge, which counter the diminishing return to capital accumulation. In addition, under 'patient' capital (long-term capital) and contingent governance, managers pursued the expansion of market shares rather than short-term profits, thus taking advantage of economies of scale.[7]

The institutional economists did not reject governmental roles, noticing that these private arrangements were subject to the problems of residual informational uncertainty and transaction costs that bureaucratic ministries sought to solve in the public policy domains of their jurisdictions. Institutional economists have shown that public policy programs (implicit government protection and low interest rate environments for the main bank system, Commercial Code provision for contingent governance, and restrictive dismissal law) solved these issues. Because these public policy programs were basically sector specific and required little inter-ministerial coordination, the bureaucratic ministries could design and implement public policy programs within their jurisdictions to complement the CME through the improved expertise and initiatives.

Among the existing insights regarding the CME, there is a missing link as to how the decentralized government could be protected from coordination failures and degeneration through bureau-pluralistic networks. Given the imperfection of ex ante and ex post monitoring, the political leadership was faced with moral hazard with regard to keeping bureaucratic behavior in check. The postwar Japanese economic success implies that such degeneration was more or less averted. Despite the lack of a central command and liberal legacy, the decentralized government in a non-liberal state successfully adjusted its public policy domains and economic institutions to the postwar liberal international order, which the prewar governments failed to accomplish.

Below I try to fill in the missing link by focusing on policy authority allocation and the politics of the governing coalition under the postwar liberal international order. I show that the CME institutions and the cross-sectoral governing coalition co-evolved under the postwar decentralized government inherited from the prewar era (Section 4.2). The CME institutions were adapted through complementary public policy programs to the liberal international order, consistent with the interests of the cross-sectoral governing coalition (Section 4.3). Intermittently, external ancillary authorities were evoked to promote coordination in conjunction with the liberalization requirements accompanied by formal treaty obligations and informal pressures (Section 4.4). Section 4.5 concludes this chapter by offering summaries and implications for Part II.

4.2 POSTWAR DECENTRALIZED GOVERNMENT AND THE GOVERNING COALITION

4.2.1 Occupation Reform and the Bureaucratic-cabinet System

In the aftermath of the surrender, postwar Japan was faced with occupation reform by the Supreme Commander for the Allied Powers (SCAP). Under the direction of US Army General Douglas MacArthur, the SCAP's mission was to transform the authoritarian state with its interwar command economy into a peace-loving liberal democracy with a market economy. The SCAP imposed sweeping liberal-democratic reforms upon the war-defeated state, including a democratic constitution, agrarian reform, taxation reform, and labor democratization, among others. To implement these reforms and govern the occupied territory, the SCAP largely maintained the Japanese bureaucracies for indirect governance, while purging a large number of politicians accountable for perpetrating the war. The SCAP's reformist mission was in part hindered by a change in the US grand strategy in East Asia under the emerging Cold War as well as by the Japanese government's reluctance to implement directives. Thus, the SCAP was an external ancillary authority that provided mixed consequences for the subsequent Japanese adjustment to the postwar liberal international order. A liberal democracy with market economy was coupled with maintaining a bureaucratic-controlled system with the remnants of the interwar command economy.

A prominent issue was the contestation between political and bureaucratic control, which ended with a victory for the latter. The new democratic Constitution of Japan, promulgated in 1946, created the principles of political control as follows:

- The emperor is redefined as a national symbol rather than the sovereign and the citizens become sovereign citizens rather than subjects (Article 1).
- Parliamentary democracy is installed based on a popularly elected bicameral Diet as the sole legislative organ of the state (Article 41).
- The cabinet is responsible for law execution and accountable for the Diet (Article 66).
- The prime minister, chosen by the Diet (Article 67), leads the cabinet. He or she has the authority to appoint and fire cabinet ministers (Article 68).
- Public officials are servants of the whole community and not any group thereof (Article 15).
- In addition, the Administrative Organization Law (Kokka Gyosei Soshiki-ho) of 1949 granted the Prime Minister's Office with the task of overseeing ministries and agencies.

Following the principle of political control, the Kishi Cabinet (1958–60) increased the number of political appointees in each ministry to two, both of whom play the role of liaison between the cabinet and the assigned ministry. With these constitutional and administrative arrangements, the prime minister could have at least ex post oversight of bureaucratic performance.[8]

In contradistinction to political control, the bureaucratic policy authority stepped up with the bureaucratization of government. Specifically, the Yoshida Cabinet (1948–54) believed a strong MOF was capable of balancing the budget by resisting parliamentarians' pressures for lower taxes and more public spending.[9] As for international trade, the cabinet found it indispensable to improve industrial competitiveness in order to reduce trade deficits and defend the state's economic sovereignty under the foreign exchange regime unfavorable to Japanese exports.[10] To do so, the cabinet transformed the Ministry of Commerce and Industry (MCI) into the Ministry of International Trade and Industry (MITI) with a specific mandate for export promotion by transferring the Ministry of Foreign Affairs (MOFA) internationalist officials to the new ministry still staffed with the officials who embraced the interwar doctrine of command economy. Furthermore, to fill the parliamentary seats vacated by purged politicians, Prime Minister Yoshida recruited elite bureaucrats as candidates of his Liberal Party for the Diet. They were known as pupils of the 'Yoshida School' and later became leading politicians.[11] Notable individuals include Hayato Ikeda, Eisaku Sato, Yoshinobu Ohira, and Kiichi Miyazawa, all of whom later became prime ministers. These arrangements, along with the bureaucratic policy delegation discussed below, led to a triumph of bureaucratic control within the postwar Japanese political system.

4.2.2 Cross-sectoral Governing Coalition and Stakeholders of Japanese-style Capitalism

A merger of the two conservative parties (the Liberal Party and the Democratic Party), creating the Liberal Democratic Party (LDP), followed the bureaucratization of government in 1955. In the midst of surging socialist popularity and labor movements, the merger was conservatives' effort to maintain a parliamentary majority in view of the prewar failure of a competitive but degenerating two-party system. In the Taisho period, as discussed in Chapter 3, the two conservative parties (the Seiyukai and the Minseito), which represented rural landlords and urban bourgeoisie respectively, vied against each other for power with the unintended effect of weakening the prime minister with respect to the Imperial Army.

The postwar merger created a predominant political party with a cross-sectoral surplus electoral coalition that cut across class lines. Although the LDP held over 60 percent of the seats in the powerful House of Representatives between 1960 and 1978, at no time (at least when opinion surveys were available) could the LDP be characterized as a catch-all party. Because of the House's electoral system known as the SNTV (single non-transferable vote – see Chapter 2), the LDP members' support bases were sector specific and cross-sectoral; opinion surveys indicate that the stable support for the LDP was derived from the respondents employed in multiple sectors, including finance, construction, agriculture, real estate, medicine, and distribution[12] (Table 4.1). In each sector, respondents with managerial positions showed stronger support than those with manual jobs (Table 4.2).

The cross-sectoral coalition was formed and developed under three pre-conditions. First, the prewar governing coalition was disbanded – the SCAP-led agrarian reform and *zaibatsu* (conglomerate) liquidation decimated the land and capitalist classes. Farmland owned by large landlords was piecemealed and transferred to the renters, while stocks owned by *zaibatsu* families were sold to managers and workers at discounted prices. Second, a new postwar coalition was formed based on tripartite cooperation among capital, management, and skilled labor that were stakeholders of the Japanese CME. Third, the cross-sectoral coalition in Japan was amplified by the general tendency toward sectoral coalitions seen across many other industrial states. Due to technological sophistication, productive factors, such as capital and labor, increasingly became non-transferable across sectors and were trapped within each sector, being

Table 4.1 Sectoral support for the Liberal Democratic Party

Industry/Year	1955	1965	1975	1985	1991
Agriculture	48.8	63.5	64.4	59.2	57.7
Construction	31.4	38.0	41.9	44.0	46.4
Retail & food services	49.8	48.6	43.4	48.8	46.2
Other services	42.3	48.7	42.5	46.4	43.0
Manufacturing	31.9	31.3	32.5	36.5	32.8
Public services	26.7	31.1	36.5	26.6	27.8
Transportation	25.0	23.4	27.8	33.1	26.4
Education & research	13.8	15.3	19.4	20.7	19.0
Retired & unemployed	44.4	38.3	32.7	43.4	36.8

Note: Numbers are the percentages of male respondents who supported the LDP.

Source: The data are based on the Social Stratification and Mobility (SSM) survey and are obtained from Miyano (1998, p. 54).

Table 4.2 Partisan support by job type, 1991

Job Type	Industrial Type	LDP	Opposition	Independence	No Response	Freq.
Specialist	1	46.1	20.6	15.7	17.8	102
	2	14.8	25.5	25.5	34.2	149
Managerial	1	63.2	10.5	8.8	17.5	114
	2	41.7	27.8	11.1	19.4	72
Clerical	1	42.7	16.9	20.2	20.2	178
	2	30.5	29.9	21.9	17.6	187

Note: Numbers are the percentages of male respondents who supported the LDP.

Source: The data are based on the Social Stratification and Mobility (SSM) survey and are obtained from Miyano (1998, p. 54).

compelled to cooperate with each other in pursuit of their self-interests (Hiscox, 2002).

These sectoral interests roughly corresponded with the policy jurisdictions of economic ministries' bureaus that have the statutory mandates for promoting the sectors' growth and stability. For instance, the MITI had sector-specific bureaus (*genkyoku*), including heavy industry, chemical industry, textiles, general merchandise, minerals, oil, and coal mining, while the MOF had bureaus such as banking, securities, customs, and tariffs. According to administrative law, bureaus set up deliberative councils (*shingi-kai*) in which sector representatives along with academics and public officials deliberate the bureaus' policy programs. As a result, sectoral interests are encapsulated within bureaus' public policy domains.

These bureaucratic arrangements are useful for defending sectoral interests. The LDP coalition members, except for farmers, were stakeholders of the Japanese-style CME. Thus, the LDP's efforts at protecting the governing coalition's interests were largely compatible with the maintenance of the CME components and could be internalized within the bureaucratic-cabinet system. Nonetheless, the bureaucratic-dependent government served as an impediment to major policy changes that came in the wake of changing international orders, as shown in greater detail in Part II of this book.

Because manual workers co-opted with management, the broad cross-sectoral coalition was basically free from class conflicts and had a stabilizing effect on society and politics, in sharp contrast to the prewar party system, which was bitterly contested along class lines (Gordon, 1988; Pempel, 1998).

Thus, eager to defend the sectoral interests for their electoral purposes, LDP officials were able to safely delegate policy authority to the bureaus due to the overlapping interests and ex post oversight through the party organizations (see Chapter 2). When adjusting the policy domains to the postwar liberal international order, the bureaus needed to design and implement policy responses to protect sectoral interests. They could do so incrementally under the international order of embedded liberalism that permitted states' policy discretion and sector-specific adjustments.[13]

4.2.3 International Comparison

Even during its high growth period, Japan was still viewed as a non-liberal state similar to Germany and Austria in continental Europe (Streeck and Yamamura, 2001). Non-liberal regimes of economic governance place relatively little trust in free markets. Instead, they rely on various hierarchical and organizational mechanisms, which require heavy injections of public authority with vertical control or horizontal collective bargaining that often overrides contractual exchanges as entered into by private agents on their own volition, discretion, and calculation (Streeck, 2001, p. 6).

Historically, state capacity has been required for the defense of non-liberal capitalism against regime incoherence and liberal erosion. To maintain a non-liberal economic regime, a consensual governance system is used because it can protect sectoral interests via a coalitional government supported by numerous sectors, including business, labor, and even agriculture. In continental Europe, non-liberal regimes are represented by multiple parties via a proportional representation system, and the government is a coalition of parties. Cabinet ministers and government policies are determined via a consensus rule. In postwar Japan, sectoral interests were represented by the LDP that formed government in close association with the bureaucracies sharing policy-making and even representational functions with the party. Government policies were determined through collaboration between the LDP and the bureaucracies. Nonetheless, as Streeck (2001, p. 35) observed, '(n)on-liberal capitalism became increasingly more liberal during the 20th century and often proved open to liberal amendments, both continuity and change of nationally embedded capitalism depended critically on state elites who were capable of strategic, autonomous, and authoritarian action'. The next section provides details on Japanese institutional reforms.

4.3 DIFFERENTIATED ADAPTATIONS UNDER THE POSTWAR INTERNATIONAL ORDER OF EMBEDDED LIBERALISM

4.3.1 Sector-specific Policy Adjustments

Essentially, embedded liberalism respects a sovereign state's policy discretion in the sense that it permits conditional sector-specific liberalization and protection upon the state's socioeconomic conditions (Evans, 1995). The idea of embedded liberalism was developed based on a combination of the prewar laissez faire experiences with theories of Keynesianism and multilateralism (Ruggie, 1982). It seeks to balance economic efficiency with social stability by permitting orderly government interventions with domestic markets and cross-border economic transactions. The postwar international economic institutions, the General Agreement on Tariffs and Trade (GATT), and the International Monetary Fund (IMF) were established based on the spirit of embedded liberalism. Japan was an ardent recipient of such institutional flexibility.

The international economic order described above provided favorable institutional environments within which the Japanese-style CME could evolve from the interwar command economy.[14] As argued earlier, the CME institutions corresponded to the bureau-controlled policy domains, while the CME stakeholders were concurrently members of the LDP governing coalition. In effect, the CME was imbued deeply within the postwar Japanese political-bureaucratic system.

As noted earlier, the Japanese-style CME depended upon specific assets, including firm-specific patient capital as well as human skills and loyalty

(Dyer, 1996). Because these specific assets entailed high transaction costs with respect to contracting, training, and recruitment, they needed to be provided by industrial organizations rather than by markets (Williamson, 1998). Yet organizations experienced intra- and interfirm coordination problems between managers, workers, suppliers, and financiers. The Japanese-style CME had to solve these problems with the help of public policy domains. Together these CME institutions and policy domains stressed systemic coordination among the government, business, and labor, resulting in improved economic efficiency and dynamic capability (Aoki, 2000, pp. 60–75; Gilpin, 2001, pp. 156–68).

In the following subsections, I focus on three major CME institutions: the main bank system, manager-centric corporate governance, and long-term employment. I seek to illuminate how a public policy domain concerning each institution assisted in (1) evolution, (2) solution to intra- and interfirm coordination problems, and (3) adaptation to changing international orders.

4.3.2 Main Bank System

Evolution

The main bank system, which was the financial core of the postwar Japanese-style CME, evolved from the preceding interwar system based on the designated financial institution via the diluted SCAP reforms (Hoshi et al., 1994). During the occupation, the SCAP abolished the designated financial institution and sought to impose liberal reform on the Japanese war-financing machine with respect to structure, bank–firm relations, and capital control. With regard to structure, the SCAP urged Japan to install a version of the Glass-Steagall Act, which separated commercial banks from brokerage firms in the United States in the aftermath of the Great Depression because financial speculations and irrational lending under unregulated markets was believed to be the cause. Second, the SCAP demanded the application of a strict monopoly exclusion law to the banking sector, a capital adequacy ratio requirement of 10 percent for private banks, and a deposit insurance scheme (Nakamura, 2012). Through these reforms, the SCAP's Economic and Scientific Section (ESS), which was in charge of postwar reconstruction and economic reform, sought to develop stock markets and loan markets for long-term capital investment and short-term capital, respectively.

The Japanese government was reluctant to implement all these reforms because of its own intent to maintain and adapt the bank-centric financial system market economy under the postwar international order for three reasons (Aoki and Okuno, 1996, pp. 316–17; Horiuchi, 1999). First, the bank system was already well developed, and Japanese officials believed it was capable of directing limited financial resources to key industrial sectors for war reconstruction and beyond. In contrast, Japan's stock markets were underdeveloped and believed to disperse resources thinly across sectors. This belief was firmly held by the Economic Stability Board (ESB; Keizai Antei Honbu), which was established in 1946 as a pilot economic agency to respond to the SCAP directives until 1952 by unifying the fragmentary Japanese economic bureaucracies in pursuit of speedy reconstruction. The ESB led policy planning for reconstruction to secure stability in production, distribution, consumption, labor, prices, finance, and transportation. It had the authority to conduct comprehensive coordination among the bureaucratic tasks and oversee their policy implementation. The ESB staff embraced the concept of economic control inherited from the interwar government, and chose to pursue the priority production method (*keisha seisan hoshiki*) with which it sought to use limited resources and foreign reserves efficiently to promote industrial shifts from coal and steel to petrochemical and manufacturing industries. The allocation scheme was implemented by public and private banks according to the guidelines on capital allocation for financial institutions (1947) that succeeded the interwar Temporary Capital Distribution Law (Rinji Shikin Chosei Ho; see Chapter 3). Although its effectiveness was problematic at best,[15] the method elevated the importance of banks in industrial finance.

Second, when US reconstruction aid ended, the Japanese government established its own reconstruction finance mechanism (the Fukko Kinyu Kinko, later the Japan Development Bank [JDB] in 1951), which led to the formation of loan syndicates and bank consortiums. The Bank of Japan (BOJ) financed the mechanism by purchasing its bonds and directing the allocation of credits to firms in accordance with the guidelines. Because it relied on bond financing, the mechanism was inflationary and disruptive to private loan markets. To lessen these negative effects, the mechanism was replaced by the BOJ's coordinated bank loan promotion program (1947–54) that authorized commercial banks to allocate credits. The program, backed by government credits, facilitated the development of private loan syndicates within which a principal bank assembled a package of long-term loans with other banks while playing a monitoring role for the loan syndicate.

Furthermore, the Long-term Credit Banking Law of 1952 designated the governmental financial institutions, including the Industrial Bank of Japan, Export-Import Bank, and JDB, as suppliers of long-term loans based on bond issuance to priority industries. Private banks, which were financed with short-term saving deposits, held the bonds. However, the private banks were unable to provide long-term loans without appropriate oversight and risk-hedging techniques. The governmental financial institutions in effect transformed the short-term private loans into long-term public loans, while performing oversight roles for the private lenders. That is, the governmental financial institutions generated a cheap-talk effect of directing private loans to priority industries under implicit government guarantees and regulatory control (Teranishi, 2005, pp. 237–44). Lastly, the government facilitated the establishment of credit unions to finance small and medium-sized enterprises (SMEs) that were unable to obtain long-term loans from private banks due to their low creditworthiness, although SMEs accounted for a large portion of Japanese business and employment. Again, commercial banking was a preferred financing instrument because of its controllability from the perspectives of public policy and electoral politics.

Third, unlike banks, Japanese stockholders, who were initially weakened by the interwar dividend control measure, were further weakened by the SCAP's 'stock democratization' measure. Consequently, Japanese stockholders were unable to provide sufficient capital and reliable external oversight for firms. Furthermore, managers were averse to stockholders' expanded influence and viewed it as a source of managerial instability since it would expose them to the risks of unreasonable speculation and hostile takeovers. Regardless, an oversight function was definitely needed. To enhance firms' managerial performance, the government enacted the Corporate Finance Rehabilitation Act (Kaisha Keiri Okyu Sochi Ho) in August 1946. This act urged private banks to send trustees to troubled firms for managerial oversight and loan rollover. Bank credits with long maturity could provide firms with protection from these risks as well as managerial oversight vitally needed for firms without the critical eye of the stockholder.

Bank–firm coordination

The main bank system, which served as the financial core of the Japanese-style CME, evolved from the interwar system protected by capital and foreign exchange into one that controlled the transition economy under IMF Article 14. Under the postwar banking system, commercial banks played a major role by providing oversight to syndicated long-term loans. Industrial firms depended on patient capital and oversight for investment and employment. In turn, commercial banks relied on low interest rate environments and protection from competition in order to play the main bank roles. The MOF provided such environments and regulatory protection via (1) interest rate regulations based on the Banking Act; (2) market segmentation that divided the banking sector into nationwide retail, regional retail, trust, debenture-based long-term investment, foreign

Table 4.3 Sources of credit for Japanese business firms

Source/Year	1931–40	1941–44	1946–55	1956–65	1966–75	1976–85
Own capital	37.0	28.8	37.0	41.1	43.8	58.8
Bank loan	27.3	41.8	45.4	43.7	45.8	32.4
Public loan	0.0	0.0	4.2	3.4	4.3	3.3
Special account loan	–0.9	1.2	2.6	0.9	0.6	1.1
Corporate bond	4.3	8.6	8.3	2.6	2.0	1.4
Stock	31.0	19.5	8.7	8.3	3.4	3.1
Other	1.3	0.1	–0.2	0.0	0.1	–0.1
Total	100.0	100.0	100.0	100.0	100.0	100.0

Source: The data are drawn from the Annual Economic Statistics of the Bank of Japan Research Bureau.

exchange, and so on; (3) regulations controlling market entry, financial products and retail locations; and (4) implicit insolvency protection to contain a systemic risk.[16]

A set of these programs constituted a unique regulatory regime, known as the 'convoy system'. These programs supplied banks with regulatory rents to offset the transaction costs that they had to bear in offering patient capital and external oversight to business firms. The convoy system was implemented under the international financial order that permitted discretionary regulation and residual capital control. Until the mid-1990s when full financial liberalization and prudential regulation were finally achieved, the convoy system was an integral part of the Japanese economic system. With their main banks underpinned by the convoy system, Japanese business firms expanded bank loans as their primary credit portfolios for investment and operation (Table 4.3).

Incremental adaptation

In the mid-1970s, a significant change in the international financial order ensued, compelling Japanese bank regulators to adapt policies. Specifically, the foreign exchange regime shifted from an adjustable peg to a competitive float. Because the Japanese yen was expected to appreciate with regard to other major currencies, Japanese export firms were pressured to relocate their production facilities in order to reduce foreign exchange risks. Many governments in the developed world sought to adapt to the float by liberalizing foreign exchange control and corporate bond markets to help reduce firms' risks. Likewise, Japanese business communities demanded the legalization of corporate bond issuance in pursuit of investment funds. In 1974, an amendment to the Commercial Code permitted the issuance of corporate bonds under restrictive conditions; only large export firms could issue bonds convertible to ordinary stocks. In the 1980s, another Commercial Code amendment reduced the remaining restrictions incrementally with respect to the issuance of non-convertible bonds with collateral.

Thus far, it seems that a complementary relationship existed between foreign exchange liberalization and the diversification of corporate finance via bond issuance. However, there were at least two profound concerns about bond issuance. One was that, given the centrality of commercial banking, financial diversification would reduce banks' profits and the stability of the main bank system as a whole. Another concern was that newly issued corporate bonds would crowd the market, which already had large public bonds, resulting in increased interest rates and government bond repayment costs. Even with these concerns, the Japanese yen appreciated sharply to unprecedented levels, accelerating the need to reduce foreign exchange risks. Moreover, the United States government stepped up its criticism against Japanese exports (steel, TV sets, cars, etc.) for threatening US jobs. Japanese firms were urged to invest in the United States in order to preserve US jobs and defend their own sales in the world's largest market. The Japanese government acknowledged that the demand for corporate bond legalization would outweigh its cost, but knew that legalization had to be gradual enough to permit loan markets to coexist with bond markets.

The speed and width of legalization was determined by the MOF in consultation with the MITI. The former took a stand in defense of banks for limited legalization, while the latter sought to protect business firms for full legalization. As a result of inter-ministerial consultation, the following measures were taken. First, corporate bond issuance was managed by main banks rather than by brokerage firms with respect to collateral management and insurance (this requirement was finally abolished in 1993). Second, various classes of bonds (convertible bonds, straight bonds, secured bonds, unsecured bonds) were instituted, depending on firms' creditworthiness. The classification and bond management schemes constrained full liberalization. The result represents an instance where inter-ministerial coordination was driven by power politics rather than by policy rationality, as argued in Chapter 2. Furthermore, it is broadly consistent with the politics of the governing coalition in that the limited legalization measures favored the 'incumbent' interests of banks and business firms much more than the interests of outsiders, such as brokerage houses and stockholders in the sense of Bebchuk and Roe's (1999) theory of path dependence in corporate ownership.

Due to the above measures, corporate bond markets were effectively embedded within loan markets as part of relational and consortium lending. Nonetheless, the effect of bond market liberalization on loan markets was profound. Bond issuance steadily reduced the need for large and competitive firms to obtain loans. However, non-competitive ones still did, leaving only risky clients with commercial banks, which was a contributing factor in the 1997–98 banking crisis in the aftermath of the asset bubble burst (see Chapter 8).

4.3.3 Contingent Corporate Governance

Evolution

A second important component of the Japanese-style CME, contingent (manager-centric) corporate governance, evolved through a path similar to the main bank system: public–private interactions based on the interwar system via the SCAP reform and postwar reconstruction. In 1943, the military government, in an attempt to direct industrial production via firm management, enacted the Corporate Accounting Control Act (Kaisha Keiri Tosei-rei), and the Munitions Corporate Control Act (Gunju Kaisha-ho) in 1943 to reduce divided payments and release managers from stockholders' control. During the occupation, the SCAP sought to recuperate stockholders' control by proposing an amendment to the Commercial Code, while promoting stockholder democratization by dissolving the *zaibatsu* (i.e., major holding companies).

Although the latter dissolution reform was aimed at transforming the Japanese corporate system into a 'diffused' one (i.e., the US model that supervises managers through a board representing a diffuse mass of external stockholders whose rights are defended by a variety of institutional rules), it had an unintended effect in strengthening contingent governance. The SCAP reform faced stiff opposition from members of the Japanese business and legal communities who viewed it as a major challenge to contingent governance already prevalent among many Japanese firms in the immediate postwar era. Because the reform encouraged workers to purchase the dissolved *zaibatsu*-held stocks, stock prices decreased while simultaneously dispersing stockholdings. Hence, firms were at greater risk of hostile takeovers. After capital control restrictions were partially removed in conjunction with Japan's IMF accession in 1952, managers felt even more prone to foreign takeovers. Consequently, they invented a system of cross-stockholding with other firms that had formerly belonged to the same *zaibatsu* oligopolistic network. The Japan Economic Research Institute, a consulting arm for the managers' associations, including the Japan Business Federation (Nippon Keidanren), the Japan Chamber of Commerce and

Industry (Nihon Shoko Kaigisho), the Japan Association of Corporate Executives (Keizai Doyukai), and the Japan Trade Association (Nihon Boekikai), requested the MITI to ease the antimonopoly law on corporate stock transactions to enhance block- and cross-stockholding and even the nationality requirements for corporate board members. A loose antimonopoly law made block- and cross-stockholding legal, but not the nationality requirements. These measures increased the average ratio of block-stockholding from approximately 42 percent in 1955 to 63 percent in 1974 (Miyajima, 2008).[17]

Interfirm coordination

The arrangements of block- and cross-stockholding led to the creation of a horizontal or vertical network of firms (*keiretsu*). Within the network, affiliated firms monitored each other's performance as both stockholders and stakeholders. In addition, managers were incentivized to improve their firms' performance through intra-network competition and reputational mechanisms: organization-based contingent governance (Aoki, 1998). Furthermore, the network internalized an industrial cluster where the affiliated firms were functionally integrated to develop supply chains and conduct joint research and development for product design and technological innovation.

However, organization-based contingent governance was susceptible to collective action in which individual rationality would discourage parent firms from monitoring subsidiaries' performance. To reduce this problem, a commercial bank was designated as a 'main bank' with a task of monitoring the borrowing subsidiaries' performance. The main bank would intervene with a subsidiary's management if it fell into liquidity trouble. Then the contingent governance would become a bank-based *relational* contingent governance. Hence, the main bank effectively substituted for stockholders' control, which was virtually absent amongst the postwar Japanese business community.[18]

Nonetheless, networked firms might not be able to rapidly shift resources from inefficient to efficient sector firms because workers and managers held firm-specific skills, were loyal to a specific firm, and disliked a shift that would threaten their careers even though it was within the same network. Insofar as product life cycles were sluggish under constrained mobility in goods and money, Japanese-style corporate governance could perform reasonably well based on long-term contracts and business planning. Again, the international order of embedded liberalism provided such preconditions.

Partial adaptation

Even before the order shifted to the neoliberal one in the 1990s for enhanced mobility, endogenous movements emerged for corporate governance reform. Negative side-effects of contingent governance were corporate fraud and managerial moral hazard. It was in the self-interest of managers to initiate board reform in order to reduce fraud and moral hazard in attempts to maintain the legitimacy of contingent governance. The 1974 Commercial Code amendment mandated that an auditor be appointed to a corporate board to reduce management fraud. The 1981 Commercial Code amendment went a bid further: (1) mandating the appointment of two or more auditors, one of whom must be full-time; (2) establishing stockholders' rights for managerial proposals; (3) legalizing convertible corporate bond issuance; and (4) repelling disruptors of stockholder meetings (*sokaiya*).

The amendments led to firms establishing audit and supervisory boards, paving the way to the Berle-Means principle of separation between ownership and management. Nonetheless, the amendments were limited in that they neither strengthened minority stockholder protection (MSP) nor reduced cross- or block-stockholding,[19] primarily because they were proposed to the Diet by the Legislative Council of the Ministry of Justice where managers were disproportionately represented compared to stockholders[20] (see Chapter 6 for details).

Therefore, the partial adaptation attempt can be understood from the politics of authority allocation and governing coalition. However, the contingent governance model lost its efficiency, as the preconditions dissipated with enhanced capital mobility, trade openness, and product life cycles under the neoliberal international order that was ushered in during the 1990s.

4.3.4 Labor Relations

Evolution

The path for long-term employment practices, the third component of the Japanese-style CME, was again similar to those for the main bank and corporate governance systems: public–private interactions based on the interwar institution, the SCAP reform, and postwar reconstruction. The difference hinges on the double standards for regular and irregular workers that evolved from the prewar practices via asymmetric adaptation processes.

As part of its economic democratization policy, the SCAP demanded the legalization of labor unions and the enhancement of workers' managerial participation. Concurrently, it dissolved the enterprise branches of the

Industrial Patriotic Society as a pro-war management–labor collaborative organization. However in practice, the Society's organizational basis was replaced with an enterprise union, while its active members assumed leadership in the widespread 'factory control' movement immediately after the end of the war in an attempt to rebuild the weakened industrial confidence. Furthermore, the management council was formed to facilitate workers' participation in managerial decisions. This led to the internal promotion of corporate management from a firm's skilled labor force. Counterfactually, if industry- or profession-based unionism had been adopted, workers might not have acquired firm-specific skills that emerged as a major feature of Japanese corporate life.

Nonetheless, the enhanced labor participation caused firms to hold excessively large labor forces. Emboldened manual workers demanded increased wages and improved working conditions, creating strong nationwide labor movements and even social unrest. To reduce the size of work force to a competitive level, corporate managers had to rely on external oversight by the firms' lenders or main banks, while the banks had their own incentives to improve the borrowers' managerial efficiency. Through bitter negotiations, workers acquiesced to the proposed arrangements of a reduced work force and bank oversight to maintain their firms' profitability and their jobs in the long run.

Management–labor coordination

In effect, the Japanese labor management model was created based on the system of tripartite collaboration between managers, bankers, and regular workers in the absence of stockholders. Managers conducted wage bargaining with firm-based unions from the viewpoints of long-term business and employment plans. Workers developed firm-specific loyalty and competencies (asset specificity) because their skills were non-transferable skills and mid-career labor markets were sluggish. Additionally, firms provided workers with stable employment in return for dedicated services and constant skills improvement.

However, there was an irrevocable uncertainty about long-term employment contracts under market fluctuations. If workers were uncertain about firms' contractual commitments, they worried about layoff risks and were compelled to find more secure jobs with other firms. As a result, workers sought to improve generalized transferable skills, weakening firm loyalty and firm-specific skills, which were sources of Japanese firms' competitiveness. Even though firms had no intentions of dismissing workers despite adverse market conditions, skepticism generated the same behavioral result.

The public policy program that had a reducing effect on labor market uncertainty was the Ministry of Labor's enforcement of the principle of 'irrational' dismissal upheld by the court decisions. Similarly, the administrative guidance for recession cartel and rationalization by the MITI's industrial bureaus aided gradual industrial restructuring. These policy programs led to the development of a rigid labor market with legal and customary constraints on dismissal. These programs enabled firms to maintain long-term employment that could in turn incentivize the workers to keep their firm-specific loyalty and skills. However, this environment permitted unprofitable firms to stay in the market for the sake of employment, creating a paradox of low unemployment and low economic growth rates that became apparent in the 1990s (Aoki and Okuno, 1996, pp. 264–5).

Asymmetric adaptation

Since the 1980s, industrial companies, including those in Japan, have undergone major changes in the labor markets. In conjunction with enhanced cross-border mobility in goods and money, strong business demands for flexibility in labor markets have emerged. In response, many governments have introduced flexible labor contract laws to enhance employers' freedom in hiring and firing workers. In Northern and Central European countries with the traditions of a coordinated market economy, improvements have been made on unemployment insurance, mid-career markets, and retraining programs to assuage workers' concerns about dismissal. These programs do not differentiate between regular and irregular workers because the labor unions are inclusive and both types of workers are well represented by a social democratic or labor party in government (see Chapter 6 for further details).

On the other hand, differentiated treatments came to fruition in Japan. A temporary work program was introduced for service sectors in 1986 followed by a flexible work-hour program across sectors. This was timed with an economic boom, rising wages, and a shortage of quality labor force. Work flexibility was generally viewed as desirable in diversifying workers' choices to meet variable professional and social needs. In the 1990s and early 2000s, temporary work programs were expanded across many sectors, while unemployment insurance, mid-career job markets, and retraining programs were not significantly improved primarily because firms were uninterested in arrangements that would discourage workers from acquiring firm-specific skills (again, see Chapter 6 for further details). Organizationally, firm-based labor unions are devoted exclusively to regular employees. Because irregular workers are not members of these unions, they form separate unions across firms and sectors. Politically, managers and associated regular elite employees are members of the governing coalition, while few of the irregular workers are. These distinct arrangements can be attributed to politics of the LDP governing coalition, which arguably generate asymmetric policy adaptation for regular and irregular workers to the increasingly liberal international order on labor.

4.3.5 Institutional Complementarity and the Bureaucratic-cabinet Government

Why could the aforementioned multiple institutional arrangements produce rapid economic growth under the decentralized bureaucratic-cabinet government? This question pertains to a missing link within the comparative institutionalist explanation of postwar Japanese economic growth stated earlier. The answer hinges on institutional complementarity between the arrangements, including relational banking, contingent corporate governance, and long-term employment. Relational banking reduces the importance of stock issuance to business firms' capital formation, contributing to the preservation of cross- and block-stockholding, which was a precondition for contingent governance. Then the contingent governance incentivized regular workers to develop firm-specific skills for career promotion up to managerial positions. Long-term employment in turn created a large pool of competent and determined candidates for future managers, making contingent governance durable.

As explained earlier, bureaus in the public policy domains of their jurisdictions separately regulate these institutional arrangements. Because of institutional complementarity, a bureau's policy action would have a complementary effect on its counterpart's irrespective of whether they consciously or unconsciously coordinated their actions. Equally important, the postwar international order of embedded liberalism allowed for constrained liberalization as well as the maximal maintenance of national rules and standards in pursuit of growth and stability.

Suppose that there are two industrial sectors, an efficient internationally competitive sector and an inefficient internationally non-competitive sector (Table 4.4). Suppose further that the former prefers trade liberalization

Table 4.4 Policy change, distributive conflict, and coordination

		Agent 2	
	Domain 1/Domain 2	Liberalization	Protection
Agent 1	Liberalization	2, 1	2, 2
	Protection	0, 0	1, 2

against which it can withstand and even facilitate its business position, whereas the latter dislikes liberalization that will undermine its domestic sales and put its survival at risk through import expansion. The opposite is true for trade protection. Under the order of embedded liberalism, the state may not have to undertake sweeping cross-sectoral liberalization and may maintain the preferred asymmetric policies for both sectors – the upper right solution in Table 4.4 (Nash equilibrium) is permitted. Separate rational decisions for the two sectors suffice to achieve the solution, without establishing a central command. This is substantially different from the case for the neoliberal order in which the asymmetric solutions are punished and the state is compelled to coordinate policies for the two sectors in pursuit of cross-sectoral liberalization (see Chapter 1). This indeed occurred in the wake of changing international orders in the 1990s and will be a topic for Part II of this book.

4.4 POLICY COORDINATION WITH ANCILLARY AUTHORITIES

Even under the international order of embedded liberalism, Japan intermittently faced enhanced liberalization obligations and pressures that imposed significant adjustment burdens on its decentralized government. These formal obligations and informal pressures ensued in conjunction with the conclusion of multilateral trade rounds, the adoption of new international treaties, or the substantial improvement of national income. While adroit at adaptation, the decentralized government was inept at inter-policy domain coordination associated with broad liberalization. Electorally, rank-and-file members of the ruling LDP sought to oppose liberalization in order to secure regulatory rents for the cross-sectoral governing coalition. In both cases, political leadership might turn to external ancillary authorities to break a domestic impasse and promote policy coordination. In this section, I focus on trade and finance.

4.4.1 Trade Liberalization

Through bitter negotiations, Japan acceded to the GATT in 1955 with US support over European objection. However, several European countries evoked GATT Article 35 (non-application of the agreement between particular contracting parties) to refuse to provide Japan with a most favored nation (MFN) status partly because they still regarded Japan as a war enemy and partly because of the economic fear that Japan, given the MFN status, would begin to send cheap exports to European markets using the mercantilist instruments of a depreciated currency, export promotion, and import restriction. European countries formed the European Economic Community (EEC) in 1957 with the goal of establishing a common market, while restoring the convertibility of their currencies to the US dollar. From the Japanese perspective, these European movements were viewed as a threat that would isolate Japan from the international economic community. In the GATT ministerial meeting of 1958 held in Tokyo, US State Secretary Lodge urged Japan to speed up its own trade liberalization to lessen the European skepticism in pursuit of the removal of the Article 35 restriction. In addition, the IMF advocated liberalization in trade and foreign exchange contingent upon stability in the balance of payments as an IMF Article 8 obligation, which was viewed as a certificate for the developed world, the removal of the GATT Article 35 restriction, and accession to the Organisation for Economic Co-operation and Development (OECD).

In response, the Kishi Cabinet established the Plan on the Liberalization of Trade and Foreign Exchange that would liberalize trade up to 80 percent mainly on industrial products until 1961. This was a major departure from the MOF/BOJ-led sector-specific import control in the immediate postwar era to balance payments constraints and protection of infant industries. Furthermore, US President John F. Kennedy sought to facilitate international trade liberalization as a means to defend the US dollar in the midst of declining trade surpluses, by enacting the Trade Expansion Act, which ultimately led to the conclusion of the Kennedy Round in 1967. Correspondingly, Prime Minister Ikeda (1960–64) decided to speed up and expand the Kishi Cabinet's plan up to the 90 percent liberalization level until 1963. Industrialists and bureaucratic officials were worried that Japanese firms still lagged behind US and European rivals and could not compete squarely without high tariff barriers. To obtain domestic consent, the Ikeda Cabinet took advantage of the Japan–US Joint Committee on Trade and Economic Problems as an external ancillary authority to persuade the opponents on the urgency for trade liberalization. The committee was held for the first time in fall of 1961 upon President Kennedy's request and met annually until 1973 with cabinet officials' participation under the norm of 'equal partnership' (see Chapter 7 for more details).

Moreover, to assuage the liberalization anxieties, the Kishi Cabinet expanded loan programs for SMEs that were likely to suffer from import injuries due to tariff cuts. For the workers whose jobs and income might be threatened by liberalization, the Kishi Cabinet established a national medical insurance system, while the Ikeda Cabinet established minimum wages and a national pension. The package of liberalization and social security programs was part of the Income Doubling Plan, the Ikeda Cabinet's primary economic policy mandate. The governing conservative party's adoption of a welfare state was fueled not just by the need for liberalization, but by a rise of progressive opposition parties, primarily the Japan Socialist Party (JSP) that attracted increasing popular support by advocating for generous social welfare programs. The Kishi-Ikeda cabinets emulated some of the JSP programs to legitimize their liberalization agenda and expand the LDP's support base further into urban workers.

Still, the GATT order permitted the protection of import-sensitive industries. Residual barriers were continuously imposed on selected agricultural products, including rice, sugar, tobacco, dairy products, and so on. Moreover, some of the US requested liberalization items (e.g., automobiles, computers, and industrial machineries) were met with reservation because these products were viewed as strategically important by the MITI industrial bureaus. While prime ministers often advocated for generalized trade liberalization, the bureaus pursued sectoral protection. Under the decentralized environment, intra-governmental negotiations produced selective liberalization outcomes.

4.4.2 Financial Liberalization

The wave of financial liberalization pressure came to Japanese shores a bit later than trade liberalization. The Treaty of the International Monetary Fund (IMF) to which Japan acceded in 1952 urged its contracting states to remove capital controls in a graduated manner, depending upon their development levels. Article 14 exempted less developed or transition economies from the full liberalization obligations stated by Article 8 for developed economies. Japan could use the exemption until 1964 when it accepted the full obligations. Even before that, the US government had demanded the gradual liberalization of Japanese financial markets through conditionality associated with war reconstruction loans. The US loans were offered conditionally upon Japan's provision of the MFN and national treatment (NT) principles for foreign investors as well as tight screening and prudential regulation. Japan needed foreign capital to reconstruct the war-torn socioeconomic infrastructure and counter the deflationary effect of the Dodge Line that imposed fiscal austerity to tackle postwar inflation.

With tenacious bargaining, the Yoshida Cabinet settled the issue with the Eisenhower Administration by accepting both the MFN and NT principles for a variety of industrial sectors, but only the MFN for the financial sector for the fear of foreign takeover. Prime Minister Yoshida obtained US approval by alluding to Japan's fragile balance of payments and geopolitical significance for the US Cold War strategy. In return, the Japanese government agreed to provide the NT principle only to the incumbent US banks that had already entered Japanese markets.[21] This *quid pro quo* arrangement kept the influence of foreign financial institutions at bay, protecting the national banking rules and standards.[22]

Even when Japan accepted the Article 8 obligations, it again placed reservations on 18 of the 37 liberalization items demanded by the IMF. Capital control was an important condition for the main bank system because the system was based on the MOF's regulatory control (interest rate control, segmented competition, implicit bank bailout guarantee, etc.), which was effective only in the absence of large foreign financial institutions and mobile capital owners who would reject the control.

Comparatively, the use of an external ancillary authority was less intense for financial than for trade liberalization because the former would produce a broader and severer effect on Japanese industrial sectors than the latter. Under the decentralized bureaucratic-cabinet government, ministerial bureaus managed trade liberalization sectorally, while few bureaus could manage financial liberalization with a far-reaching, cross-sectoral distributive effect. As a result, financial liberalization lagged behind, impeding the development of capital markets and risk diversification techniques in the postwar Japanese financial community.

4.5 CONCLUSION: VARIOUS ADAPTATIONS AND INSTITUTIONAL MISALIGNMENT

In this chapter, I explained how the postwar political-economic system evolved from interwar authoritarianism to political democracy and eventually to a market economy, while maintaining bureaucratic policy delegation and stakeholder capitalism. Newly added arrangements were patient capital with bank oversight, industrial networks with reputational mechanisms for managerial competence, firm-centric unions and pension schemes for firm-specific skills and loyalty. These newly layered arrangements made the postwar economic system internally coherent, compatible with agents' individual interests, and consistent with the principle of a market economy. The transition was mediated by occupation command that provided mixed foundations for the postwar political economy. While removing the authoritarian elements, the SCAP kept the bureaucratic-controlled system and the associated public policy domains that entailed interwar arrangements. With their strong organizational and individual missions, postwar bureaucracies administered their distinct policy domains appropriately because the governing party willingly delegated policy authorities to them and because the international order of embedded liberalism permitted sectoral policy adjustments, making their policy tasks largely complementary to one another.

The CME stakeholders whose interests were protected by the policy domains were generally members of the LDP governing coalition. Many provided the LDP with stable support insofar as the LDP-led government had the policy domains administered adequately by bureaucratic ministries through delegation and monitoring. Thus, the governing party and the ministries held shared interests in protecting CME stakeholders and promoting CME institutions in order to pursue electoral gains and organizational tasks, respectively. In effect, the systems of bureaucratic-cabinet and CME were complementary under the international order of embedded liberalism based on the compatibility of interests held by the governing party, bureaucracies, and governing coalition.

The microfoundations of incentive compatibility and institutional complementarity are the keys to the postwar Japanese political economic system as these distinguish it from the macro-structural models of Gerschenkron's late developer and Johnson's developmental state. The distinction is crucial to preventing the phenomenon of middle-income trap. More recently, states known as 'emerging states' have replicated the developmental state model, but, despite their initial successes, some have failed to boost their industrial and income levels beyond middle thresholds. A cause of the middle-income trap might be found in the absence of microfoundations, which should be prevalent across all sectors to realize sustainable growth.

Nonetheless, even the Japanese decentralized government is susceptible to policy degeneration, characterized as bureau-pluralism. To avert degeneration, the LDP government occasionally coalesced with the external ancillary authorities to reduce the bureau-pluralistic practices and promote internal coordination for institutional adjustments to meet changes in international orders in pursuit of efficiency and competitiveness. Despite the occasional use of external ancillary authorities, Japan lost its adaptive efficiency and experienced low growth in the 1990s and 2000s in part because external ancillary authorities collaborated with Japanese political leadership only in the policy domains of their interest and would not intervene in other domains that might be crucial for furthering efficiency. This may be in part because the extent of adjustment to the newly emergent neoliberal order is beyond the limited coordination capability of the decentralized government.

As indicated in this chapter, an early sign was observed in the wake of accelerated trade and foreign exchange liberalization in the 1980s. Since then, Japan has been exposed to comprehensive adjustments to an increasingly liberal international order. The bureaucratic-cabinet system has been ineffective in the inter-ministerial coordination necessary for comprehensive adjustments, thus engendering an institutional disequilibrium. As its electoral foundation has gradually eroded, the governing party has become more disposed towards protecting the non-competitive sectors of the governing coalition as reliable supporters.

In the realm of security and foreign policy, the principle of defensive defense became subject to revision in the 1990s as the Cold War paradigm lost influence during the first decade after the demise of the Soviet Union. Increasingly, the bilateral alliance started to reinvent itself, developing a new strategic concept in the mid-1990s that broadened the alliance's mission. Reformists within defense policy communities in Tokyo and Washington want the alliance to play a more prominent role in regional security, not just the defense of Japan from external aggression (Article 5 contingencies).[23] More specifically, they want the alliance to meet a broader set of challenges that include deterring military confrontation over the Korean Peninsula and the Taiwan Strait, combating the proliferation of nuclear, biological and chemical (NBC) weapons, and providing counterterrorism and missile defense. In their view, the US–Japan alliance should be an enforcer of liberal values and a contributor to maintaining the liberal international order. Stated differently, the reformists see that joint interests could be better served through Japan's deeper integration into US grand strategic considerations. This change in Japanese security and foreign policy has generated additional impetus for adjusting its economic policy to the newly emerging neoliberal economic order.[24] From a slightly different perspective, it appears that Japanese political leadership has been using security cooperation with the United States as a diplomatic leverage to promote economic policy adjustment. This security–economy linkage will be elaborated in Chapter 7 of this book.

In Part II, I will analyze how contemporary Japan has been dealing with the problem of adjusting its CME system to the neoliberal international economic order with an emphasis on specific policy domains – corporate governance and labor relations, international trade, and banking from the viewpoints of authority allocation, coalitional politics, and leaders' political strategies as well as ancillary authorities to ameliorate structural dilemma and manipulation.

NOTES

1. There was a major debate concerning the robustness of the Yoshida Doctrine in post–Cold War Japanese foreign and defense policy. See Heginbotham and Samuels (1998) for the continuous influence of the Yoshida Doctrine in post–Cold War Japanese foreign policy, Green (2003) and Pyle (2008) for its dilution, and Samuels (2007) for an intermediate position.
2. Japan relied on the US nuclear shield and needed no nuclear weapons of its own, but several LDP politicians claimed that it was not unconstitutional for Japan to possess them.

3. This defense budget ceiling was set by a cabinet order in 1967 (Japan Defense Agency, 1976, p. 129).
4. Internationally, as suggested in the text, the issue of security and defense was effectively removed from the adjustment agenda because of the adoption of the Security Treaty of 1951 with the United States and the principle of defensive defense. However, within domestic politics, the issue remained highly contentious between the conservative and the progressive parties.
5. Likewise, Calder (1995) showed strategic credit allocation by public financial institutions, including the Industrial Bank of Japan (IBJ) and the Development Bank of Japan (DBJ), under the auspices of the MOF.
6. Although Hall and Soskice (2001) did not refer directly to the postwar Japanese economy, their CME model can easily be applied to it.
7. The argument relies on the theory of endogenous economic growth advanced by Uzawa (1965), Romer (1986), Lucas (1988), and Rebelo (1991).
8. However, since bureaucracies held greater information and expertise than the cabinet ministers, it would still be difficult for the political leadership to control bureaucratic behavior on an ex ante basis.
9. In order to deal with hyperinflation fueled by the reconstruction finance scheme, the SCAP directed the Japanese government to adhere to the principle of balanced budget through fiscal austerity measures (known as the Dodge Line). The measures included cutbacks on public work projects and industrial subsidies, freezes on income tax cuts and turnover tax abolition.
10. This meant a shift from double exchange rates (depreciated yen for export and appreciated yen for import to balance the trade account) to a single fixed exchange rate (later, 360 yen per US dollar agreed), under which Japan would incur large trade deficits: the optimal exchange rate based on purchasing power parity was about 440 yen per dollar at the time, rather than the official 360 yen per dollar.
11. The recruitment from bureaucracies was the response to the SCAP-led purge of politicians during the occupation. Candidates without interwar political experiences needed to be recruited to fill vacant seats.
12. An SNTV system was used for the House of Representatives elections from 1928 to 1942. Its effect on prewar party politics was unobservable because party governments were swiftly replaced by a bipartisan bureaucratic government in 1932 that effectively removed inter-party competition. SNTVs were reintroduced in 1947 and continued till 1993.
13. LDP leaders initiated distributive programs to maintain support from inefficient sectors of the governing coalition. Prime Minister Hayato Ikeda's program was to achieve the doubling of the average citizen's income, Prime Minister Nobusuke Kishi for social security for the sick and elderly, and Prime Minister Kakuei Tanaka for rural development. These programs were aimed at expanding the fruits of economic growth to the members of the inefficient sectors who might otherwise have felt wary about Japan's participation in the liberal international order. In addition, the programs constituted a major part of the Japanese-style social welfare regime, thus helping the LDP obtain popular consent to its economic policy (Calder, 1995; Estévez-Abe, 2008).
14. This point is consistent with the theory of interest groups developed by Rajan and Zingales (2003) in which they argue that the postwar Bretton Woods system permitted states to keep closed financial markets favorable to the incumbent stakeholders such as bankers and managers and the maintenance of the national economic systems.
15. Coal and steel constituted engines of industrial growth but were unable to increase their production because of close interdependence between the two sectors – an increase in the production of one sector would have to come from an increase in another, creating circularity. The priority production method sought to solve this coordination dilemma by distributing steel to the coal industry and coal to the steel industry through non-market transactions (Okazaki and Okuno-Fujiwara, 1999).
16. Until the late 1990s, Japan had not established a formal deposit insurance scheme.

Instead, an informal protection mechanism had been operative – when a bank became insolvent, a healthy bank that accumulated large rents would be asked by the MOF to rescue the failing one through a merger or acquisition. Because of this implicit protection mechanism known as the 'convoy system' (*goso sendan hoshiki*), officially, no single bank became insolvent between 1950 and 1997.

17. The explanation for the block-stockholding model in Japan stresses the importance of contingent governance that filled the vacuum created by the dissolution of *zaibatsu* holding companies. This differs from Gourevitch and Shinn (2007) who attribute block-stockholding to a multi-party system that creates a coalition government based on sectoral interests. The authors also try to attribute the rise of stockholder capitalism (or a diffused model) in the late Meiji era of the 1880s to the two-party system. But, as argued in Chapter 3, multi-partyism prevailed during the period, while the Meiji government was viewed as oligarchic. A competitive two-party system emerged in the brief period of parliamentary democracy between 1920 and 1932.
18. The unique CME institutions of cross-stockholding, industrial networks, and main banks produced the unintended effect of the underdevelopment of auditing and rating agencies. According to Gourevitch and Shinn (2007), auditing and rating agencies are important reputational intermediaries for a diffused model and minority shareholder protection that are the key to robust stock markets, but they were virtually unnecessary for the postwar Japanese corporate community because of main banks' oversight. More recently, the lack of reputational intermediaries has hindered the government's attempt at buttressing stock markets (see Chapters 6 and 8).
19. Furthermore, the development of a diffused model in Japan has been hindered by the weak administrative independence of the Securities and Exchange Surveillance Commission (SESC) and the national pension and insurance funds with high dependence on government bonds rather than on stocks.
20. Intriguing was the MITI's survey asking managers of several hundred large firms about their opinions on corporate reform. This indicated a typical bureaucracy's decision-making style in which it takes the regulated industry's preferences into consideration.
21. Similarly, the World Bank demanded that Japan meet the conditions for loan agreements, non-inflationary monetary policy, market economy, trade promotion, public investment plan, and domestic saving promotion through tax reform in pursuit of steady economic growth and loan repayability.
22. The discretionary bailout scheme, another important component of the convoy system, emerged in the aftermath of the financial crisis in 1965. The Sato Cabinet (1964–72) urged the Bank of Japan to bail out the Yamaichi Security House by injecting public funds derived from the issuance of government bonds. While the cost of the bailout was levied on taxpayers, the rescue led to a quick economic recovery that precipitated the longest boom in postwar Japanese history. The discretionary bailout scheme became part of the convoy system that the MOF had used to maintain financial stability for the next 30 years until another major financial crisis occurred in 1998.
23. See Suzuki (2010) for details from the perspective of coordination theory similar to the approach taken in this book.
24. Indeed, as shown in Part II of this book, policy reforms designed to adjust the Japanese economy to the post–Cold War neoliberal international order have been promoted by prime ministers, including Hashimoto, Koizumi and Abe, who shared a relatively strong pro-US foreign policy stance.

PART II

Contemporary analysis

5. Authority reallocation under the neoliberal global order – an overview

5.1 GLOBALIZATION AND CENTRALIZATION

5.1.1 Comprehensive Liberalization

A neoliberal global order has emerged since the 1980s, gradually replacing the post–World War II order of embedded liberalism. Under the new order, states are urged for cross-sectoral, sweeping liberalization, as opposed to sectorally limited, incremental liberalization under the preceding order. The scope of openness has expanded from conventional commodity trade to trade in services and agriculture. Enhanced regulatory rules on corporate governance and labor relations are pushed for the promotion of international investment. Last and not least, global standards for commercial banks' minimum capital requirements are necessitated for financial prudence and stability.

On the one hand, the implementation of these market-consistent rules and standards stimulates global competition, but on the other it generates a major distributive problem between domestic economic sectors (battle of the sexes game; see Chapter 1). The distributive effect is substantial, particularly for states with non-liberal origins whose national rules and standards are qualitatively different from those of liberal states. The solution to the distributive problem requires the coordination of the policy actions of multiple ministries and agencies in charge of different policy domains and economic sectors. As put forward in Part I of this book, the decentralized government structure and the related approach of bureaucratic delegation under the bureaucratic-cabinet system are unsuited to inter-ministerial coordination on the issue of a major distributive problem. The continuous use of bureaucratic delegation would cause structural dilemma and manipulation. Therefore, adjustment to the global order and a solution to the coordination problem require the centralization of the government structure and the establishment of political command.

5.1.2 Majoritarian Consumerism

Globalists argue that, with the political and administrative reforms in the 1990s, contemporary Japan has become capable of responding appropriately to comprehensive liberalization and regulatory reform under the neoliberal order. First, the reforms have contributed to the centralization of the government structure and the strengthening of the prime minister's political power and policy authority. The old electoral system, the single non-transferable vote (SNTV) system for the House of Representatives, was replaced with a mixed system that combines first-past-the-post (FPTP) votes with proportional representation (PR) votes. Among the 475 seats of the lower house, 295 are chosen through FPTP votes in single-member districts (SMDs), whereas the remaining 180 seats are chosen through PR votes in nine regional blocks (with non-binding party lists). According to Duverger's Law, FPTP votes will produce a two-party system in which two parties compete for power and either one can capture a majority of seats in a parliamentary house with minor third parties being ineffective and defunct because of strategic voting or rational candidate withdrawal or both (Cox, 1997).

In FPTP elections without primaries, a single candidate must be chosen by a party to run for each SMD to avoid vote fragmentation and to win a seat. This electoral arrangement shifts candidate nomination authority from factional to party leadership. Similarly, a PR election gives party leadership the opportunity to rank party candidates on a party list. Each of the two electoral schemes compels rank-and-file party members to be subservient to their party leadership to solicit nomination. Thus, the mixed system that combines both schemes empowers party leadership's nominating authority and helps centralize party organizations, thus diminishing intra-party factional politics that had a fragmentary effect on government under the previous SNTV system (Cox et al., 1999).[1]

Second, the FPTP vote-centric mixed system is said to produce a majoritarian-consumerist effect on the state's economic policy (Rosenbluth and Thies, 2010, pp. 184–5, 192). Under the assumption of a two-party system with centripetal competition, candidates of major parties are expected to appeal to the interests of the median voter in the electorate, or consumerist interests, in order to win the office. Having assumed power, the victorious party leads a majoritarian government to cater to consumerist interests by improving market efficiency through regulatory policies, including competition laws, property rights protection laws, free trade policies, and so forth. This is in direct contrast to the distributive policy programs that are earmarked for narrowly defined sectors of society and are often pursued by parties under a consensual democratic system based on proportional representation (including SNTV). PR produces a multi-party system in which small parties vie for seats by representing sectoral interests in business, labor, agriculture, and so on. A government has to be formed by a coalition of parties and maintained through a coordination of sectoral interests that are represented by the parties in the coalition (Rogowski and Kayser, 2002; Persson and Tabellini, 2004; Iversen and Soskice, 2006, p. 616).[2]

In sum, the preceding line of argument suggests that a liberal market economy co-evolves with a majoritarian political system within which government leadership has a strong electoral incentive to improve market efficiency and satisfy consumerist interest. Several analysts contend that the Japanese political system has become increasingly majoritarian under the FPTP-centric mixed electoral system and consequently favorable for a liberal market economy. This means a major departure of the Japanese economy from the prior coordinated market system that evolved under the SNTV system.

5.2 PUBLIC PREFERENCES, ELECTORAL POLITICS, AND POLICY MANIPULATION

5.2.1 Constrained Majoritarian Consumerism

Contrary to the aforementioned hypothesis, majoritarian consumerism is moderate at best under the post-reform Japanese political system. Without strong electoral pressure for majoritarian consumerism, government officials may not be incentivized to reduce the vested sectoral interests that have been locked in the prior decentralized government arrangements and public policies. The following three reasons are cited to account for constrained majoritarian consumerism.

Mixed electoral system with the resurrection rule

First, the mixed system, which combines FPTP votes with PR votes and entails the resurrection rule (to be explained shortly), is not a genuine FPTP system and produces an imperfect two-party, or even multi-party, system within the House of Representatives. As shown in Table 5.1, contrary to Duverger's Law, the number of effective parties (i.e., parties that acquire more than 5 percent of total candidate votes) has not decreased after the shift from the SNTV to the mixed system.[3] Elections yielded two effective parties only once – in the 2009 general election in which the Democratic Party of Japan (DPJ) triumphed over the Liberal Democratic Party (LDP) for the first time. The other six general elections under the mixed system constantly produced effective third parties, including the

Table 5.1 Number of effective parties under the SNTV and the mixed system

Year	1990	1993	1996	2000	2003	2005	2009	2012	2014
Number of effective parties	4	5	4	3	3	4	2	5	4

Note: An 'effective party' is a party that acquired more than 5 percent of aggregated votes across all districts in a general election. The figures for the elections in 1990 and 1993 are based on SNTV, while those for the following elections are based on the FPTP votes of the mixed system.

Source: The numbers of effective parties are computed based on the data on party votes from the Bureau of Statistics of the Ministry of Internal Affairs and Communications (http://www.stat.go.jp/english/index.htm; accessed 24 October 2015).

Japanese Communist Party (JCP) and the Ishin no To (Japan Innovation Party, since 2012), which attracted ideological voters and dissatisfied urban voters in western Japan, respectively. The Clean Government Party (the Komeito), a continuous coalition partner of the LDP, could have been another effective third party with loyal followers of the Buddhist group, the Soka Gakkai, had it terminated electoral cooperation with the senior partner. Furthermore, third-party candidates are able and willing to enter SMD elections to seek PR seats by exploiting the resurrection rule of the mixed system. The rule means that even though they are defeated in the SMD races, candidates still can win PR seats given their parties' sufficiently large PR votes plus their own sufficiently small margins of losses in the SMD races (known as the *sekihai-ritsu*). Voters in turn have incentives to cast their FPTP votes for such candidates to promote their resurrections in PR elections by diminishing their margins of losses. Thus, the resurrection rule pre-empts rational withdrawal by third parties, which is a logical facilitator of a two-party system.[4]

Consequently, the share of the largest party's votes in general elections has been far below 50 percent (Figure 5.1), suggesting that the largest party in recent general elections conducted under the mixed system could never be qualified as 'majoritarian'. With multi-party races, even candidates of the largest party were not pressured to pursue the median voter's preference because they could win seats with less than a majority of the FPTP votes.

Bicameralism with electoral malapportionment

A second reason for the non-centrist policy tendency hinges on the constitutional arrangement of symmetric bicameralism.[5] This means that the House of Representatives and the House of Councillors [sic] have almost

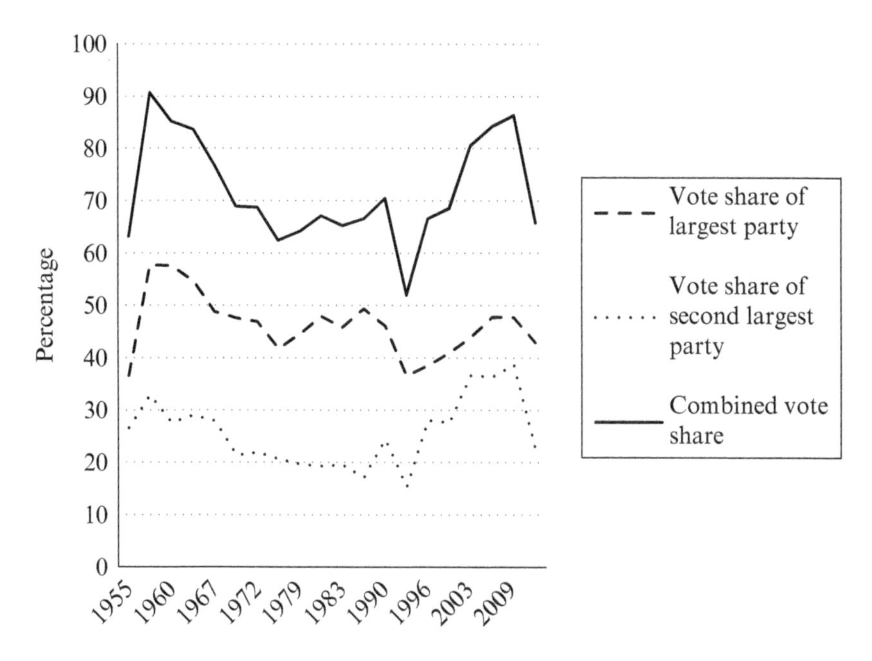

Source: The data are provided by the Bureau of Statistics of the Ministry of Internal Affairs and Communications (http://www.stat.go.jp/english/index.htm; accessed 24 October 2015).

Figure 5.1 Combined vote share of the two largest parties in the House of Representatives

equal power in enacting a bill to set forth a new public policy program. The two houses hold popular elections under different electoral schemes and constituencies with different time intervals, possibly producing different parliamentary majorities. In the recent past, this arrangement has created a 'twisted Diet' (*nejire kokkai*) in which the governing majority coalition (or party) chosen by the lower house did not have a majority of seats in the upper house.[6] Thus, the cabinets, formed by the majority coalitions, had enormous difficulties passing cabinet bills through the bicameral Diet and conveying the preference of the median voter in the lower house, not just because they lacked overall control in the upper house, but also because they had a limited access to procedural decisions based on the parliamentary rule.[7]

Furthermore, both houses have suffered from chronic disparity in seat allocation across districts (see Figure 5.2 for the House of Representatives). Disproportionate shares of seats are given to rural districts at the expense of urban districts despite the latter's population increases due

Source: The figure is based on data from the Bureau of Statistics of the Ministry of Internal Affairs and Communications (http://www.stat.go.jp/english/index.htm; accessed 24 October 2015).

Figure 5.2 Electoral malapportionment in the House of Representatives

to continuous migration. In spite of repeated lawsuits by lawyers' groups and civic organizations, the judicial system has been unwilling to strike down the existing electoral rules for both parliamentary houses as being unconstitutional for contradicting the principle of a single vote per person. Instead, the Supreme Court handed down rulings declaring a 'state of unconstitutionality' for the 2009 and 2012 general elections for the House of Representatives due to a 2.30 and 2.43 disparity in vote weights between the most populous and the least populous district, respectively. For the House of Councillors, the Supreme Court ruled a state of unconstitutionality for the 2010 election (5.00 disparity ratio) and the 2013 election (4.77 disparity ratio). These acts of judicial restraint hinge on the conviction of popular sovereignty and parliamentary supremacy that have consistently been upheld since the promulgation of the democratic Constitution in 1947. With the ambivalent rulings, the Supreme Court has effectively delegated reform responsibility to the Diet. Of course, because it is dominated by members chosen from rural districts, the Diet has been extremely cautious about revising the existing electoral rules and the seat allocation arrangements in accordance with the geographical distribution of voters. Because rural districts often have high concentrations of inefficient sectors that are susceptible to import pressure, electoral majorities in these rural districts are rarely liberal consumerist and oppose economic liberalization, defying majoritarian consumerism at the national level. In the bicameral Diet, it has become increasingly difficult for a single party to control a majority in both houses because of the lingering malapportionment and increasing popular preference heterogeneity. Thus, Japanese governments since 1993 have continuously been coalitional ones. This is in sharp contrast to a single coherent majority party consistently in power postulated by the Westminster model. These coalition governments in recent Japan are formed between the largest LDP (DPJ between 2009 and 2012) and the smaller Komeito or other small, ideologically moderate parties (the Sakigake, the Social Democratic Party, the Liberal Party, or the Conservative Party). Because of power asymmetries, intra-coalition bargaining over policy has shifted toward the conservative or business direction preferred by the LDP, thus failing to capture the preference of the median voter in the electorate (Suzuki, 2005).

Party organizations

A third and last reason for the sectoral tendencies hinges on party organizations with strong sectoral connections. Here, I focus on the LDP since it has continually been in power and is the most important party for modern Japan. The LDP holds three important organizations, including the General Affairs Committees, the Policy Affairs Research Committees (PARCs), and individual members' support organizations (*koen-kai*), which were created and developed to seek SNTVs through strong connections with sectoral interests. These organizations still prove useful for gathering political contributions and electoral support even under the mixed system (Krauss and Pekkanen, 2010).

Yet the adoption of the mixed system has produced some limited 'desectorization' of the LDP's support structure. Changes in occupations and industrial affiliations of LDP supporters are identified based on longitudinal survey data provided by the Social Stratification and Mobility (SSM) study that has been conducted systematically every ten years since 1955 by groups of Japanese sociologists (Table 5.2). The share of LDP supporters who work in agriculture or are self-employed (owner-managers of small and medium-sized enterprises [SMEs]) has declined sharply. As a result, supporters in 2005 were slightly more spread across occupational categories than in 1955, but with some residual concentration on agricultural workers and the self-employed. This partial desectorization of the LDP support structure can be attributed to the electoral reform of the House

Table 5.2 Political supporters of the LDP by occupation, 1955–2005

Job/Year	1955	1965	1975	1985	1995	2005
Professional	28.6	32.8	23.7	33.8	16.5	26.2
Supervisors	45.2	66.4	61.0	55.4	34.7	35.3
Clerk	25.3	32.4	34.6	32.5	22.3	24.1
Retail	54.5	53.4	44.4	54.5	29.7	34.9
Skilled	38.8	35.1	36.5	37.7	24.6	26.6
Semi-skilled	33.3	24.0	27.8	37.9	19.0	29.0
Unskilled	28.4	26.0	30.1	41.1	23.2	31.5
Agriculture	51.6	63.1	65.6	60.5	39.2	37.3
Self-employed	49.0	58.4	59.6	56.0	36.2	39.0
All	42.1	42.1	40.2	41.9	25.2	29.6

Note: Each figure represents the percentage ratio of respondents who supported the LDP to all respondents in a particular occupational category.

Source: The data are from SSM surveys and Tanabe (2011, p. 52).

of Representatives, partially consistent with the majoritarian hypothesis. Nonetheless, if majoritarianism were really robust under the mixed system, support for the LDP would be more evenly distributed across sectors and occupations.

Furthermore, these old party organizations at the national level are linked closely to regional chapters at the prefectural and municipal levels where SNTVs have continued to be employed for assembly elections. Thus, regional SNTV elections transmit sectoral influence to the party headquarters in Tokyo through organizational ties, constraining the major party's shift toward the median voter at the national level.

The limited desectorization of the LDP's support structure means that when in power the LDP may pursue policy adjustments to the global economic order to variable extents, depending on the strength of sectoral interests within its governing coalition. More specifically, agricultural policy may still be susceptible to strong protectionist pressure because of strong political support from the agricultural sector and electoral malapportionment in favor of rural districts (see Chapter 7). Likewise, the SME policy may tend toward protectionism, including generous subsidies and accounting rules for bank lending (Chapter 8). Last, reduced support from clerical and unskilled workers compared with peak levels in 1985 suggests that the LDP's labor policy for contractual flexibility has become less favorable for these groups (Chapter 6).

The decline in the influence of labor within the LDP support structure means a reciprocal increase in business influence that may be translated into the market-consistent neoliberal policy pushed by recent LDP-led governments. Thus, it is incorrect to ascribe such policy single-mindedly to majoritarian consumerism that is registered only weakly in the party system. Neoliberal policy may rather be a consequence of the expanded influence of business and private finance – increasingly powerful sectoral interests within the governing coalition.

5.2.2 Administrative Reform and Structural Manipulation

In this section, I shift the analytical focus to the bureaucracies that should never be ignored when analyzing public policy in Japan. In 2000, the Basic Act for Reforming the National Government Organizations (Chuo Shocho to Kaikaku Kihon Ho) streamlined bureaucratic organizations and arguably contributed to the improvement of central political command. The number of ministries and agencies was halved through mergers, while political appointees to the ministries were increased. In addition, the number of deliberative councils was halved from 211 to 105 in 2000 by the law. By definition, a deliberative council is a policy-proposing institution of a ministry or agency,[8] whose legal status, jurisdiction, and members are determined by a ministry's establishment act. In reality, however, the council is often used to pursue negative agenda-setting, or to delegitimize new policy ideas in order to maintain the existing policy administered by the ministry (Kusano, 1995; Ogawa, 1997). It is expected that, by reducing the number of councils, political leadership can weaken the councils' negative agenda-setting power and increase its ability to replace existing policy with new policy, which would amount to positive agenda-setting power.[9]

The effects of these reforms are felt by elite bureaucratic officials who responded to the longitudinal opinion surveys taken by Muramatsu and his associates (Muramatsu, 2010) in the years 1980, 1994, and 2003–04. A majority of the respondents in the 2003–04 survey said that their overall policy influence had decreased in favor of elected officials[10] (Muramatsu, 2010, pp. 108–9). More importantly, the survey results suggest changes in multifaceted bureaucratic roles rather than an across-the-board decline of bureaucratic influence.

Specifically, the survey questions asking about bureaucratic tasks show that information processing and communication with elected officials have become more important, while balancing sectoral interests and interministerial coordination have decreased in importance (Figure 5.3). In addition, bureaucratic officials said they gain information from contacting representatives of private groups, but are concerned about a distortionary effect on their policy visions. These survey findings corroborate the

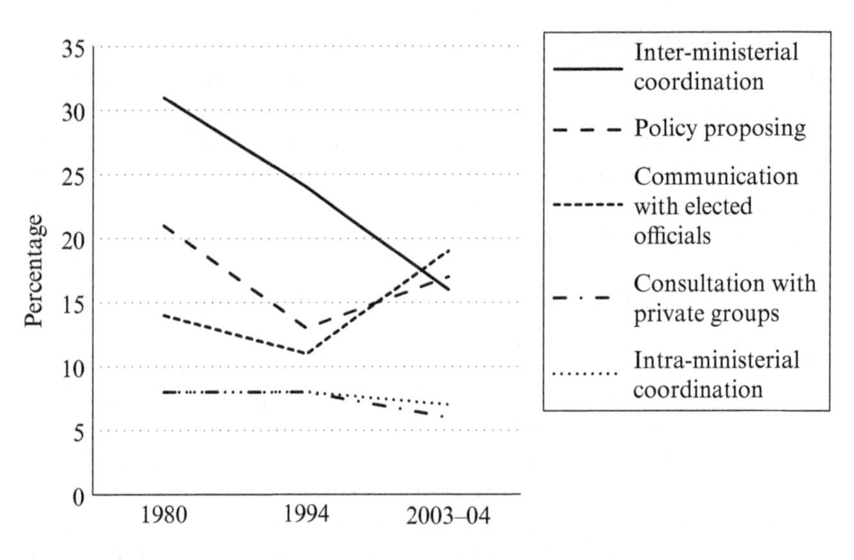

Note: The figure indicates the percentage ratios of the respondents who rated the suggested role as important. The survey respondents were elite bureaucratic officials, including vice-ministers, bureau directors, director-generals, and division directors of the Economic Planning Agency, the Ministry of Finance, the Ministry of Health and Welfare, the Ministry of International Trade and Industry, the Ministry of Labour [sic], the Ministry of Construction, the Ministry of Agriculture, Fishery and Forestry, and the Ministry of General Affairs. Officials holding equivalent positions were surveyed after the administrative reform in 2000. The sample size of the surveys was 251 in 1980, 252 in 1994, and 290 in 2003–04.

Source: Based on data reported in Muramatsu (2010, p. 65).

Figure 5.3 Bureaucratic officials' tasks

main theme of this book with respect to a strengthening of bureaucratic officials' informational and communicative role, and a weakening of their coordinating role at times of major policy reform.

The survey data indicate a general tendency toward enhancing bureaucrats' role in information processing and policy proposal-making. Nonetheless, the data do not deny officials' continued, albeit reduced, concerns with promoting and balancing sectoral interests, which is still ranked as the second most important determinant of bureaucratic policy decisions (Figures 5.4 and 5.5). Corroborating the survey findings, ministries have increased the number of deliberative sub-councils, totaling 863 in 2005,[11] perhaps in attempts to counterbalance the reduced number of deliberative councils. Thus, the reduced number of councils does not mean reduced bureaucratic influence to the advantage of the cabinet or the prime minister.

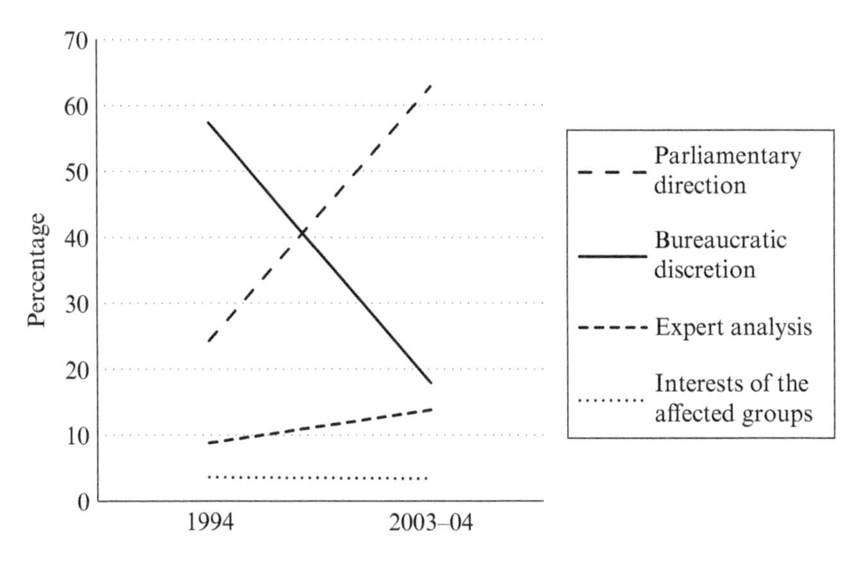

Note: The figure indicates the percentage ratios of respondents who rated the suggested factor to be important. See the descriptions in Figure 5.3.

Source: Based on data reported in Muramatsu (2010, p. 75).

Figure 5.4 Determinants of bureaucratic policy decisions

Furthermore, the regulatory reform toward the neoliberal global order has arguably increased the influence of bureaucratic organizations because regulatory complexity enhances the need for policy information and expertise that are unavailable to politicians, let alone the general public (Vogel, 2006). This is paradoxical in that political leadership has sought to adjust public policy to the neoliberal global order by reducing bureaucratic resistance, which in turn increases the need for policy expertise and its bureaucratic reliance. This buttresses the thesis that globalization is associated with the ascendancy of the regulatory state, observed ubiquitously across advanced industrial states (Peters, 2001).

Whether or not the emergence of the regulatory state has resuscitated a bureau-pluralistic government is a highly empirical question. Supporters of the hypothesis predict that a regulatory state enables bureaucratic officials and supervising elected officials to coalesce in manipulating regulatory policy for sectoral interests, rather than for public interests (Mattli and Woods, 2009a). Highly technical regulatory environments provide regulated private sectors with access and opportunities to buy off bureaucratic and political officials for lenient supervision (i.e., 'regulatory

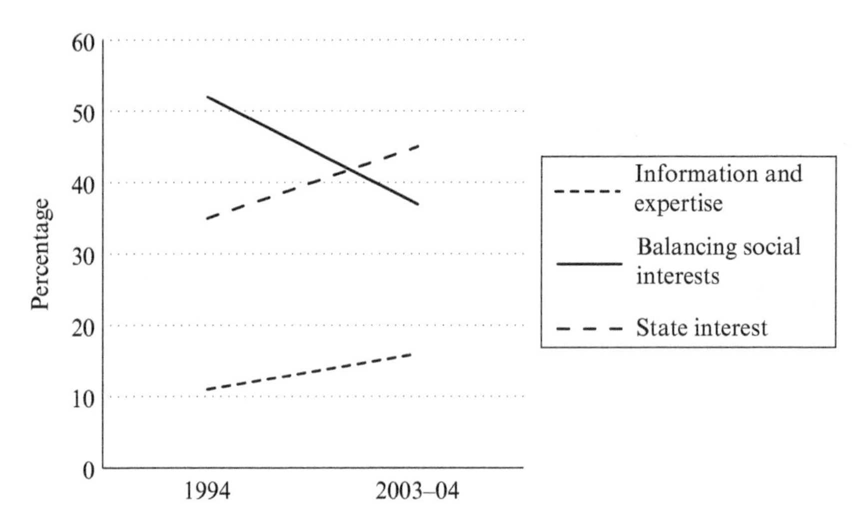

Note: The linked data points are the percentage ratios of the respondents who answered yes to the importance of the suggested determinant. See the descriptions in Figure 5.3.

Source: Based on data reported in Muramatsu (2010, p. 77).

Figure 5.5 Determinants of bureaucratic policy discretion

capture') in pursuit of rents. Such regulatory capture is considered a primary cause of the banking crisis in the late 1990s after the financial big-bang reform that divided the comprehensive regulatory regime, known as the convoy system, into separate entities with supervising and stabilizing functions (see Chapter 8 for details).

5.3 POLITICAL LEADERSHIP AND STRATEGIES FOR POLICY CHANGE

5.3.1 Leadership's Policy Scope

In general, political leadership has an intrinsic interest in catering to public interests because of the nature of its office. This may not differ substantially between the mixed electoral and the SNTV system. Even under the SNTV system, several prime ministers initiated new public policies against political opposition in attempts to cater to the 'public interests' they defined. In doing so, they employed central political command approaches because their bold policies evoked major coordination problems and stiff domestic opposition.

Evidence that substantiates the claim is ample. As discussed by Kitaoka (2008), Prime Minister Shigeru Yoshida invented the principle of defensive defense, backed by US security guarantees, to concentrate the state's limited resources on postwar economic recovery by rejecting the claim of pacifists and textualists that a security treaty would be in violation of the Constitution. Prime Minister Nobusuke Kishi established the national pension and medical care system as a basis for good labor relations by arguing against fiscal conservatives within his party who pressed for the maintenance of small government. Prime Minister Hayato Ikeda launched fiscal expansion and trade liberalization (together known as the 'Income Doubling Plan') to create an affluent society with a large middle class, persuading industrialists and economic bureaucrats who demanded continuous fiscal austerity and trade protection. Prime Minister Yasuhiro Nakasone (1982–87) pushed for the privatization of inefficient state enterprises to improve public services and national economic efficiency, dividing the opposing labor unions into submission.

Without these leaders' policy initiatives evaluated by the bureaucratic-cabinet government and the governing party, postwar economic growth might have been less rapid and less widespread than it turned out to be. Given these precedents, it is empirically incorrect to argue that political leadership can gain a nationwide perspective only under an FPTP system. Even under the SNTV system, LDP party presidents (then prime ministers) were chosen either through closed discussions among faction leaders or through party members' votes, in both of which the selection criteria focused on candidates' policy or ministerial experiences as well as their abilities to unite the party and win parliamentary and local elections (Sato and Matsuzaki, 1982). Individuals with these qualities would often, if not always, have strong commitments to catering to 'public interests', as summarized above.

5.3.2 Political Strategies for Central Command and Policy Change

Faced with globalization and an ailing national economy, contemporary Japanese political leaders might well intend to make policy changes, because of their office's intrinsic tendency to pursue the 'public interests' they envision. Nonetheless, in order to initiate policy change, it is necessary to break with existing policy practices deeply embedded in the party and bureaucratic organizations (as shown in the sections above) and employ powerful central command mechanisms. Such mechanisms have to be capable of coordinating competing social interests as well as policy tasks of multiple bureaucratic organizations.

For policy change, the following political strategies, including council, issue-dimensional, and crisis politics, are useful, and will be central concerns of the empirical analyses in the subsequent chapters of this book.

Council politics

If political leadership and a concerned bureaucratic organization share similar policy preferences, then the leadership can safely delegate policy authority to the bureaucracy, which in turn consults with its deliberative council (*shingikai*) for making a specific policy proposal consistent with the shared preference. Council members are appointed by the ministry based on its internal rules and are often representatives of stakeholders of ministerial policy. However, if their interests differ substantially, the bureaucracy-sponsored deliberative council will exert negative agenda-setting power, or the ability to reject new policy ideas that challenge the existing policy. Then the leadership has to take recourse to referring to a separate advisory council (*shimon i'inkai*) within the Cabinet Office (formerly the Prime Minister's Office) whose members the prime minister can choose at his or her discretion.

Such an advisory council is said to have positive agenda-setting power – the ability to put forward a policy agenda and deliberate on the prime minister's policy proposal with a group of eminent persons with expertise and loyalty to the latter. Of course, even by holding such a council, the prime minister cannot supersede parliamentary debates and consultation with the governing party insofar as the proposal requires enactment. Yet an advisory council can provide the prime minister's proposal with legitimization and publicity, which helps persuade party and bureaucratic officials, while reducing the legitimacy of existing policies or rival proposals endorsed by the deliberative councils under the auspices of ministries. In addition, an advisory council at the cabinet level may have an overarching policy scope that cuts across ministries' policy domains, with the ability to coordinate their policy tasks. In Chapter 6 of this book, council politics will be discussed in the context of corporate governance and labor relations.

Issue-dimensional politics

A second strategy for policy change is one of persuasion with linguistic or rhetorical manipulation – political leadership can manipulate a policy debate by adding or subtracting issue dimensions (Riker, 1986). In doing so, leadership tries to break the dominant political coalition underpinning the existing policy and create an alternative coalition to embrace a new policy it promotes. In the context of Japanese politics, a policy issue is normally classified as part of a single or a handful of ministries' jurisdictions. If a new dimension of the policy issue is added, however, it will draw other ministries into the policy debate, altering the balance of power among the ministries and creating an opportunity to change the existing policy.

A prominent example of linguistic manipulation or 'heresthetics' cited by Riker (1986) is the abolition of the Corn Law in nineteenth-century England. Before the consumerist Liberals seized power, Tory Prime Minister Robert Peel chose to abolish the Corn Law by manipulating issue dimensions to counter staunch opposition within the conservative party. He used linguistic manipulation – unless the Tories abolished the law, the Whigs would win the next election under the expanded suffrage and abolish not just the law, but also the subsidies and other perks given to landlords, the Tories' principal clients. Peel thought that the Tories' pre-emptive abolition of the Corn Law could eliminate the issue of tariff protection and high cereal costs unfavorable to urban workers from the forthcoming election campaign, thus discouraging the Whigs from abolishing the subsidies. Prime Minister Peel's rhetoric added a new dimension, 'subsidies', to the issue of tariff reduction and divided the Tories' protectionist coalition, creating a temporary marriage of convenience between the 'strategically minded' Tories and Whigs for the abolition of the Corn Law. More recently, an architect of the contemporary neoliberal international order, Prime Minister Margaret Thatcher, used a similar rhetoric to undertake painful structural reforms in order to reinvigorate the ailing British economy (McLean, 2001). Thatcher's repeated reference to the claim that 'there is no alternative' (TINA) was meant to weaken the existing coalition resting on the theory of Keynesian welfare economics. While the credibility of the theory was already eroding over ongoing stagflation, a combination of stagnation with inflation, the TINA claim drove the final nail in the coffin, leading to the creation of a new coalition that embraced the neoliberal idea as a new policy alternative. In Chapter 7, a similar case will be discussed in the context of contemporary Japanese trade politics.

Crisis politics

A catastrophic event, such as an acute economic downturn, a systemic banking crisis, or a national security threat, is a major facilitator for policy change. The reason is that a crisis often enables reformists to argue credibly that the existing policy and the associated policy-making mechanism are no longer effective in ensuring stability and growth, hence calling for a new policy and a new policy-making mechanism.

Successful reformists are usually new entrants, rather than incumbents, who are disassociated from the failed existent policy and policy-making mechanism. They are typically members of an opposition party or a renegade group of the governing party. A crisis reverses the balance of power between the new entrants and the incumbents by undermining the credibility of the existing policy embraced by the latter and creating an opportunity for the former to claim the superiority of their new policy. Aoki (2000, pp. 53–9) stresses the importance of expectational change under a crisis that reallocates policy authority from the incumbents to the new entrants. Of course, authority reallocation and policy change are politically contentious. In attempts to change the present policy, reformists take advantage of popular discontent that intensifies against incumbents who have continued the inappropriate policy. At the same time, the incumbents try to disassociate themselves from the crisis and maintain their power by claiming that the crisis is fortuitous and exogenous to the existing policy. In Chapter 8, the case of a banking crisis will be discussed with respect to reforming regulatory policy over commercial banks in conjunction with the Basel minimum capital requirements that has had a profound effect on the main bank system, the financial core of the Japanese-style market economy.

5.4 CONCLUSION: POLITICAL STRATEGY AND POLICY CHANGE

These political strategies have important implications on the government structure and the allocation of policy authority. The strategies enable and even legitimize political leadership to utilize the cabinet-level central command entities – the Cabinet Secretariat, the Cabinet Office, and associated advisory councils – for policy change. These entities at the top of the government hierarchy represent a renewed partnership between political and bureaucratic elites to facilitate policy adjustment to the global order. In using the central command entities extensively, contemporary Japanese political leaders differ from their predecessors who relied on the bureaucratic-cabinet system with the occasional use of external ancillary authority. Furthermore, in disassociating themselves from the majority party and even the public, they differ from leaders in the Westminster and the presidential models who rely for the governance foundation on the voter-majority–party-cabinet connection and the public–populist connection, respectively. Yet the reduced policy process in contemporary Japan is double-edged: on the one hand, it helps circumvent political and bureaucratic opposition to their efforts at adjusting public policy to the global order for economic efficiency and popular interest, but, on the other, it undermines the institutional mechanisms to evaluate leaders' policy initiatives and prevent the pursuit of particularistic interests. Thus, the risk of political monopoly coexists with the adjustment gains within the system of central command with the weakened institutional mechanisms.

In Part II of this book, I will analyze these strategies separately in the context of corporate governance and labor relations (Chapter 6), trade policies (Chapter 7), and banking policies (Chapter 8). In the conclusion of this book, I will revisit the nature of political leadership in the age of globalization and its implications in greater detail.

NOTES

1. Party leadership's empowered nominating authority was manifest in the 2005 general election, in which Prime Minister Koizumi as Liberal Democratic Party (LDP) president refused to nominate members who had opposed his postal privatization bill in the preceding plenary session. Instead, he nominated handpicked candidates who pledged to endorse the bill if elected. This incident was a watershed that turned rank-and-file LDP members into loyal followers to the party leadership.
2. This line of research has attracted substantial scholarly interest. More sophisticated studies (Iversen and Soskice, 2006; Cusack et al., 2007; Persson et al., 2007) consider coalition formation along with electoral rules and obtain results that are slightly different from those cited in the text by Rogowski and Kayser (2002).
3. The scholarly definition of an 'effective party' being a party with 5 or more percent of total votes (Lijphart, 1994, p.69) is roughly consistent with the legislative rule in the Japanese House of Representatives that says a parliamentary group with 20 or more members (4.2 percent of all lower house members) is eligible for proposing a legislative bill.
4. Duverger's Law has been called into question even in parliamentary democracies with more genuine FPTP votes, including Great Britain and Canada as well as the prewar Japanese experiences (see Chapter 3). See Grofman et al. (2009).
5. Article 59 of the Constitution states that the enactment of all non-budgetary bills requires consent of both the House of Representatives and the House of Councillors [sic], suggesting symmetrical bicameralism in which the two houses share equivalent legislative power.
6. A twisted Diet is different from a hung parliament in the Westminster model in which a governing party fails to obtain a majority of seats in the powerful lower house. In recent Japan, a twisted Diet occurred for the years 1998–99, 2007–09, and 2010–13.
7. The National Diet Act states that the steering committee of each house decides procedures for bills submitted to the house as well as members of standing and special committees that deliberate the bills.
8. Article 8 of the National Government Organization Act (Kokka Gyosei Soshikiho, 2006) establishes deliberative councils. According to the act, a deliberative council is given the role of listening to a variety of opinions in society, legitimatizing a ministry's policy based on the opinions, and balancing social interests. Deliberative councils had existed before World War II, but were formally established by the Act after the war as part of bureaucratic democratization.
9. See Cox and McCubbins (2005, pp. 13–15) for negative and positive agenda-setting with respect to the US congressional system.
10. This survey questionnaire may be problematic because politically appointed ministers often make their own policy initiatives compatible with the assigned ministries' positions: they know that their reputations would be tarnished if they put forth policy proposals that diametrically oppose the ministries' positions. There are several instances in which newly appointed ministers were forced to resign because their policy initiatives

were rejected vehemently by the ministries. The cases in point are the short tenures of Foreign Minister Makiko Tanaka of the LDP and Health, Labour [sic] and Welfare Minister Akira Nagatsuma of the DPJ.

11. 'Kaikakugo no Chuo Shocho Shingikai' [Post-reform ministerial deliberative councils], *Asahi Shimbun*, 27 February 2005 [in Japanese].

6. Council politics for regulatory reforms on corporate governance and labor relations

6.1 THE NEOLIBERAL INTERNATIONAL ORDER AND REFORM AGENDA

Regulatory reform is a prominent aspect of the globalization agenda in the early twenty-first century. As the international order has shifted from embedded liberalism to neoliberalism, non-liberal states with arrangements of coordinated market economy (CME) are pressured to adjust their policy domains to market-oriented ones in order to enable their firms to operate competitively in international markets where liberal practices are increasingly common (Gilson, 2001; Hansmann and Kraakman, 2001).

The United States and the United Kingdom, major liberal market economies (LMEs), have strengthened stockholder-centric corporate governance and flexible labor contracts based on the principle of profit maximization since the 1980s. Germany, which has long embraced the CME principle of co-determination, underwent market-consistent reform under the Schröder Social Democratic government in an attempt to revive its stagnant economy after unification. It adopted a liberal Corporate Governance Code stressing managerial transparency and stockholder rights, while legalizing work sharing and dismissal with severance pay. Finally, the Organisation for Economic Co-operation and Development (OECD) adopted the OECD Principles of Corporate Governance in 1999 (revised in 2004), which stressed stockholder rights and disclosure, and pushed for a reform for flexible labor markets to accommodate rapid technological changes and enhanced production cycles.

In Japan, regulatory reform was the central political agenda for the period between the late 1990s and early 2000s, following the political and administrative reforms that have presumably strengthened Japanese political leadership, as discussed in the previous chapter. The regulatory reform sought to refurbish Japanese industrial sectors whose competitiveness was decreasing under intense global competition.[1] Arguably, the reforms have had strong transforming effects on the Japanese-style capitalist economy, known as CME or stakeholder capitalism. As discussed in Chapter 4, the Japanese-style CME solves coordination problems inherent in a market economy through complementary institutional arrangements of long-term capital and stable employment (Hall and Soskice, 2001). The principal institutional arrangements include (1) a bank-centered financial system that provides long-term lending (or patient capital) and external monitoring, known as the main bank system; (2) long-term employment relationships (LTERs) for firm-specific loyalty and skills; (3) vertical and horizontal industrial networks (or *keiretsu*) composed of banking, brokerage, insurance, trading, manufacturing, and transport firms; and (4) insider-led corporate management or contingent management pursuing interests of stakeholders, including managers, workers, suppliers, clients, bankers, and local communities. Private practices have been complemented by public policy domains: (1) regulatory regimes for commercial banks (implicit deposit guarantees, segmented competition, administrative guidance, etc.); (2) legal restrictions on 'irrational' dismissal of workers; (3) the Commercial Code supporting managerial autonomy; (4) restrictions on holding companies, mergers and acquisitions (M&As), and stock options for managerial stability, and so forth.

These unique regulatory regimes helped the Japanese-style CME system evolve from the interwar command economy to the post–World War II international economic order of embedded liberalism. Thus, CME is a product of inter- and postwar government-led reforms that promoted tripartite cooperation among bankers, managers and skilled regular workers. Large parts of the institutional arrangements described above have lasted until today because of the vested interests of stakeholders who are also members of the governing coalition and have offered consistent electoral support to the LDP that has governed Japan from 1955 to the present day, except for the period between 2009 and 2012. The institutional arrangements are a stable self-enforcing equilibrium for two reasons. First, the stakeholders have no rational incentives to defect unilaterally from the arrangements because they hold non-transferable or firm-specific human assets, based on patient capital, manager-centric corporate governance, and long-term labor relations. Second, they pressure the governing party and bureaucracies against an adverse regulatory reform that would upset the institutions.

The Japanese CME differs from an LME that shapes the capitalist systems of the United States and Great Britain. In sharp contrast to the CME, an LME entails its own complementary arrangements, including the predominance of equity markets in capital formation, stockholder-centric corporate governance, flexible labor markets, and limited government intervention in business activity to ensure the efficiency of markets and the protection of property rights. By comparison, an LME upholds stockholder capitalism based on a coalition between stockholders and managers, while CME espouses stakeholder capitalism with a coalition between managers and workers (Gourevitch and Shinn, 2007).

Therefore, even a small regulatory reform would incur a major reverberating effect on the entire CME system, shifting the distribution of benefits from stakeholders to stockholders. Predictably, the stakeholders who have benefited disproportionately from the existing regulatory regimes would oppose the reform by coalescing with tribal parliamentarians and rank-and-file bureaucratic officials through bureau-pluralistic networks. They would seek to maintain the decentralized policy-making mechanism within which they are well represented and have institutional opportunities to veto the reform. Hence, the historical institutionalist hypothesis of 'non-reform' seems to apply to the decentralized bureaucratic-cabinet government in postwar Japan (Katz, 1998).

Contrary to the non-reform hypothesis, some regulatory reforms have taken place in the domains of corporate governance and labor relations. Yet the reforms are limited in promoting market-consistent private practices. An international comparison based on the corporate governance quality (CGQ) index developed by De Nicolò et al. (2008) suggests that Japan scores low compared to other G7 countries.[2] Even in the latest available data of 2012, the CGQ dynamics suggests that although Japan's corporate governance quality has improved since the early 1990s, it is still the second lowest in the G7 after Italy (Aoyagi and Ganelli, 2014, p. 9). Similarly, in the domain of labor relations a temporary staffing services (TEMP) program was introduced for service industries in 1982 and was expanded gradually to cover most industrial sectors until 2010. Nonetheless, Japan is still known as one of the countries with the most restrictive labor practices among OECD countries. Analysts attribute Japan's sluggish business performance in recent years to problems with market-inconsistent contingent management and rigid employment practices.

Legal scholars (Shishido, 2000; Gilson and Milhaupt, 2005) have noticed the limited effects of regulatory reforms on Japanese business practices and attributed them to the adoption of the enabling approach or menu-based law that permits optional rather than mandatory adoption of independent board membership.[3] Having observed the process of the Commercial Code revision in 2002, Gilson and Milhaupt (2005, p. 17) argued that '[t]he approach is distinctive, but that distinctiveness owes much to the need to cabin the scope of reform within prevailing political and social limitations'. They seem to claim that the enabling approach was a result of compromise between competing political interests and a lack of judicial review of regulatory enforcement.

As legal scholars, Gilson and Milhaupt did not analyze the politics of the regulatory reform closely. From the perspective of political science, the reform is viewed as a bit more than a compromise or business decision. As discussed in Chapter 5 of this book, the electoral and administrative reforms in the mid-1990s that have arguably empowered political leadership had preceded the regulatory reforms in the late 1990s and 2000s. The core-executive model stresses the elitist political–bureaucratic partnership to coordinate bureaucracies' policy tasks. The Westminster model views a coherent majoritarian party as a driving force for reform,[4] and the presidential model points to leadership's populist technique. However, the empowered political leadership postulated by the three models seems discordant with the mediocre reforms and the limited efficiency improvements in corporate governance and labor markets.

In the rest of this chapter, my analysis looks into how prime ministers use deliberative and advisory councils to enact regulatory reforms on corporate governance and labor relations. Following the committee analysis (see also King, 1997), I focus on the politics of counseling with respect to referral, jurisdiction and membership, assuming that deliberative councils in the Japanese legislative process are equivalent to congressional committees in the United States.

6.2 REGULATORY REFORM OF CORPORATE GOVERNANCE

6.2.1 Demands for Reform

Under global competition and capital requirements, fewer and fewer Japanese banks are able and willing to provide relational banking services of patient capital and external monitoring. In addition, fewer and fewer Japanese business firms are able to and willing to provide long-term employment contracts. This means that key agents provide less institutional input to the CME system, thus undermining its efficiency, stability, and continuity. An increasing need to reform the CME system emerges as it begins to suffer from disequilibria in the wake of changing external environments. This situation is characterized by three major traits:

International competition

Many Japanese firms are engaged extensively in international trade and investment. In the wake of the yen's appreciation and trade protectionism abroad in the 1980s, many firms began to relocate productive facilities abroad via foreign direct investment. Japanese firms' subsidiaries had to comply with local corporate governance rules – stock exchanges in New York and London require independent board membership, independent auditors, financial statements based on international accounting standards, the use of rating services for stock valuation, and so on. Thus, firms with substantial dealings in LME states needed to adapt their corporate governance practices to these rules. Moreover, the percentage of foreign investors holding stocks of Japanese listed firms has increased considerably from 5 percent in 1991 to 27 percent in 2012. Half of all stock trading is done by foreign investors.[5] Despite Japanese firms' closed stockholder meetings, foreign investors have increasingly been demanding market-oriented corporate governance, generous dividends, independent board membership, managerial transparency, and so on. Therefore, Japanese firms with international dealings are under strong pressure to adapt their corporate governance practices to international standards.

Organizational complexity

Large domestic firms with high levels of organizational complexity need to develop a governance mechanism for efficient intra-firm communication and flexible reorganization. As they become internationalized and diversified, Japanese companies' organizational complexity has increased, with many divisions requiring varying managerial styles, a range of human talent, a work force made up of diverse nationalities, and so on. This organizational complexity calls for improved corporate governance techniques that are consistent with the principles of individual rationality and market economy. In addition, rapidly changing business environments have enhanced the need for flexible organizational restructuring techniques, such as M&As and organizational splits.

Erosion of the main bank system

Under the Japanese-style CME, the main bank system has provided the key mechanisms of patient capital, external monitoring, and private dissolution – a main bank's patient capital is a long-term investment linked to the firm's business performance. A bank that held a block of a client firm's stocks could also monitor its managerial performance and promote the dissolution of the company or a merger with other, more viable corporations if the firm became insolvent.

However, Japanese firms have recently been in need of alternative monitoring mechanisms. The banking crises in 1997–98 and 2003–04 and the subsequent lending retrenchment reduced the credibility of the main bank system as a mechanism of long-term finance and external monitoring.

More specifically, Japanese banks are subject to at least two kinds of pressures that undermine their traditional functions. First, some main banks are discouraged from providing long-term lending to client firms (short-termism) in order to reduce risk assets in their portfolios under the Basel minimum capital requirements (see Chapter 8 for details). Other banks have to continue 'irrational' lending to client firms whose borrowing accounts for large parts of the banks' assets in order to dress up their own balance sheets (soft-budget constraints). The termination of lending will lead to the firms' bankruptcy and increase the banks' non-performing loans. Both short-termism and soft-budget constraints incapacitate the banks' monitoring function. Second, the banking crises revealed that banks had their own governance problems. Large portions of bank stocks were held by mutual insurance companies that were owned not by stockholders who contributed capital, but by policyholders who paid insurance coverage premiums and had limited managerial interests. The pressures led to specific reforms. These reforms effectively reversed the corporate reforms of the interwar and post–World War II periods – the abolition of holding companies, manager-centric governance, dividend control, the abolition of performance-based remunerations for managers, and so on (see Chapter 4 for details).

Prominent comparative institutionalist economist Aoki (2010) has advanced an 'evolutionary' hypothesis in which corporate governance reform has evolved primarily from changes in external market environments and the related rational business calculus. As noted in Chapter 4, the financial liberalization movements in the 1980s and 1990s enhanced capital mobility and improved bond markets, making major Japanese firms less reliant on bank loans and reducing the importance of main banks. There was an increasing concern that reduced bank oversight might lead to managerial moral hazard and soft-budget constraints on banks.

6.2.2 Conventional Referral Approach to Regulatory Reform

Suppose that a prime minister wishes to put forth a regulatory reform on labor relations through 'conventional referral'. To execute the reform, the prime minister has to obtain consent from his or her party (i.e., the majority party in the Diet) and the jurisdictional bureaucracy (the Ministry of Health, Labour [sic] and Welfare [MHLW]) that is needed to enact the reform in the Diet and implement it through an administrative process. As prescribed by administrative law, the prime minister refers it to the ministry, which then convenes deliberative council meetings. The statutorily determined council members are representatives of the stakeholders, including workers, employers, bureaucrats, lawyers, and academics, deliberating on the existing law and, if necessary, formulate a policy proposal (*kengi*) as an amendment to the Labor Standards Law or other related laws, based on a consensus rule. The proposal is then sent to the ministry for codification, the cabinet for approval and the Diet for enactment, where the prime minister's party or the party-led coalition holds a majority.

Without consent of any single actor – the stakeholders, the ministry, and the governing party (or the governing coalition of parties) – a council proposal could not be enacted as new law. To avoid a loss of credibility, the deliberative council has an institutional incentive to create a proposal that is compatible with the interests of all the concerned actors. Only such a proposal is enforceable as a political-bureaucratic equilibrium under the conventional referral approach. Thus, the deliberative council holds the key to the enactment and implementation of regulatory reform and often performs *negative agenda-setting* to kill new proposals that contravene stakeholders' interests.

However, from the prime minister's perspective, conventional referral will be inefficacious if his or her planned regulatory reform is incompatible with the interest of any of the stakeholders noted above. If he or she uses conventional referral, his or her reform proposal will be either rejected or amended to a large extent by the deliberative council, leading to a loss of the original intent. In such a case, the prime minister may use 'strategic referral' to an advisory council within the Cabinet Office (formerly the Prime Minister's Office), if he or she is determined to pursue his or her original reform idea even at the expense of the stakeholders' interests. The major advantage of referring to an advisory council is that the prime minister can determine its members, often a group of eminent persons with expertise, public recognition, and loyalty to the prime minister. Without facing opposition or stakeholders' influence directly, the council members provide the prime minister's proposal with legitimacy and publicity for enactment and implementation. In this case, an advisory council is said to perform *positive agenda-setting*. Nonetheless, the prime minister may not use strategic referral if he or she believes that it injures the interests of the governing coalition, tarnishes the ministry's reputation or portrays him or her as authoritarian. Accordingly, the use of strategic referral depends on his or her political judgment based on an analysis of expected costs and benefits.

In what follows, I analyze how political leadership pursued the reforms on corporate governance and labor relations with either of the two referral strategies. I also compare and contrast two cases, the legalization of holding companies and the regulatory reform of corporate boards. Finally, I evaluate which of the three leadership models – core executive, Westminster, and presidential – were used to legitimize and accomplish the reforms.

6.2.3 Legalizing Holding Companies: Strategic Referral

The amendments to the Commercial Code and the Antimonopoly Law in 1999 set up the legal framework for establishing holding companies that could own shares of multiple business firms.[6] The amendments in 2000 eased legal procedures for corporate mergers, stock swaps, and corporate divisions. The change embodied the notion of organizational structure as a major strategic variable of corporate governance. Using the holding company scheme to reorganize their structures, firms can shift or concentrate their limited resources into productive tasks. This also transfers corporate authority from individual firms' managers to the holding's top executives who are in a position to ensure the efficient distribution of financial and human resources across the firms. The need for this type of central command has been increasing under intense global competition in conjunction with rapid technological changes, variable consumer preferences, and rapid product life cycles. This market-consistent concept of 'strategic' governance challenges the spirit of company community that underpins the traditional Japanese-style 'contingent' governance. In addition, it may fuel the fear of prewar oligopolistic firms (*zaibatsu*) that were holding companies by definition and accelerated social stratification and class conflict.

The contingent governance scheme evolved in post–World War II Japan when holding companies had been outlawed by the Supreme Commander for the Allied Powers (SCAP) in conjunction with the liquidation of the *zaibatsu* as culprits of the war. The prohibition of holding companies had been inscribed in Article 9 of the Antimonopoly Law enforced by the Japan Fair Trade Commission (JFTC). With the strong anti-*zaibatsu* norm, the JFTC successfully resisted the business community's repeated requests to reinstate holding companies. To be organizationally efficient, a large Japanese conglomerate would build a vertically and horizontally integrated network of firms through the sharing of stocks. The network, known as *keiretsu*, would have a parent company with its own core business, while providing subsidiaries with nearly full managerial authority and external oversight in accordance with the concept of company community. However, conflicts of interest would often arise between the core business of the parent company and the subsidiaries.

In contrast, a holding company would have fewer conflicts of interest since the holding company has no core business. As an owner of the subsidiaries, a holding company would be able to take the commanding authority to shift the firm's financial, managerial, and labor resources across the subsidiaries in pursuit of maximum profitability. Seemingly, the holding company scheme would promote LME-consistent strategic governance through rapid organizational restructuring. However, counter-intuitively, the holding company scheme could be used to help protect contingent governance from market forces. This point can be made clear by summing up the legalization process that began with the conventional bureaucracy-led regulatory reform approach noted earlier, but which changed to central command in the process.

In the early 1990s, the request to legalize holding companies was submitted to the Ministry of International Trade and Industry (MITI) by corporate managers' associations, including the Keidanren (Japan Business Federation) and Keizai Doyukai (the Japan Association of Corporate Executives – JACE), as well as by industrial associations of large firms such as the Japan Automobile Manufacturers Association (JAMA). The reasons provided by the Doyukai were mixed: the holding company scheme could (1) promote strategic restructuring of firms through transfer of human, financial, and technological resources from one subsidiary to another; (2) manage industrial networks flexibly through corporate mergers, acquisitions and splits; (3) monitor subsidiaries' managerial performance; and (4) maintain stable ownership of shares and combat irrational share speculations at a time of declining cross-shareholding practices among Japanese firms (RIETI, 2013b, p. 298).[7] While reasons (1) to (3) were related to strategic governance, reason (4) meant a continuation of contingent governance.[8]

Responding to the requests, the Industrial Policy Bureau of MITI reviewed the problems of Japanese-style corporate governance and released the interim report, *The Industrial Structure in the Twenty-first Century* (Industrial Policy Bureau, 1994), to suggest future prospects for industrial structure and industrial policy. Likewise, the MITI's Deliberative Council on Industrial Structure[9] evaluated the changing behaviors of banks and business firms. It found that (1) large firms used equity markets rather than bank loans to raise new capital; (2) banks had to withhold lending to meet the minimum capital requirements, thus reducing their external monitoring functions; and (3) Japanese labor markets with long-term contracts were increasingly rigid and inefficient against the backdrop of rapid technological changes and shorter product cycles. Based on these findings, the council stressed the need for an alternative external monitoring mechanism and flexible labor markets.

The same deliberative council issued another interim proposal in February 1995, in which it recommended that Article 9 and Article 9.2 of the Antimonopoly Act be amended to legalize holding companies and permit them to possess large volumes of the subsidiaries' shares. The holding company scheme would provide an alternative authoritative structure to improve the existing Japanese-style contingent governance relying on cross-shareholding networks and main banks. The proposal cited the evidence showing *keiretsu* firms' declining influence in the Japanese economy and the absence of a positive correlation between corporate ownership and business transaction, then arguing that holding companies would not lead to excessive market control. The business environment in the late 1990s differed substantially from that in the prewar era. Holding companies, if legalized, would hardly be oligopolistic under intense international business competition. In other words, under the existing Antimonopoly Act, Japanese firms were handicapped in international competition where Japan was the only advanced industrial country that prohibited holding companies. Evidently, the report was meant to fore-close the JFTC's antimonopoly claim.

However, the legalization momentum stalled when it was confronted with intra-bureaucratic and intra-coalition disagreements. As for the former, the JFTC claimed that holding companies, if legalized, would acquire monopolistic market control and thus should be constrained. Likewise, labor unions and the Ministry of Labor were concerned that workers would be fobbed off with labor contracts with subsidiaries that would be inferior to those with parent companies. The largest labor union, the Rengo, demanded that, if holding companies were legalized, the Labor Union Act be amended to allow subsidiaries' labor unions to negotiate directly with their parent firms' management.[10] The Social Democratic Party, a coalition partner of the first Hashimoto (LDP-led) Cabinet (January 1996–November 1996), opposed it for fear of monopolization and large welfare losses to consumers and workers. In a nutshell, opponents claimed that the legalization of holding companies would undermine antimonopoly jurisprudence and stable labor relations that postwar Japan had embraced based on its bitter prewar experiences.

In the midst of the controversy between stability and efficiency, the legalization issue was picked up by the Hashimoto Cabinet, which rede-fined it as part of its regulatory reform initiative to boost the ailing Japanese economy. No longer relying on conventional referral, the cabinet referred the issue to the Administrative Reform Council (Gyosei Kaikaku Kaigi), an advisory council within the Prime Minister's Office (Kantei) where business leaders were represented disproportionately (see Table 6.1). In effect, the cabinet avoided the Legislative Council in the Ministry of Justice where amendments to the Commercial Code and the Antimonopoly Act were typically deliberated with limited business representation. The Administrative Reform Council had the broad statutory mandate of advising the prime minister regarding 'necessary reforms to realize appro-priate and rational administration under the changing socioeconomic environments' (an excerpt from its establishment act) and could use the top bureaucratic office's bargaining power to dilute the opposition.

First, the office obtained the JFTC's consent to fully legalize holding companies by establishing a stringent guideline for the prevention of excessive concentration of business control power (RIETI, 2013b, p. 308).[11] Second, it assuaged labor's contractual concern by promising the strict enforcement of the Labor Standards Law to ensure the succession of contracts from parent to subsidiary firms. In addition, the political hurdle was removed by the SDP's withdrawal from the coalition cabinet in November 1996. The council proposal was approved by the cabinet and was enacted by the Diet in June 1997. As sketched thus far, the legalization process started with the conventional referral approach but turned to a strategic variant to overcome intra-bureaucratic disagreements through the political-bureaucratic finesse of the Prime Minister's Office. Prime Minister Hashimoto presumably used strategic referral because business support for the legalization was overwhelming and because the aforementioned clauses to the bill could resolve the bureaucratic, political, and labor disagreements.

6.2.4 Reforming Corporate Boards: Conventional Referral

A second case of regulatory reform on corporate boards entails a slightly different process. The case started with an unusual phase of a newly elected DPJ government's bold reform idea that conflicted with incumbent interests. However, because of its political candor or inexperience, the DPJ government chose to take the conventional referral approach, in effect diluting the original spirit of the reform under harsh legislative realities.

A traditional Japanese firm relies exclusively on an internal management team, or contingent governance, with no clear separation between management and monitoring. Both directors and officers are insiders at the top of the corporate hierarchy, promoted from rank-and-file employees or representatives from parent firms and the main bank, while statutory auditors are given no votes and are usually retired executives. They can maintain their autonomy provided the firm performs well – the firm's parent company or main bank might intervene as soon as the firm performs worse than a certain benchmark or experiences financial distress. Because of the erosion of the main bank system and network monitoring, the traditional governance scheme needed to be revised.

An amendment to the Commercial Code in 2002 (Companies Act 416) enabled Japanese firms to adopt a US-style board with committees. The US system differs from the Japanese one with respect to clear separation between management and monitoring, or between officers and directors.

Independent board members or directors are divided into audit, nomination, and remuneration committees to perform monitoring roles, while delegating day-to-day management to officers. The Japanese Commercial Code neither mandated the US-style committee system, nor required the strict independence of external directors. Thus, the law left the traditional scheme largely unchanged since firms could appoint ex-employees or the parent firms' managers as 'external directors'.

This corporate governance problem attracted attention from the DPJ, which upholds economic liberalism and embraces interests of stakeholders, including workers, urban voters, and local communities, separate from the LDP's close association with business managers. DPJ members and supporters were discontented with Japanese businesses' performance, given their decreasing profits, declining international competitiveness, and the worsening general economic climate. The DPJ formed a project team, which returned a proposal for the establishment of a Public Company Act in July 2009. The proposal called for financial disclosure, improved independence of directorship, and employees' representation in the statutory auditing board (*kansa yaku*), inspired by the German CME model of co-determination, as measures to improve corporate governance. It still fell short of demanding increases in dividend payments, possibly at the expense of wages. Thus, the DPJ did not intend to overturn the existing contingent governance scheme or form a new coalition between workers and stockholders.

Having won the general election in the summer of 2009, the DPJ assumed power for the first time and was committed to change the LDP's bureaucratic delegation approach and clientele politics. In February 2010, the DPJ Cabinet referred its reform proposal to the Ministry of Justice (MOJ). It can be speculated that the DPJ chose conventional referral as a means to change the existing law because it thought that the MOJ, the most politically independent ministry among all the bureaucracies, could provide a fair deliberation on the issue. The ministry referred it to the Legislative Council in which several members found that the lack of binding directorial independence was a legal defect of the Companies Act and established the Companies Act Subcommittee to discuss it in detail.[12] In December 2011, to solicit public opinion, the subcommittee issued an interim proposal on legal reform[13] with several options. One option urged the institution of directorial independence as a legal obligation for all listed businesses with capital of more than 500 million yen, and that upper limits be imposed on block-shareholders' managerial influence for the protection of minority shareholders.

The subcommittee argued that it has been the international norm that major firms have independent directors to enhance their corporate performance through the improvement of transparency, managerial oversight, and governance. Japanese business communities, according to them, need to be encouraged to adjust their governance practices to international norms by mandating directorial independence by public law. Several subcommittee members stated openly that government had to make it legally binding because Japanese stock exchanges had no legal authority to enforce private rules against listed firms.[14] Furthermore, they insisted on the need for independence by pointing out the fact that directors were often managers of affiliated firms.[15]

However, the mandatory independence clause met with strong opposition from business circles. As predicted, the Keidanren,[16] Keizai Doyukai[17] and the Japanese Association of Commercial Banks[18] strongly opposed it, arguing that a uniform obligation was irrational given the varying objectives and organizational structures of Japanese firms. They claimed that what counts is not independence, but a board member's ability to give appropriate managerial advice based on expertise and knowledge about the firm. They also argued that no objective data exist showing that firms with independent directors have higher profitability than those without.[19] Furthermore, the Ministry of Economy, Trade and Industry (METI, formerly the MITI) recognized the need for corporate governance improvements but argued for external, not independent directorship – if members of the main bank and parent firms were to be excluded, the board would not have the necessary expertise and information required for oversight. Finally, the Financial Services Agency (FSA) raised two objections. First, independent board membership would undermine commercial banks' oversight functions that are still needed for small and medium-sized enterprises (SMEs). Second, regional banks would have difficulties recruiting appropriate individuals for the role.[20]

In August 2012, given the intra-bureaucracy disagreements and managers' objections, the subcommittee and the parent Legislative Council adopted the final proposal recommending at least one independent external director with a comply-or-explain clause – a firm needs to provide a substantive explanation in the case of non-compliance at the annual meeting. It is unclear as to whether the DPJ attempted to overturn the council's proposal. Yet the DPJ permitted the council to announce the proposal without pressing for mandatory directorial independence. Without changing the council's composition or superseding the conventional bureaucratic process, even the governing party with a parliamentary majority could not accomplish its intended regulatory reform.

However, the council proposal was not submitted to the Diet because of the DPJ's internal turmoil and the subsequent snap election for the House of Representatives in December 2012. The election returned power to the

LDP, which has closer business associations than the DPJ. The LDP led by Prime Minister Shinzo Abe, despite his reformist pledge, avoided taking a strong position on mandatory directorial independence. Recognizing that growth had to come from regulatory reform, including corporate governance improvements,[21] Prime Minister Abe knew that his party's strongest support came from business managers.[22]

In April 2014, the DPJ and three smaller parties submitted a bill mandating directorial independence, which was voted down by the LDP-led majorities in both parliamentary houses. In the plenary session, LDP Justice Minister Sadakazu Tanigaki acknowledged that council members did not reach agreement on the appropriateness of legal obligation, but stressed that the proposed enabling approach would provide firms with opportunities to build best practices for their business goals in varying organizational and social environments. He stressed that mandatory independence might not be good for all Japanese companies,[23] predicting variable effects among firms.[24] A legally binding liberal reform that produced adverse business outcomes would be politically costly. Consistent with the principal–agent theory (Huber and Shipan, 2008), under informational uncertainty the governing LDP effectively delegated policy authority to the bureaucracy that recommended the enabling approach serving its own interest. The approach helped elected officials to avert responsibility by transferring critical corporate governance decisions to private agents. With the LDP-led coalition's parliamentary majority, the bill for optional directorial independence with the comply-or-explain clause was enacted as an amendment to the Companies Act on 20 June 2014.[25]

The second Abe Cabinet (2012–present) has deferred a 'soft law' version to the Financial Services Agency (FSA) and the Tokyo Stock Exchange (TSE). Prime Minister Abe has been strongly committed to refurbishing the Japanese economy through his platform known as the 'Abenomics', composed of monetary ease, fiscal expansion, and regulatory reform. Abenomics includes corporate governance reform, with the belief that directorial independence will promote stockholders' interests and boost stock markets, thus speeding up economic recovery. Acting as a joint secretariat, the FSA and the TSE adopted the 'Corporate Governance Code' in March 2015, based on the recommendation by the Council of Experts Concerning the Corporate Governance Code, yet another deliberative council of the FSA that is housed within the Cabinet Office.[26] The code requires two independent directors for major listed firms without specifying their qualifications and the enforcement procedures. As a consequence of the reforms, the Japanese corporate governance system has become multilayered based on the public Companies Act and the private Corporate Governance Code, arguably providing corporate managers with a high level of discretion under the reduced oversight of main banks.[27]

6.2.5 International Comparison

The aforementioned corporate governance reform in Japan can be juxtaposed with similar reforms in France and South Korea during the same time period, both of which represent institutional reforms via supranational processes. France embraced corporate governance reform, financial deregulation, and open capital flows to promote French industrial modernization. Although, like the Japanese government, the French government remained fragmentary because of cohabitation arrangements during much of the period (1993–95, 1997–2002), the framework decisions were firmly embedded within a pact with Germany and the strategy of the European Commission to accelerate EU integration (Tiberghien, 2007). Even in the aftermath of the major financial crisis in 2008, France and other European Union countries have not deviated from neoliberal policies and the related fiscal austerity. It is primarily because neoliberal ideas have been imbued firmly within the supranational institutions, including EU law (particularly the Single European Act), the European Commission, the European Court of Justice, and the European Central Bank. During the 1980s, neoliberalism was institutionalized by conservative leaders to release markets from states' ownership and regulatory constraints, and was confronted with the social democratic ideals to reduce social spending and reform the welfare state in pursuit of market efficiency (Schmidt and Thatcher, 2013). Among many reforms, corporate governance reform has been promoted to emulate the Anglo-American stockholder (diffused) model that showed superior profitability with regard to the stakeholder model prevalent in continental Europe (Vitols, 2013). The European Commission adopted the Action Plan on European Company Law and Corporate Governance in 2003 and issued related directives for implementation by member states based on expert advice from the European Corporate Governance Institute (ECGI).

The South Korean story slightly differed from this. The country started corporate governance reform under its first civilian president, Kim Young-sam (1993–97), who unified three political parties, in order to modernize the Korean economy that was increasingly faced with global competition from advanced industrial nations as its income level rose. President Kim's conservative New Korea Party lost the 1996 National Assembly election to the liberal National Congress Party led by Kim Dae-jung who was skeptical about the reform. With some backing by the US Treasury, however, financial deregulation could be partially achieved in 1997. The process was completed by the post-currency crisis IMF-sponsored structural adjustment reform, including the elimination of industrial subsidies, which compelled Korean business and labor communities to adopt more competitive practices.

Both European and South Korean experiences show that external authorities – Germany/the European Commission and the United States/IMF respectively – exerted intense pressure for comprehensive corporate governance reforms, providing the states with technical information and expertise for adaptation as well as with coercion for coordination. Contrastingly, in the case of Japanese corporate reform, no external organizational pressures existed. Japan was neither a member of a powerful supranational integrating body nor did it make use of the IMF's structural adjustment facility (it did not request an IMF rescue for its own banking crisis). Although the reforms undoubtedly entail some characteristics of marketization and financialization that are consistent with LME practices, Japan is still permitted to continue its politics of governing coalitions and create a menu-based multilayered law favorable to corporate managers. In effect, the agenda for public companies has been diluted.

6.3 REGULATORY REFORM ON LABOR RELATIONS

The recent labor relations reform on skilled regular employees approximates that on corporate governance, while the reform on unskilled temporary workers does not. The difference hinges on the membership of the governing coalition and the extent of representation in bureaucratic processes. Skilled regular employees as well as corporate managers are both members of the governing coalition and represented in several important deliberative councils, while temporary workers have neither. The labor reform – the introduction and expansion of the temporary staffing services (TEMP) program – was undertaken in a non-consensual manner through joint political-bureaucratic authorities as a measure to reduce rigid labor contracts, whereas reforms for flexible dismissal and equal treatments have stalled, in effect protecting regular employees and the Japanese-style CME system that rely on firm-specific human capital.

6.3.1 Japanese Labor Practices and Changing Economic Conditions

Origins of long-term employment relationships

Long-term employment relationships (LTERs) are a major feature of post–World War II employment practices in Japan, but are not rooted in Japanese culture or society. Prior to the evolution of LTERs, there had been competitive labor markets and weak labor law that failed to protect workers' rights and safety. The war evoked a sweeping change in labor practices. In attempts to increase industrial production, the military government sought to enhance cooperation between managers and workers by setting out labor law to improve work conditions through regulations on working hours, minimum wages, and hazardous works. During wartime, when young and able males were conscripted as soldiers, firms needed to introduce long-term contracts to secure the quality work force. However, labor unions were continuously banned as anti-state communist sects that would disrupt industrial production and war efforts.

In the immediate postwar era, labor regulations were vastly strengthened by the SCAP as a means to promote democracy. Labor unions were legalized and additional improvements were made upon the interwar safety standards, work-hour restrictions, child labor prohibition, and so on. LTERs were maintained privately to satisfy a massive war reconstruction demand for labor and were even reinforced during the high growth period when staff were constantly in short supply.

More importantly, LTERs were used to promote firm-specific loyalty and skills that are essential for complex product designs and production with which Japanese companies sought to create a competitive edge with regard to their international rivals (Shishido, 2008). Because LTER employees were hired for 'general' positions, firms could use them at low cost for various positions that were needed to serve corporate goals at times. With long-term labor contracts, employees were willing to develop firm-specific skills and loyalties. The joint interests of employees and managers were the linchpins of LTERs as a self-enforcing economic institution. However, the interests are not shared by outsiders – the skills specific to a particular firm might not be valued by other firms. This non-transferability of specific assets accounts for the absence of viable mid-career labor markets in postwar Japan.

LTERs nurture the willingness to rotate among various types of jobs depending on the economic environment or the process of on-the-job training (OJT), and the willingness of senior employees to train young employees on the job (Tsuneki and Matsunaga, 2008, p. 14). The classical human capital theory holds that a competitive labor market does not ensure an efficient level of investment in firm-specific human capital. Because of the firm-specific nature, companies do not have an incentive to pay for employees' training efforts, and, given this expectation, employees lose their incentive to invest. Even explicit contractual arrangements cannot solve the problem due to a lack of third-party verifiability – courts cannot observe the level of human capital investment. The logic of moral hazard predicts that employees will not invest if they are paid prior to investment. In addition, they will not be motivated to invest either, if they doubt a firm's promise to pay later for the same reason of verifiability.

To solve the problem of underinvestment in firm-specific human capital, it is necessary to provide incentives for employees to invest and for firms to pay appropriately for employees' efforts; that is, an LTER should be a self-enforcing implicit contract that does not involve verifiability problems. The coordination of expectations between two players is necessary for attaining an efficient reputation equilibrium. More concretely, firms should build a good reputation for keeping their promises to employees.

There is no legal mandate for a good reputation or LTER, yet legal precedents that regulated abusive dismissal ensued in the 1970s. The freedom of dismissal has been strongly restricted under the doctrine of abusive dismissal that has been formed by case law. This doctrine has been codified on an *ex post facto* basis as Article 16 of the Labor Contract Act[28] and has its foundation in the basic principle of Civil Law, which prohibits the abusive exercise of rights. The doctrine of abusive dismissal accords with LTERs but does not mandate the principle: the doctrine still allows fixed-term employment. Long-term employment is based on an economic demand for firm-specific skills. LTERs evolved because of joint interests of firms and employees under the prevailing economic conditions and legal arrangements.

However, in the long deflationary period of the 1990s and 2000s, oversupply became chronic and widespread across industrial sectors. Thus, many firms were pressured to reorganize their productive structures by dismissing parts of the work force or shifting employees from unprofitable to profitable business. In this vein, LTERs have increasingly been viewed as a major barrier to flexible reorganization. Furthermore, the international economic order after the 1990s is partly characterized by drastic technological progress led mainly by the development of information technology and financial engineering. When new businesses and industries came into existence, old technologies became obsolete within a short span of time. As the merit of LTERs lies in the accumulation of firm-specific knowledge in the long run, they are more effective in an economic environment growing at a stable rate and with relatively small technological changes. It is said, therefore, that Japan needs a new system of labor relations and labor markets to cope with this change. The changing economic environments go against the protective scheme for employment in Japan.[29]

6.3.2 The Expansion of Temporary Staffing Services: Strategic Referral

To improve labor market efficiency, the Temporary Staffing Services (TEMP) Act (Haken Rodo Ho) was enacted in 1986 with a 'positive list' for 16 sections of the service sector where seasonal or temporary demands were prominent.[30] The act was amended by the Hashimoto Cabinet in 1996 to cover 26 clerical jobs and was redefined by the Obuchi Cabinet (1998–2000) in 1999 with a 'negative list' that designated the industrial sectors where the TEMP program did not apply.[31] Then, it was expanded again by the Koizumi Cabinet (2001–06) in 2003 to all sectors except construction and port facilities. The legal changes prompted a steadfast increase in the share of temporary workers, accounting for approximately 15 million, or 36 percent of total work force, in 2012.[32]

While this Japanese labor market reform accords with the international trend, the dual structure of labor relations is hardly a new development in Japan's labor history. Since its inception in the prewar era, LTERs have been limited to skilled employees in major firms as a means to secure the high-quality work force. They are also given special treatment in promotions, payment, and employment guarantees. In contrast, unskilled workers have rarely received long-term contracts even in periods of rapid growth when Japanese courts established the legal precedent of rational dismissal. Thus, Japan's labor market has been of a dual nature, wherein regular workers are internalized within the firm, while non-regular workers participate in an outside spot market and experience higher turnover rates. While this dual nature is universally observed in developed capitalist countries, it is characteristic of the Japanese economy to clearly distinguish regular and non-regular workers at the time of recruitment (Figure 6.1).[33]

In most cases, temporary workers have been dismissed before regular workers at the time of recession and therefore served as buffers. The proportion of life-time contracts fluctuated throughout business cycles: the recessionary periods such as the aftermaths of the two oil crises were associated with decreases in life-time employees. Likewise, the long-lasting deflationary economy of the 1990s and early 2000s produced a substantial increase in temporary workers. Prior to the reform, the distinction between the two groups had been informal. The TEMP program has made a clear legal distinction.

In 2001, the Koizumi Cabinet took up the TEMP expansion issue and referred it strategically to the Council for Regulatory Reform (*Sogo Kisei Kaikaku Kaigi*) (see Table 6.1) within the Cabinet Office (formerly the Prime Minister's Office) that had the statutory mandate of advising the prime minister regarding 'the regulatory reform needed to facilitate the structural transformation of the economic society'.[34] The council members included economic ministers, business leaders, and academics, but no labor representatives, substantially different from the Regulatory Reform Committee within the Prime Minister's Office under the Hashimoto and the Obuchi Cabinets as well as the deliberative councils within the Ministry

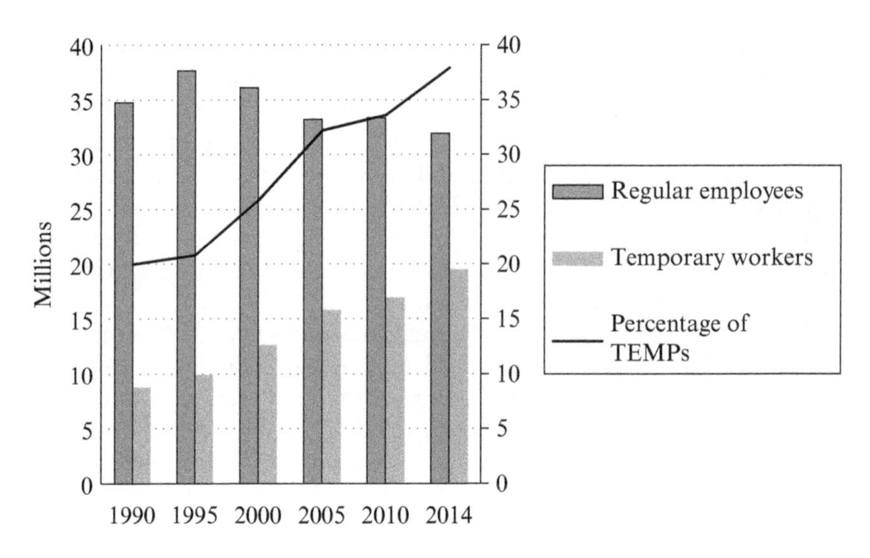

Source: The figure is constructed from the Workforce Statistics, MHLW.

Figure 6.1 Trends in the work force

Table 6.1 Deliberative councils on regulatory reform

Name of Council	Duration	Labor	Business	Total
Administrative Reform Council	November 1996–December 1997	1	4	13
Headquarters for the Promotion of Administrative Reform	February 1998–March 2001	1	3	7
Council for Regulatory Reform	April 2001–March 2004	0	10	15
Council for the Promotion of Regulatory Reform	April 2004–January 2007	0	6	13
Council for Regulatory Reform	January 2007–March 2010	0	6	15

Note: The data was obtained from minutes of the above councils.

of Labor (Table 6.1). Without labor objection, the Council for Regulatory Reform deliberated on the issue smoothly and proposed to the cabinet the abolition of the existing restrictions on the TEMP program with respect to industrial sectors, contract terms, employment agencies, and so on. This strategic referral approach superseded the conventional approach of bureaucratic delegation that the Koizumi Cabinet believed would be time-consuming and unable to reach agreement between business and labor representatives because of the deliberative council's consensus rule.[35]

With the recommendation, the Koizumi Cabinet sent the bill for the expansion of the TEMP program to the Diet for enactment without referring it to the conventional Deliberative Council on Labour [sic] Policy. Nonetheless, the issue was debated by the council's Subcommittee on Equal Employment, even though the deliberations had no legal consequences. The subcommittee's labor representative urged for the enforcement of the equal treatment principle, pointing out the risks of job substitution and increasing income inequality between regular and temporary workers who would perform virtually the same duties under the newly expanded TEMP program. Yet business representatives opposed the legalization because of the difficulties involved in evaluating occupational duties and enforcing the principle. As predicted by the Koizumi Cabinet, since both sides were unable to reach agreement, the subcommittee did not issue a recommendation on the legalization of the equal treatment principle.

Neither the Cabinet Office nor MHLW paid close attention to the institutional improvements on mid-career job markets, unemployment insurance and vocational retraining programs that would be useful safety nets for TEMP workers. Furthermore, the government failed to develop mid-career job markets, because it could not obtain cooperation from Japanese firms that value firm-specific skills and have limited interest in mid-career recruitment and perhaps because temporary workers are not members of the LDP's governing coalition. Hence, temporary workers have experienced deteriorating employment conditions without proper protection. This point is explored further in the next section.

6.3.3 Stalled Reforms on Regular Employment: Conventional Referral

Initially, the TEMP program was not expected to affect present-generation regular employees with long-term contracts. Nonetheless, it has begun to affect next-generation skilled employees. Under the globalizing economic order, human skills are quickly outdated because of rapid technological innovation. Exogenous market fluctuations have made business cycles more volatile, compelling firms to revise the size of their work force more frequently. Moreover, through global economic networks, companies relocate their productive or even managerial facilities across national borders, depending on shifting competitive advantages. Hence, Japanese firms are increasingly unable and unwilling to maintain LTERs at home that are supposed to protect employees from dismissal due to technical innovations or business cycles.

Under intense cost-cutting competition, Japanese firms are pressured to switch employment contracts from regular to non-regular workers. The TEMP program effectively provides Japanese firms with an option to fill skilled positions with (qualified) temporary workers for lower wages. Japanese firms are practically immune from legal penalties even if they pay less to temporary workers than to regulars for virtually the same work because the Japanese government has not enforced the principle of equal pay or treatment for equal work strictly. As a result, the ratio of regular employees in the entire work force has declined markedly over time. Among many other candidate causes (recession, technological change, import pressure, etc.), the expanded TEMP program can be viewed as a major culprit. Reforms aiming for flexible dismissal and equal treatment have faced stiff opposition, even though they would reduce the pains and costs concentrated on TEMP workers and improve labor market flexibility.

Dismissal with severance pay

Corporate executives and METI officials have attempted to further labor market reforms for flexible business reorganization through timely dismissal and hiring of workers with appropriate skills and experiences. They argue that dismissal with severance pay should be legalized to reverse the effects of the restrictive labor law under which they are unable to dismiss redundant regular workers and thus have to transfer them to subsidiaries for meager jobs that need no costly retraining or human capital investment (Fukao, 2012). This 'internal unemployment' has been an unintended consequence of the rigid labor law and the LTERs.

Dismissal with severance pay has become a widely used method to improve labor market efficiency in many advanced industrial countries. However, in Japan, the idea had not found strong bureaucratic or political support until recently. The MHLW sought to enact dismissal with *ex post facto* severance pay in order to prevent contractual disputes and promote efficient court settlements. Labor representatives in the Subcommittee on Equal Employment of the MHLW Deliberative Council on Labour [sic] Relations opposed it, arguing that it would upset long-standing Japanese labor practices.[36] The subcommittee was unable to reach agreement, compelling the ministry to drop the severance pay clause. However, with the Koizumi Cabinet's approval, the ministry sent a bill to amend the Labor Standards Act on irrational dismissal to the Diet in the 2003 plenary session. Members of opposition parties as well as the governing parties in the Committee on Health, Labour [sic] and Welfare of the House of Representatives raised the concern that the bill might be interpreted in a way that puts the burden of proof concerning the irrationality of their dismissal on the dismissed employees.[37] The committee passed an amendment with unanimity to ensure that the burden of proof should reside with employers without altering the Supreme Court precedent and Civil Code practices.[38] The amended clause states that 'dismissal shall, if it lacks objectively reasonable grounds and is not considered to be appropriate in general societal terms, be treated as an abuse of right and be invalid'.[39] Because the issue involved regular employees who have become important members of the electoral coalition for the LDP in the wake of the urbanization of its support base, political leadership was unwilling to take central command to press for dismissal with severance pay.

In April 2013, the issue re-emerged in the Roundtable on Industrial Competitiveness, Prime Minister Abe's advisory council, in which Keizai Doyukai President Yasuchika Hasegawa brought it up as a regulatory reform measure to enhance the competitiveness of Japanese firms.[40] However, afraid of being held accountable for an abuse of the dismissal rules, Prime Minister Abe decided not to introduce the proposal in the 2013 plenary Diet session just before the upper house election scheduled for the summer of the same year.[41] The prime minister, however, said that he would continue to deliberate on dismissal with *ex post facto* severance pay.[42] The roundtable scaled down the idea and redefined it as a measure implementable only within special economic zones,[43] one of Abe's pet projects known as 'Abenomics' to revive the ailing Japanese economy. In September 2013 even after he was victorious in the upper house election, the prime minister again decided not to legalize dismissal with severance pay in special economic zones. This time, not just labor unions but corporate managers opposed it because their firms would be handicapped with the existing restrictive dismissal rules outside the special economic zones, while foreign firms and new venture firms inside the zones would benefit from the flexible rules. In addition, the MHLW opposed it because it would diversify the dismissal rules and make their enforcement difficult.[44] In effect, Prime Minister Abe has chosen not to further labor reforms on regular employment because they are a highly divisive topic amongst the governing coalition, rendering coordination politically costly.

Equal pay for equal work

A similar deadlock has ensued in the case of strict implementation of equal treatment. More sympathetic to temporary workers than the LDP, the DPJ was committed to strict enforcement of the equal treatment principle. However, having known that it would have a severe enforcement problem, the DPJ Cabinet led by Prime Minister Yoshihiko Noda (2011–12) amended Article 18 of the Labor Contract Act in 2012 to mandate firms to rehire temporary workers who have worked for the company for five or more years as regular employees. The DPJ's insistence on regular employment could be attributed to the fact that the party has gained electoral support from labor unions for regular employees with an intrinsic interest in expanding their support base by turning temporary workers into regular employees with union membership. However, the amendment generated the unintended effect that many firms terminated contracts with their temporary workers just before the fifth year in order to circumvent the legal obligation.[45] The stalled reforms have left the restrictive dismissal and equal treatment issues unresolved, leading firms to use the TEMP program extensively in attempts to reduce labor costs and reorganize corporate structures. The abuse of the TEMP program has worsened working conditions for temporary workers.

Nonetheless, this trend may be reversed to some extent by two forces. First, the chronic shortage of skilled labor has become apparent in the wake of population aging. A census study indicates that the population has been decreasing by approximately 200 000 per year since 2010 through natural attrition and will continue to decrease for the foreseeable future, elevating the importance of LTERs as a measure to secure a high-quality work force. Second, when a small economic boom followed the Bank of Japan's reflationary monetary policy in 2013, a number of firms predicted that demand would pick up, and felt the need to expand their work force and re-contract their qualified temporary workers as regular employees. In this instance, companies have voluntarily undertaken rehiring for purely business reasons, unlike the DPJ-led mandatory rehiring program after the five yearly contracts.

The succeeding Abe Cabinet has sought to alter the DPJ labor policy by revising the Temporary Staffing Services Act. The revision will eliminate the three-year limit for temporary workers in all job categories and allow firms to keep using temporary staff for the same jobs as long as individual workers are replaced every three years.[46] Under the revised law, firms will be required to hear the opinion of their labor unions to do so, but the unions are not given the power to veto the companies' decision.[47] The opposition parties, JIP, DPJ, and SDP, tabled a bill to counter the government's TEMP bill in order to establish the equal treatment principle. However, an amended version of the bill jointly approved by the ruling LDP–Komeito coalition and Ishin no To (Japan Innovation Party), the second largest opposition party in the lower house – which the ruling coalition agreed to support in exchange for Ishin agreeing to put the government bill to a vote – substantially watered down the provisions of the opposition bill. While the original bill sought to equalize the pay for temporary and regular workers engaged in the same work, the amended bill calls for 'balanced' wages in accordance with the 'content of the work, the degree of the worker's job responsibility and other circumstances', effectively paving the way for firms to use temporary staff at lower pay than their regular employees. The requirement that the government take 'legislative measures within a year' to correct the wage disparity proposed by the opposition bill was reworded so that the government would need to take 'necessary measures, including legislative steps, within three years'. Again, the equal treatment principle has failed to be established appropriately.

6.3.4 International Comparison

As examined thus far, in contemporary Japan the introduction and expansion of TEMP programs have been executed in the absence of significant improvements in equal treatment, mid-career employment markets, and unemployment insurance. In contradistinction, the Netherlands, Austria, Germany, and Scandinavian countries with similar traditions of long-term employment relationship, have successfully introduced programs relating to temporary work, work sharing, and dismissal with severance pay as well as improved human capital investment and employment subsidies, under the notion of active labor market policies (ALMPs). These countries have 'shifted emphasis from income maintenance to employment promotion and from full employment to individual employability' (Martin, 2013, p. 233). ALMPs comprise flexible labor contracts and the equal treatment of permanent and temporary workers to reduce labor market segmentation and enhance economic growth, with some interpretative ambiguities on the principle of non-discrimination (Rönnmar, 2011).

ALMPs hinge on the solidaristic coalitions that are appropriate for the empowerment of a group of individuals to achieve collective benefits. These coalitions are derived from political-economic institutions based on proportional representation and inclusive labor organizations. Both regular and non-regular workers join inclusive labor unions that have strong representation in parliaments as well as in bureaucracies. Through political coalitions and work councils, workers and employers are enticed to adopt the ALMPs that minimize negative impacts on marginal workers (Martin, 2013, pp. 239–42).[48]

In contrast, Japanese labor unions are firm specific, with separate arrangements for regular and temporary workers. Employers have cooperative working relations with regular employees but unfriendly relations with non-regular workers. Politically, while the LDP has close relations with business associations, the DPJ relies on the unions for regular employees and is interested in protecting regular employees with limited interest in improving temporary work conditions. Bureaucratically, union representatives in ministry-sponsored deliberative councils pay limited attention to the well-being of unskilled workers who are affected most by the reforms for flexible contracts, while seeking to block the reforms deemed unfavorable to regular employees. Even though Japan shares coordinated market economy arrangements with the continental European countries, its labor reforms have undergone processes and produced outcomes that differ substantially from those of its European counterparts because of its distinct party support and coalitional structures.

Within Japan, compared with reforms on corporate governance and regular labor relations, the TEMP reform seems more coercive in that both political and bureaucratic officials expanded the TEMP program without improving mid-career job markets and retraining programs. As a result, the Japanese experiences accord with the Freeman hypothesis that, without synchronized reforms, temporary work programs alone increase income gaps between skilled and unskilled workers (Freeman and Katz, 1995). In this respect, contemporary Japanese politics shares characteristics with majoritarian democracies such as the United States and Great Britain. In both, Japan and these LME countries, irregular workers without appropriate organizations and access to major parties have not generated unified political power.

6.4 CONCLUSION: THE POLITICS OF COUNSELING

In this chapter, I have analyzed how contemporary Japanese prime ministers have sought to facilitate the adjustment of Japanese firms' corporate governance and labor relation practices to the neoliberal international order by reforming the relevant public policy domains. The logic of global competition and efficiency enhancement alone cannot persuade opponents within the governing party or the jurisdictional bureaucracy, because the reform generates a distributive effect, upsetting sectoral interests represented by the party or the bureaucracy. To execute the reform, the prime minister needs consent from both the governing party and the bureaucracy by employing a creative political strategy. In this chapter, I have focused on referral to an appropriate council in pursuit of consent. Which council to refer to is the prime minister's strategic decision in view of not just expected efficiency gains, but the politics of governing coalitions and the bureaucracy (see Table 6.2).

I have found that, first, for reforms with a peripheral coalitional interest

Table 6.2 Regulatory reform and referral to deliberative councils

Issue	Deliberative Council Referred To	Type of Referral	Interest Protected
Holding companies	Administrative Reform Council	Strategic	Managers
Directorial independence	Legislative Council	Conventional	Managers
Temporary staffing services	Council for Regulatory Reform	Strategic	Employers
Dismissal with severance pay	Labour [sic] Policy Council	Aborted	Regular employees

and bureaucratic opposition, the referral procedure and outcome may be coercive and legally binding. Procedurally useful is strategic referral to an advisory council within the Cabinet Office whose membership the prime minister can determine. The prime minister can exploit an advisory council's positive agenda-setting power, getting his or her reform idea legitimated by eminent council members and disposed to bureaucratic consent through the Cabinet Office's administrative finesse. A prominent example is Prime Minister Hashimoto's referral to the business-dominated Administrative Reform Council within the Prime Minister's Office to resolve the reluctant bureaucracies' reservations on the legalization of holding companies as part of the cabinet's financial big-bang mandate. Another example is the Koizumi Cabinet's expansion of the temporary work program through referral to the Council for Regulatory Reform within the Cabinet Office to supersede labor opposition – temporary workers are not part of the LDP's governing coalition.

Second, for reform with a major coalitional interest and bureaucratic opposition, the referral procedure and outcome have to be consensual and non-coercive. The prime minister has to refer a reform idea to a deliberative council sponsored by a jurisdictional ministry with substantial representation of the related sectoral interests. This case is most difficult and entails a dilemma between executive and coalitional-bureaucratic politics. Within a deliberative council, substantial revisions are made to balance coalitional and bureaucratic interests. An amended bill is submitted to the Diet where the governing party will approve it. However, if appropriate revisions fail, the reform will suffer from the council's negative agenda-setting effect.

Third, recent prime ministers have been faced with the above-mentioned case more frequently than their predecessors were. Under globalization pressure, they are urged to implement market-based reforms of the

Japanese-style CME, while the governing party and bureaucracies often seek to maintain the existent policies and institutions. In this case, the prime minister has to use a creative political strategy – his or her referral procedure and its outcomes may be non-coercive but market based. A case in point is the corporate governance reform for which, having obtained a non-binding law with the comply-or-explain clause from the Legislative Council, Prime Minister Abe directed the FSA and the TSE to adopt the Corporate Governance Code that requires two independent directors for major listed firms. With this move, the corporate governance reform shifts from the public policy domain to private spheres where enforcement is problematic, providing corporate managers with high levels of discretion.

These findings have implications on rival leadership models. It appears that the presidential model has some explanatory power for prime ministers' 'presidential' efforts to promote their own policy platforms (e.g., holding company legalization for Prime Minister Hashimoto's financial big bang, the expansion of temporary staff services for Prime Minister Koizumi's universal structural reform) through strategic referral to advisory councils in the Cabinet Office. However, unlike a president, a prime minister is still constrained by the politics of the governing party's electoral coalition. This becomes obvious when he or she cannot use strategic referral to an advisory council in the Cabinet Office because within the constraint of parliamentary democracy, he or she has to have the governing party's support to enact reforms without relying instead on opposition parties, a strategy available to a president.

The Westminster model is also inconsistent with the observed regulatory reforms. A parliamentary majority under a competitive party system may not be enough to break a bureaucratic impasse in government based on a legacy of a bureaucratic-cabinet system involving multiple veto gates. The prime minister has to pay careful attention to the jurisdictional bureaucracy and determine his or her referral strategy to enact a reform idea, even though it may promote the median voter preference. This bureaucratic constraint may distinguish Japanese executive politics in Nagata-Cho from their British counterpart with civil services largely loyal to Downing Street.

The frequent use of strategic referral by Japanese prime ministers indicates the emergence of a new partnership between political leaders and elite bureaucrats at the cabinet level, giving some empirical support to the core-executive model. The model has been utilized by British prime ministers with the intent of improving the efficiency of policy coordination by creating policy networks (Rhodes, 2007, pp. 1247–8). In contrast, a Japanese prime minister is motivated to use a core-executive system in order to circumvent middle bureaucratic and party processes entrenched with vested interests, by taking advantage of his or her office's enhanced power under the centralized government structure. However, without network creation, the Japanese core-executive system can be used to promote another particularistic interest, rather than the public interest. This might have been different if Japan had been faced with strong external pressure to enforce rapid and deep reforms uniformly across policy domains. International comparisons indicated that, even in the absence of reform-minded domestic political leadership, bold liberal reforms were pushed for in France and South Korea by coercive external institutions. Immune to such an external authority, Japanese political leadership still has the luxury to take differentiated reforms that are consistent with a particularistic interest.

In the next two chapters, I will analyze reforms on trade and finance under intense external pressures. In Chapter 7, trade policy changes will be analyzed in relation to external market opening pressures and national security imperatives. In Chapter 8, the banking reform will be analyzed in light of substantial pressures from minimum capital requirements abroad and a major financial crisis at home.

NOTES

1. Specifically, major regulatory reforms include (1) a Japanese version of financial big bang (cross-entry between banking and investment, legalization of financial holding companies, deregulation on stock transactions, and the like); (2) Commercial Code reforms for the facilitation of market-consistent corporate governance; (3) the expansion of the temporary work program to office work and manufacturing industries; (4) the abolition of the large retail store control law; (5) the abolition of the fare-route control regimes in trucking and civil aviation; (6) the privatization of the postal service and highway corporations; (7) the abolition and mergers of other public corporations, and so on (see Vogel, 2006 and Tsunekawa, 2010 for detailed descriptions).
2. The CGQ index is constructed at the country level using accounting and market data of samples of listed non-financial firms. The index is a simple average of three proxy measures of outcomes of corporate governance in the dimensions of accounting disclosure and transparency on a de facto rather than de jure basis.
3. Menu-based corporate governance law is increasingly common and has been adopted by several continental European countries with CME arrangements (Overbeek et al., 2007).
4. Aoki (2010, pp. 166–8) argues that the recent corporate governance reform has co-evolved with the change in the political system that has improved the power of political leadership at the expense of tribal parliamentarians and bureaucratic officials, but he has not analyzed precisely how the political change has induced the reform.
5. See the Tokyo Stock Exchange at http://www.jpx.co.jp/english//; accessed 20 September 2014.
6. In 2005, the Companies Act was branched off from the Commercial Code as a separate legal body.
7. For designing and implementing regulatory reform, the Japanese government has relied on business communities, such as the Keidanren and the Keizai Doyukai, composed of large firms that are typically internationally competitive. These associations and their member firms have first-hand experience with and detailed information on the existing regulations that inhibit their business activities, while having business ties with their

foreign rivals and foreign governments. The Keidanren has submitted a list of regulatory reform requests based on its member firms' opinions to the government every year since 1993. There are direct channels of communication between the government and the business associations. President Yoshihiko Miyauchi of the Orix Corporation, a JACE member, had chaired the Committee on Regulatory Reform under multiple LDP-led cabinets. In addition, Keidanren President Hiroshi Okuda of Toyota Motor Co. and JACE advisor Jiro Ushio of Ushio Electronic Co. were members of the Council on Economic and Fiscal Policy under the Koizumi Cabinet. Yoshimatsu (1998) argues that the Keidanren has had considerable influence on the government's regulatory reform agenda. The Keidanren (2008) reported the likelihood of its recommendations leading to policy actions: 48 percent in 2003 and 30 percent in 2005 out of more than 200 requested items. There is no direct English translation of the original report in Japanese but a summary is provided in the document, 'The Keidanren's Proposal: Growth Strategy 2010', accessed 27 October 2015 at http://www.keidanren.or.jp/english/policy/2010/028proposal.pdf.

8. Among firms listed on the Tokyo Stock Exchange, nearly 30 percent had taken advantage of the holding company arrangement by 2009. The major reasons given by these companies in a survey were to promote efficient corporate governance, flexible reorganization, and defense against hostile takeovers – antithetical to the spirit of marketization. The last survey response suggests that the holding company scheme is a mixed blessing for the spirit of corporate governance reform, indicating that the reform might be used to protect management. This point is stressed throughout this chapter.
9. The Deliberative Council on Industrial Structure has been created based on the Ministry of Economy, Trade and Industry (METI) Establishment Act (see Chapter 5), and its members include a dozen business leaders, a labor union representative, and a few academics.
10. The Japan Federation of Employers' Associations (the Nikkeiren, merged with the Japan Business Federation, or the Keidanren, in 2002) objected to the Labor Union Act reform suggested by the Rengo because, under the existing act, direct negotiations between subsidiaries' labor unions and parent firms' management were possible, as shown in legal precedents. The business association was concerned that the amendment would constrain holding companies' managerial discretion (Mochikabu 'Gaisha Sakiokuri' [Holding companies postponed], *Asahi Shimbun*, 27 April 1996).
11. Earlier, the JFTC upheld the partial legalization of holding companies under highly restrictive standards: the proscription of holding companies with a capitalization of 10 trillion yen or more and a reporting requirement for 100 billion yen or more.
12. The subcommittee members included judges, lawyers, academics, business managers, labor union representative, legal specialists of the MOJ, the METI, the Financial Services Agency and the Cabinet Legislative Bureau, a representative of the Tokyo Stock Exchange, and an auditor association representative, but no representatives from investor associations and brokerage firms.
13. *Kaisha-ho Minaoshi no Chukan Shiron* [*Interim Report on the Revision of the Companies Act*], Companies Act Section of the Legislative Council, Ministry of Justice, 7 December 2011.
14. Since March 2010, the Tokyo Stock Exchange has required external board membership for listed firms.
15. Kato, H., 'Kaisha-Ho Kaisei Secchuan de Matomaru' [A compromise on Companies Act reform], *Ho to Keizai no Janaru* [*Journal on Law and Economics*] in *Asahi Shimbun*, 20 August 2012, accessed 5 November 2015 at http://judiciary.asahi.com/articles/2012081700001.html.
16. For the Keidanren's opinion on the interim report, see https://www.keidanren.or.jp/japanese/policy/2012/007.pdf [in Japanese]; accessed 20 September 2014.
17. For Keizai Doyukai's opinion on the interim report on 20 January 2012, see http://www.doyukai.or.jp/policyproposals/articles/2011/pdf/120130a.pdf [in Japanese]; accessed 20 September 2014.

18. For the Japanese Association of Commercial Banks' opinion on the interim report, see http://www.zenginkyo.or.jp/abstract/opinion/entryitems/opinion231020.pdf [in Japanese]; accessed 20 September 2014.
19. They opposed the idea of making directorial independence a binding rule for the Tokyo Stock Exchange, although approximately 50 percent of firms listed on the Tokyo Stock Exchange had already had outside board members in 2010. Several prominent Japanese firms refused to have independent board members because they said they needed board members to have detailed knowledge of the firm's unique production and management styles. In addition, the Japanese business community viewed the council's proposal as a measure to prevent corporate fraud in the midst of scandals surrounding major Japanese companies, such as Olympus, Daio-seishi, Yakult, etc. They (wrongly) claimed that, although these firms had independent board members (in loose terms), the illegal practices could not be stopped or even uncovered.
20. Testimony by Assistant Vice-Minister of the FSA in charge of the General Planning Bureau, Tadakazu Ikeda, before the Judiciary Committee of the House of Representatives on 23 April 2014.
21. The average revenue to equity ratio for a US firm was approximately 15 percent, while that for a Japanese firm was approximately 8 percent.
22. The LDP's Japan Economic Revival Headquarters revealed its policy proposal, *Japan Revival Vision* in May 2014. See its English version on the LDP's website: http://jimin.ncss.nifty.com/pdf/english/news/Japan_Revival_Vision-Provisional_Translation20140523.pdf; accessed 19 September 2014.
23. Justice Minister Taniguchi's testimony before the Judiciary Committee in the House of Representatives, 23 April 2013.
24. This point is vindicated by the result of scholarly analysis, showing that the Japanese firms that adopted a committee system with external directors are not performing significantly better than those without (Saito, 2010).
25. It is widely speculated that the Abe Cabinet assuaged managers' discontents about the proposal by promising a corporate tax cut.
26. See the final draft of the Corporate Governance Code on the FSA's website: http://www.fsa.go.jp/en/refer/councils/corporategovernance/20150306-1/01.pdf#search='tokyo+stock+exchange+stewardship+corporate+governance; accessed 11 May 2015.
27. This point is evidenced by a major corporate scandal. When I was finishing this book, Toshiba, a leading Japanese electronics manufacturer, announced that it was involved in a major accounting fraud. The internal investigating commission said it had discovered 'systematic involvement, including by top management, with the goal of intentionally inflating the appearance of net profits.' The firm, earlier considered a role model in corporate governance, had adopted a committee system and reportedly complied with the Corporate Governance Code. In addition, several Toshiba managers were members of the Councils on Economic and Fiscal Policy and Industrial Competitiveness that influenced the multilayered law on corporate governance. Toshiba stockholders, both foreign and domestic, were preparing for lawsuits against the Toshiba corporate managers for the losses due to fraud and mismanagement.
28. See note 39 for an additional explanation of the law.
29. Approximately 40 percent of the 3440 responding firms in the Research Institute of Economy, Trade and Industry (RIETI) corporate survey in 2012 reported that LTERs were a barrier to their flexible reorganization efforts; see Morikawa (2012).
30. The formal name of the law is the Act for Securing the Proper Operation of Worker Dispatching Undertakings and Improved Working Conditions for Dispatched Workers.
31. The excluded sectors were port facilities, construction, home security, medicine, and manufacturing.
32. Ministry of Health, Labour and Welfare (2012), *Rodo Keizai no Bunseki 2012* [*Analysis of the Labor Economy*], p. 120. An English summary of the Japanese report is available at http://www.mhlw.go.jp/english/wp/l-economy/2012/summary.pdf, accessed 5 November 2015.

33. The dual structure of the Japanese labor market has long been a major focus of labor economists. See, for instance, Ishikawa (1999). The gaps used to be attributed to the size of firms but more recently the gaps have been attributed to the legal classification between regular and temporary workers.
34. The Council for Regulatory Reform was established within the Cabinet Office by the Act for the Organization of the Cabinet Office in 2001.
35. This belief appeared to be derived from the Obuchi Cabinet's experience that a negative list for expanding the TEMP program was faced with strong labor objections in the Deliberative Council on Labour [sic] Policy of the Ministry of Labour [sic]. The council failed to reach agreement because labor representatives refused to participate in the council meetings. However, a bill for a negative list was submitted to the Diet. This instance showcased the reduced efficacy of the deliberative council as a policy-making entity.
36. The composition of the Deliberative Council on Labour Relations was statutorily determined: it had 24 members with equivalent representation of labor, management, and the public (academics, lawyers, and bureaucrats). In contrast, the composition of the Subcommittee on Equal Employment was chosen by the ministry on a discretionary basis (it had 13 members, including three labor union representatives, five managers, and five public representatives at the time of deliberation).
37. Statement by MP Masamitsu Jojima of the DPJ in the hearing of the Committee on Health, Labour and Welfare, the House of Representatives, on 23 May 2003.
38. The legislative intent of the approved amendment to the Labor Standards Act as summed up by chair Nariaki Nakayama at the hearing of the Committee on Health, Labour and Welfare, the House of Representatives, on 4 June 2003.
39. This clause was formally Article 18.2 of the Labor Standards Act and is currently Article 16 of the Labor Contract Act that was branched out from the Labor Standards Act in 2007.
40. See the summary of the meeting of the Roundtable on Industrial Competitiveness on 23 April 2013 at http://www.kantei.go.jp/jp/singi/keizaisaisei/skkkaigi/dai7/gijiyousi.pdf [in Japanese]; accessed 22 September 2014.
41. 'Kaiko no Kinsen Kaiketsu Keizoku Giron' [Debate on dismissal with severance pay postponed]' *Asahi Shimbun*, 25 April 2013.
42. The Keidanren has supported dismissal with *ex post facto* severance pay to speed up court settlements. See its opinion on regulatory reform issued on 17 June 2008, at http://www.keidanren.or.jp/japanese/policy/2008/041/11.pdf [in Japanese]; accessed 22 September 2014. For an English text explaining its position on labor contracts see Keidanren, 'New directions for the Japanese-style employment system', accessed 27 October 2015 at http://www.keidanren.or.jp/english/policy/2007/109.html. The Deliberative Council on Labour Policy discussed dismissal with *ex post facto* severance pay and did not reach agreement (*Nihon Keizai Shimbun*, 24 August 2014).
43. The proposed special economic zones include business districts in Tokyo, Osaka, and other major cities.
44. 'Gov't to shelve key employment deregulatory items', *The Japan News*, 18 October 2013.
45. In the 2012 plenary session, this legal loophole was criticized by the Social Democratic Party (SDP) and the Japanese Communist Party (JCP), which eventually opposed the DPJ amendment to the Labor Contract Law.
46. Under the previous law, a company could not use workers from temporary staff dispatch agents on the same job for more than three years, except for those assigned to do jobs in 26 categories that require special skills, ranging from computer programming to translations, product development, marketing and research.
47. 'Lower house OKs workers' dispatch bill', *The Japan News*, 20 June 2015.
48. Martin (2013, p. 242) notes that Germany is less successful than Scandinavian countries in rallying business to the aid of marginal workers and in maintaining relative equality.

7. Issue-dimensional politics for trade liberalization

7.1 JAPANESE TRADE POLICY AND WTO-PLUS AGREEMENTS

Trade liberalization is an extremely effective instrument to promote economic growth through competition and efficiency improvements. Despite limited natural resources, Japan was able to build world-class manufacturing industries by importing natural resources from overseas, processing them into intermediary and finished products through industrial fine-tuning associated with its coordinated market economy (CME), and exporting them to markets abroad. Unrestricted cross-border transactions have been the key to Japan's economic success.

The post–World War II trade regime of the General Agreement on Tariffs and Trade (GATT) helped Japan achieve postwar reconstruction and phenomenal growth. Nonetheless, the liberal trade order provided the country with a potential dilemma: it had to open its markets to stay firmly within the order in pursuit of overseas markets, while preserving the Japanese-style CME in pursuit of long-term employment and social stability. Japanese trade policies had to achieve multiple purposes at once through careful planning and collaboration among government, management, and labor officials. Such a multipurpose policy proved possible under the GATT order of embedded liberalism in which contracting states still could implement incremental or sector-specific liberalization. In addition, the states could reduce import-related injuries to domestic industries through safeguards or trade adjustment subsidies or both.

Yet multipurpose trade policies have become increasingly difficult to maintain under the succeeding World Trade Organization (WTO) that has begun to promote not just industrial tariff reductions, but also liberalization in agricultural and service trade, regulatory reforms, investment protection, and intellectual property rights protection. Furthermore, even though the WTO-sponsored multilateral trade rounds stalled after the conclusion of the Uruguay Round, contracting states have been negotiating bilateral or regional free trade agreements (FTAs) that are deeper in liberalization and broader in regulatory reform than what the WTO originally called for.

Hence, these agreements, named 'WTO-plus', urge contracting states to reach cross-sectoral coordination as well as regulatory adaptation. A state wishing to conclude FTAs has to solve the joint problems of adaptation and coordination to adjust its economic system further to the neoliberal international order. This means that the state needs an appropriate combination of central command with bureaucratic delegation, evoking a fundamental dilemma in setting forth the appropriate authority allocation scheme.

Until recently, the Japanese government had been extraordinarily cautious about trade liberalization, in part because it believed the Japanese economic system needed to nurture firm-specific human and organizational assets and in part because inefficient sectors of the ruling Liberal Democratic Party's cross-sectoral coalition were highly sensitive to liberalization. If it failed to preserve these coalitional interests, the LDP might have experienced a coalitional realignment and suffered an electoral defeat.

As discussed in Chapter 4, the political reforms in the mid-1990s have had a transforming effect on the Japanese government toward centralization and a two-party majoritarian system. This Westminster tendency, arguably, has distilled domestic political constraints and paved the way for broad trade liberalization in pursuit of majoritarian-consumerist interests (Rosenbluth and Thies, 2010). However, domestic political constraints still seem to be entrenched in contemporary political Japan, and thus the country lags behind in the global FTA contest.

Why has Japan, as the most vigorous exporter in the postwar world, fallen behind in the recent FTA competition? What kind of authority allocation scheme did Japan use to overcome bureau-pluralistic protectionist forces in order to promote trade during the high-growth period? What was the ruling party's coordination strategy when its political coalition was cross-sectoral rather than majoritarian under the single non-transferable vote (SNTV) and factional party politics systems? Why has the conventional strategy failed to work in recent times? What can be done to adapt to the global trade order? In what follows, I will address these questions.

7.2 JAPANESE-STYLE MARKET ECONOMY, IMPORT CONTROLS, AND EXTERNAL PRESSURE

7.2.1 Conventional Explanation for Japan's Trade Policy

Endogenous growth and import controls

One of the most sophisticated explanations about steady economic growth such as Japan's postwar high growth is derived from the theory of endogenous economic growth (Romer, 1986; Lucas, 1988; Rebelo, 1991). The theory postulates that steady growth stems from continuous industrial innovation through human capital improvement, research and development, and positive externalities of knowledge that can counter the diminishing return of capital accumulation.[1] Steady growth in postwar Japan was possible because the Japanese-style CME system contributed to the enhancement of such innovation. Within the system, managers and workers were embedded in firms through long-term relational contracts and were incentivized to develop firm-specific human capital and knowledge. Organizationally, companies were connected with one another through horizontal and vertical networks to reduce interfirm transaction costs and develop efficient supply chains as well as joint research and development programs. Corporations relied on main banks' patient capital and oversight for long-term investment and competent management. These arrangements motivated firms to expand market shares rather than short-term profits, thus taking advantage of economies of scale and increasing returns.

To maintain institutional complementarity, the private arrangements were complemented by public policy interventions, including the rational dismissal principle for long-term employment, regulatory rents for patient (long-term) capital, and a commercial code for blockholding and contingent corporate governance. More importantly in this chapter, import controls were part of the public policy interventions as a measure to provide stability and predictability for long-term relational contracts and yield rents for research and development (i.e., strategic trade policy; Krugman, 1986). They also helped dynamic rationalization to relocate human and material assets from inefficient to efficient sectors.

Bureau-pluralism

In principle, import controls need to be reduced in the wake of the improvement of economic efficiency in order to achieve dynamic reallocation of human and material assets between industrial sectors. However, in reality, it is difficult to evaluate sectors' competitiveness and judge the validity of import control. Under informational uncertainty, members of the governing party may prevent market liberalization for a particular sector in collaboration with bureaucratic officials in order to maintain the sector's electoral allegiance, even though import control is no longer appropriate for the sector. This is an archetypical case of 'protection for sale' (Grossman and Helpman, 2002). In a political world, the extent of import control is determined not just by an industrial sector's competitiveness, but also by its proximity to the governing party and bureaucratic organization. Hence, the actual trade policy regime is often inconsistent with the logic of endogenous growth or comparative institutionalism.

7.2.2 External Pressure for Trade Openness

As argued above, despite their potential economic rationale, import controls could easily turn out to be a bureau-pluralistic instrument for protectionist rents. As the rents persist and even proliferate across industrial sectors, national economic growth stagnates to the detriment of the general public and productive sectors. Political leadership attentive to the worsening of national economic well-being would explore means to reduce inefficient import controls entrenched deeply within the policy portfolios of the governing party and bureaucratic organizations.

In order to remove such import controls, external pressure (*gaiatsu*) by a powerful foreign government or international organization is useful. Such an actor effectively constitutes an ancillary external authority to oversee a state's trade policy. In fact, Japan's postwar trade policy history entails several cases of trade liberalization following external pressure on the constrained political system. These cases may be interpreted as a result of the conscious use of external pressure by Japanese political leadership to reduce inefficient import controls (Schoppa, 1997). Under the decentralized political system, liberal groups scattered across the governing party, the bureaucracies, the business community, and the public were often unable to gather sufficient political momentum to eliminate inefficient import controls through ordinary policy channels because of multiple veto gates or collective inaction or both. Thus, political leadership, cognizant of the general well-being and backed by liberal domestic groups, coalesced strategically with external forces, such as the United States as the largest importer of Japanese products and the guarantor of national security, in order to circumvent the domestic veto gates and improve economic efficiency. Successful liberalization ensued when interests overlapped sufficiently to form a transnational alliance capable of exerting substantial coordinating pressure upon the constrained domestic political system.

7.2.3 Coordination Strategies for Trade Liberalization

External pressure provided the Japanese government with a potential external ancillary authority to promote selective regulatory reforms that were needed for efficiency improvements. However, external pressure alone was not enough to execute liberalization against strong domestic opposition. It had to be met with the government's own coordination effort at securing domestic consent. Below, I outline such arrangements pertaining

Table 7.1 Trade liberalization under the Kishi-Ikeda Cabinets

Year	Month	Liberalization (%)	Number of Protected Items
1960	April	41	–
	July	42	–
	October	44	–
1961	April	62	–
	July	65	–
	October	68	–
	December	70	–
1962	April	73	492
	October	88	262
	November	88	254
1963	April	89	229
	June	89	227
	August	92	192

Note: The liberalization rate is defined as the percentage of imports under the automatic approval (AA) system. A horizontal bar indicates unavailability of data.

Source: The table is constructed from *Zeikan Hyakunen Shi* [*A Hundred Years' History of Tariff Policy*], Tariff Bureau, Ministry of Finance, 1972, p. 330.

to the Kishi-Ikeda liberalization agenda (Table 7.1) in the early 1960s and the Structural Impediments Initiative (SII) in the late 1980s.

A first strategy was to provide 'compensation' or a subsidy to an inefficient sector that would lose regulatory rents from liberalization. If the loss was severe, compensation would be effective in obtaining consent from the inefficient sector that would be able to improve its competitiveness or cover up the import injuries. The compensatory strategy relies on the logic of credible commitment that posits that effective compensation requires government's guarantee based on budgetary readiness and a low probability of government turnover: these factors were obtainable during the long tenure of the LDP government between 1955 and 1993.

More specifically, in order to assuage public anxieties about liberalization, the Kishi Cabinet expanded loan programs for small and medium-sized enterprises (SMEs) that were most vulnerable to import injuries due to tariff cuts. For workers whose jobs and income might be threatened by liberalization, the Kishi Cabinet established the first national medical insurance and pension system in Japan. The two systems were introduced to build a liberal-democratic welfare state and reduce the US and European criticism of social dumping practices by Japanese firms that allegedly formed wage cartels to lower production costs. Equally important, the package of open trade and social welfare hinged on the foreign policy goal of integrating Japan deeply within the liberal international order at a time when the public was still divided between market economy and socialist planned economy. Prime Minister Ikeda said in front of the Diet in 1960 that a combination of a strong economy with robust social security would help promote the liberalization of Japan's economy, while a social security regime would need a strong economic foundation that could be promoted through a viable private sector and small government.[2] Ikeda's 'Income Doubling Plan' in pursuit of growth and stability accorded perfectly with the spirit of embedded liberalism that underpinned the GATT regime (Nakakita, 2001, pp. 823–4).

As for the SII, the relaxation of the Large Retail Store Control Act was accompanied by a compensatory measure – commercial loans to small retail stores that would suffer losses from the regulatory reform. The law prohibited opening large retail stores in close proximity of small retail store districts under the auspices of the Ministry of International Trade and Industry (MITI). The US government criticized the law for unfairly protecting small stores that distributed Japanese products disproportionately, albeit inefficiently, restricting the opening of large retail stores that would distribute substantial amounts of imports. The law harmed the interests of both Japanese consumers and foreign exporters. To support small retail storeowners, the Japan Chamber of Commerce, the MITI, and rank-and-file LDP members were initially opposed to the abolition of the law, but conceded because of the loan program and local governments' ordinance on zoning as a regulatory means to constrain, rather than prevent the opening of large stores.[3]

A second coordination strategy hinges on the 'manipulation of issue dimensions' in a policy debate that alters opponents' preference structures. This linguistic strategy was conceptualized as 'heresthetics' by William Riker (1986). Using rhetorical skills, a political leader either adds or subtracts an issue dimension from the policy debate in order to realign the participants' preferences and obtain consent from opponents. This is a type of agenda-setting through which a setter manipulates not committee jurisdiction or decision-making procedures, but the dimension of issues that organizes a policy debate.[4] In what follows, I describe two instances where Japanese leaders appeared to use issue-dimensional politics for market opening.

Prime Minister Kishi, in a statement before the Diet in January 1960, said that Japan should not fall behind in the international trend of liberalization of trade and foreign exchange in order to benefit from the enhanced mobility of goods across borders and obtain international recognition as a legitimate member of the free world. The liberalization was important with respect to Japan's acquisition of an IMF Article 8 status, OECD accession, and equal partnership with the United States against the backdrop of the Cold War. As for the SII, Prime Minister Kaifu (1989–91) stressed before the Diet in January 1991 that the key issue was 'to improve the US–Japan global partnership and contribute to the world economy as part of Japan's international responsibility'. Both prime ministers' rhetoric was meant to shift the public concern from the agonizing domestic structural reforms to the fulfillment of international responsibilities appropriate for a developed state.

To acquire domestic consent to liberalization, 'attrition' is a third strategy to reduce the influence of an opposing camp. The Kishi-Ikeda market-opening project included the attrition of the coal mining industry that had been an engine of Japanese industrial growth in the pre- and postwar era but became non-competitive in the late 1950s. Because petroleum became widely available and the industry's structural problems pushed production costs up, the LDP cabinets at last decided to reduce the protective policy for coal, issuing a rationalization protocol with subsidies and tax incentives to reallocate human and material assets from mining to manufacturing sectors in urban areas. The muted political influence of coal led to a substantial increase in petroleum imports and the expansion of an oil refinery industry that made coal mining fade into oblivion (Nakamura, 2012, pp. 596–99).

The three strategies could be employed separately or jointly in conjunction with external pressure, providing effective instruments to promote liberalization even under a decentralized government. However, in practice, few of the strategies were used to promote the emergent FTA policy in the 2000s: the Japanese government relied primarily on bureaucratic delegation, or the four-ministry co-chair system, for its FTA policy for the reasons discussed in the next section. With the bureaucratic delegation approach, Japan was unable to increase the limited share of import in its economy that was almost equivalent to that in the larger US economy (Table 7.2) and was viewed as a contributor to the lack of domestic competition and Japan's relative decline in international competition (Figures 7.1 and 7.2).

7.3 FREE TRADE AGREEMENT DESIGNS AND FOUR-MINISTRY CO-CHAIR SYSTEM

7.3.1 Japanese FTA Policy under Bureaucratic Delegation

In the late 1990s, US pressure receded as the Japanese economy underwent a long recession leading to a declining in its importance for US firms.

Table 7.2 Ratio of import to real GDP in selected states (percentage)

State/Year	1985	1990	1995	2000	2005	2010	2011	2012	Ranking in 2012
South Korea	33.31	27.66	26.11	30.09	31.67	41.9	47.06	46	40
China	13.67	13.19	17.45	18.78	29.25	23.54	23.88	22.1	111
Japan	9.57	7.7	6.3	8.02	11.26	12.6	14.48	14.85	125
United States	8.36	8.91	10.06	12.24	13.25	13.16	14.59	14.38	126

Source: The table is constructed from the data provided by Kokusai Boeki Toshi Kenkyujo [Research Institute for International Trade and Investment, Tokyo].

Source: The figure is constructed from the United Nations National Accounts Main Aggregates Database.

Figure 7.1 Share of major states' GDP in global GDP

The end of the Cold War can be viewed as another factor that reduced US interest in maintaining bilateral solidarity. Almost concurrently, the WTO multilateral trade negotiations deadlocked, propelling the member countries to resort to concluding FTAs for trade expansion. To keep up with the change in the international trade order, Japan had to launch its own FTA strategy, relying on the system of bureaucratic delegation for negotiating FTAs.

The reasons were twofold. First, the conceptual change toward FTAs in Japan was heralded not by political leaders, but by middle-echelon

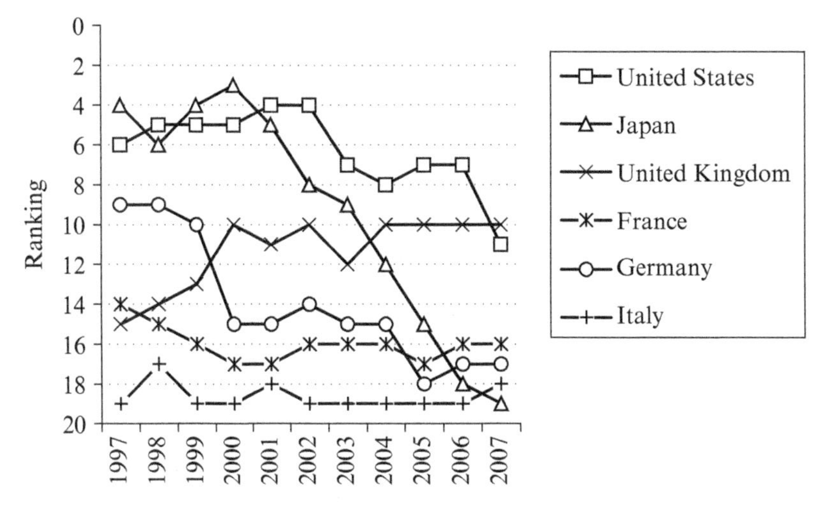

Source: The figure is constructed from the United Nations National Accounts Main Aggregates Database.

Figure 7.2 Global rankings of major states' GDP per capita

bureaucrats in the Division of International Trade Policy Planning within the MITI Trade Policy Bureau (RIETI, 2013a, p. 196). This is consistent with the theory of adaptation: bureaucratic officials have the ability to adapt to change in the international order because of their superior information and expertise. Division officials have constantly analyzed foreign states' trade policies and noticed clear shifts toward FTAs by major players, including the United States and the European Union. In the meantime, another MITI department, the Division of International Economy within the Trade Policy Bureau firmly supported the multilateral approach and opposed the proposed shift to trade bilateralism that officials feared might upset the multilateral WTO order and return Japan to the pre-war regime of trading blocs and postwar isolation. The intra-bureau conflict was resolved in favor of FTAs by external trade-related events, including (1) the failed Seattle Conference for initiating WTO-sponsored new multilateral trade negotiations in 1999; (2) the conclusion of FTAs outside Japan that began to generate negative externalities for Japanese firms; and (3) requests from South Korea, Mexico, and Singapore to conclude FTAs with Japan. In addition, the East Asian currency crisis in 1997–98 prompted Japanese bureaucratic officials to realize the risk of regional economic interdependence and the need to refurbish economic ties with East Asian states through regional trade and investment agreements.

The conceptual change in the International Trade Bureau led to the release of the 'Promotion of Strategic Trade Policy' in October 1998 that indicated (1) the existence of more than 160 FTAs in the world; (2) institutional complementarity between the FTAs and the WTO; and (3) the resilience of multilateralism in trade. The multilateralists within the bureaucratic and political circles who were still concerned about the FTAs' bilateralism were comforted by the possibility of enlargement. Despite their fragmentary FTA initiatives, several East Asian states also mentioned in both bilateral and multilateral forums that they were optimistic about transforming bilateral FTAs into a regional agreement. For instance, the final report of the East Asia Study Group, presented at the ASEAN Plus Three (APT) Summit in November 2002, asserted that:

> the establishment of an EAFTA (East Asia FTA) could be achieved by adopting a building block approach, and consolidating the existing bilateral and sub-regional FTAs in the region. . . In this regard, the ongoing progress in the discussions of establishing many bilateral and sub-regional FTAs could pave the way for establishing an EAFTA.[5]

Thus, the prospect for FTA enlargement provided a rationale for concluding bilateral FTAs, which became a formal trade policy objective for the Japanese government.[6] The conceptual change within the Ministry of Economy, Trade and Industry (METI) traversed to the Ministry of Foreign Affairs (MOFA) and resolved a similar conceptual conflict between the Division of Developing Economic Regions supporting FTAs and the First Division of International Organizations within the Economic Bureau supporting the WTO order.

The key ministries' conceptual change was echoed by the Obuchi Cabinet, an LDP-led coalition government that had already shifted from the structural reformist approach of the preceding Hashimoto Cabinet to a growth approach of revitalizing the recessionary Japanese economy through a stimulus package. The Obuchi Cabinet found that FTAs would provide a better prospect for immediate growth than the WTO regime because the conclusion of the former would be less time-consuming than the latter's multilateral trade round. Even for structural reformists, FTAs were yet another external pressure for regulatory reform at home that would promote growth in the medium term. Moreover, in the early 2000s, China's economic ascent and active FTA policy became a political motive for the Koizumi Cabinet with an international outlook to accelerate its FTA initiative in Southeast Asia. The different political leaders found the FTA-centric trade approach useful for furthering their different political economic objectives.

With the conceptual change, the Japanese government began to pursue

Table 7.3 Bilateral FTAs/EPAs and liberalization rates

Counterparty	Date of Agreement	Liberalization Rate (%)
Singapore	January 2002	84.4
Mexico	January 2004	86.0
Malaysia	December 2005	86.8
Chile	March 2007	86.5
Thailand	April 2007	87.2
Brunei	June 2007	84.6
Indonesia	August 2007	86.6
Philippines	September 2006	88.4
ASEAN	April 2008	NA
Vietnam	December 2008	86.5
Switzerland	February 2009	85.6
India	February 2011	86.4
Peru	March 2012	87.0
Australia	January 2015	88.4

Note: The liberalization rate in Table 7.3 means the percentage of imports free from tariffs within ten years. This differs from the liberalization rate in Table 7.1.

Source: The table is constructed from data in various issues of the *Diplomatic Bluebook*, MOFA.

the East Asia–centric building-block approach by negotiating a bilateral FTA with Singapore in January 2001. The negotiation went relatively smoothly because Singapore had already had zero-tariff rates covering numerous industrial products and an insignificant agricultural sector that was often a stumbling block for Japanese trade liberalization. The FTA with Singapore took the form of an economic partnership agreement (EPA) with an emphasis on investment liberalization and intellectual property rights protection that served as a model for subsequent negotiations with other foreign governments (Table 7.3).

A second reason for the bureaucracy-led FTA strategy hinges on the fact that the negotiation and conclusion of an FTA requires considerable administrative and legal skills to create treaty arrangements that should be mutually beneficial for Japan and its counterparts while consistent with WTO law and other international regulatory agreements. This calls for the involvement of bureaucratic officials with information and expertise as well as transgovernmental connections. Contrastingly, the GATT/WTO trade round negotiations had been led largely by the United States and Europe (Drezner, 2007). Other, smaller members, including Japan, played limited roles in setting the agenda and simply chose to adopt, amend, or reject proposals already on the table. As for an FTA, contracting states are directly and solely responsible for proposing, negotiating, and concluding a treaty.

7.3.2 Institutional Arrangements of EPAs

Four-ministry co-chair system

A trade liberalizing agreement needs to be an equilibrium for the contracting states. It has to be a self-enforcing or mutually beneficial agreement from which neither side wishes to defect unilaterally. Such an agreement requires meticulous adaptation techniques by specialized bureaucratic agencies. Each agency administers narrowly defined policy issues: tariffs, safety standards, intellectual property rights, labor laws, trade-related investment, and so on. Furthermore, to be qualified as an FTA, contracting states have to achieve high levels of liberalization prescribed by the WTO: 85 percent or more of tariff items or trade volumes must be covered by the agreement. These prerequisites mean that an FTA requires both adaptation and coordination techniques.

To negotiate and conclude an FTA, the Japanese government has used the four-ministry co-chair system (*yon shocho kyodo gicho taisei*), which has been the standard decision-making body on trade since the Kishi-Ikeda initiative. The four ministries include the MOFA, the Ministry of Finance (MOF), METI, and the Ministry of Agriculture, Forestry and Fisheries (MAFF). The representatives at the deputy director-general level from the four ministries form the government negotiating team (GNT, *seifu kosho dan*). In determining its negotiating strategy with regard to a foreign government, the GNT adopts a consensus rule and has to consult with the four ministries, giving each of the four ministries veto power. Hence, the four-ministry co-chair system is basically a decentralized one and is a prototype of the bureaucratic-cabinet system on trade.

The GNT's weak central command constrains its ability to coordinate inter-ministerial tasks and its bargaining power regarding a foreign government. This differentiates the GNT from the United States Trade Representative and the European Commissioner for Trade, both of whom combine the negotiating with the coordinating authorities based on the notion of central command. However, in Japan, an FTA concluded with a foreign government through the GNT is typically an aggregated outcome of ministries' separate negotiation efforts, rather than a politically orchestrated coherent agreement. The institutional arrangements discussed below are characteristic of such efforts.

Investment protection

Recent FTAs are wide in scope, including non-trade arrangements with respect to investment, intellectual property rights, labor standards, and so on. These arrangements pose considerable administrative difficulties for some governments. A precise and binding agreement needs to be backed by strong domestic regulatory agencies that can ensure interpretive and procedural accuracy as well as policy transparency and compliance. Such agencies need to operate on the basis of rules and be staffed with highly skilled policy specialists and lawyers. Once the agencies are put into place, compliance becomes self-enforcing. Developed states often stress the importance of a strong regulatory regime to enforce non-trade clauses (concerning the liberalization of investment and the protection of intellectual property rights) that they prefer to include into trade agreements with developing states. Developed states insist that regulatory ineffectiveness in developing states prevents them from entering into mutually beneficial agreements because ineffective regulatory regimes generate markets that are not transparent as well as the kind of inefficient economic systems (dubbed 'crony capitalism') that presumably precipitated the Asian financial crisis of 1997–98 (Krugman, 1999).

The agreements with Singapore, Mexico, and Malaysia allow for international arbitration under the International Centre for Settlement of Investment Disputes (ICSID) or the United Nations Commission on International Trade Law (UNCITRAL) rules in the event of an investment dispute. The Japan–Malaysia EPA (JMEPA) also permits arbitration under the rules of the Kuala Lumpur Regional Centre for Arbitration, in addition to the ICSID and the UNCITRAL. Third-party arbitration ensures impartiality, predictability, and consistency of settlement outcomes.

The Japan–Philippines Economic Partnership Agreement (JPEPA), signed in September 2006, is the fourth EPA that Japan has entered into. It offers a range of rights and protections to foreign investors, including national treatment, most-favored nation treatment, and protection against expropriation. It does not contain a mechanism to settle investment disputes.[7] The Philippines resisted, including a provision that would allow investment disputes to be settled through international arbitration,[8] because 'arbitration is very costly and partial to developed countries'.[9] Both sides have committed to search for an expedient mechanism that is within the resources of the Filipino government. The exceptional nature of the JPEPA implies that a cooperative agreement can be concluded even with a state of low regulatory capacity by setting forth a consultative procedure that can diminish the domestic cost of that state's regulatory weakness.

Intellectual property rights protection

Most EPAs/FTAs signed by Japan have clauses that are consistent with the WTO's trade-related intellectual property rights (TRIPS), with two additional clauses. First, one TRIPS-plus clause in Japanese EPAs is extrapolated from the Japanese Unfair Competition Prevention Law enacted in 1993 that stresses the prevention of product design imitation or 'dead copy', Internet domain protection, and so on. Another clause is that the Japan–Indonesia EPA compels Indonesia's accession to the International Convention for the Protection of New Varieties of Plants (UPOV Convention).[10] Basically, Japanese EPAs make a multilateral treaty signed by either party non-binding to other parties – a Japanese EPA/FTA respects only the multilateral treaties on intellectual property rights signed by both parties.

Market segmentation

The Japan–Malaysia EPA (JMEPA), for instance, permits the Malaysian government to maintain tariffs on completely built units (CBUs) of automobiles but must remove the tariffs on auto parts. The arrangement promotes the downstream phases of auto production in Malaysia and provides learning and employment opportunities for locals. In the meantime, it enables Japanese firms to set up assembly plants in the country, thereby taking advantage of cheap Malaysian labor and expanding their sales networks across Southeast Asia.

Development

The Japan–Indonesia EPA (JINDEPA) and the JPEPA promote trade and investment between Japan and the Southeast Asian countries and assist them in developing human capital. Under the arrangements, Japan annually accepts Indonesian and Filipino students who study nursing and elderly care practices and work for medical institutions in Japan conditional on their passing achievement exams.

Agriculture

During the 2000s, the Japanese government chose small economies with limited agricultural exports or some agricultural exports that do not compete with Japanese producers because of divergent product lines, seasonal differences, or meticulous import control arrangements. For instance, there is little direct competition in agricultural products between Japan and Mexico because of geographical and climatological differences. Nonetheless, one agricultural product from Mexico, pork meat, is disputed. The Japan–Mexico Economic Partnership Agreement (JMEPA) contains a protective measure that is a quota-based graduated tariff rate, prescribing the minimum rate below a certain threshold of import volumes and higher rates beyond the threshold. This mechanism helped overcome the required levels of liberalization in terms of trade volumes and tariff items, set forth for an FTA by the WTO. It would produce a substitutive effect in replacing pork imports from elsewhere with those from Mexico.

7.3.3 Effects on the Japanese-style CME and Limits of the Four-ministry Co-chair System

As argued in Part I of this book, institutional reform needs varying extents of adaptation and coordination, depending on the nature of change. From the perspective of rational institutionalism, the appropriate government structure needs to be chosen based on the relative importance of the two in a given policy domain. The choice of bureaucratic delegation in the case of FTAs with small economies is rational insofar as the importance of adaptation outweighs that of coordination. The aforementioned treaty arrangements with relatively small Asian and Latin-American economies are either regulatory or sector-specific with limited coordination needs. This is a rational reason behind the use of the decentralized four-ministry co-chair system for negotiating the FTAs with limited effects in expanding trade volumes and in creating efficiency improvements.

However, the same delegation approach is inappropriate for an FTA with a large economy. In general, the government of a large foreign economy will agree to conclude an FTA with the Japanese government only if Japan reduces trade barriers against its exports substantially and vice versa. Thus, the FTA will generate substantial gains to consumers as well as export opportunities to competitive industrial sectors, yet creating major losses to non-competitive domestic sectors (e.g., Japanese agriculture). Thus, the conclusion of the FTA will require government to achieve major coordination between competing domestic interests.

Because of this coordination difficulty, the LDP that conducted FTA policy in the recent past was extraordinarily cautious in choosing co-signing states. Until recently, the LDP government had avoided negotiating an FTA with a large economy for fear that it would jeopardize coalitional interests and considerably reduce electoral support for the party. As a result, FTA-based trade accounts for a mere 20 percent of Japan's total trade, whereas the share of FTA trade in total trade in South Korea, the United States, and the European Union is 40 percent, 45 percent, and 40 percent, respectively. In addition, the average rate of liberalization for the FTAs ratified by Japan is approximately 86 percent, barely exceeding the WTO threshold, and is lower than nearly 100 percent for the United States, the European Union, and South Korea (see Table 7.3).[11] By the late 2000s, the Japanese FTA strategy had included most small economies among its East Asian trade partners; competitive liberalization could not go any further without involving larger economies. This implies that the four-ministry co-chair system has effectively become a veto gate that hinders the conclusion of FTAs with large economies, failing to reverse the Japanese decline in international competition shown in the previous section.[12]

Outside Japan, deep and broad FTAs are becoming the global standard in the wake of enhanced competition and regulatory sophistication because they are believed to improve welfare more than small ones. Accordingly, FTA forerunners, such as the United States, the European Union, South Korea, and so on, have established central authorities to coordinate the relevant bureaucracies' policy tasks and negotiate directly with foreign governments. The question is whether Japan can adjust its trade policy to global standards by establishing central command and reallocating the trade policy authority.

7.4 COORDINATION STRATEGIES FOR A LARGE FTA

The decade of the 2010s has ushered in a dramatic change in the Japanese FTA policy. In March 2013, Prime Minister Abe announced Japan's participation in the ongoing negotiations for the conclusion of an expanded Trans-Pacific Partnership (TPP) and established the TPP Headquarters within the Cabinet Secretariat. This effectively shifted the decision-making authority from the four-ministry co-chair system to the cabinet level. In this section, I discuss the Japanese leadership's most recent attempts at negotiating large FTAs.

Originally, the TPP aimed at achieving a liberalization ratio of over 95 percent for four Asia-Pacific states – Singapore, Brunei, Chile, and New Zealand – in 2005. In March 2010, the Obama Administration became interested in expanding the TPP as a measure to reinvigorate the financial-crisis ridden US and global economy by reversing the emergent protectionist tendency and strengthening the liberal economic order in the Asia-Pacific region, where growth was most prominent. The expansion negotiations were joined by Australia, Peru, Vietnam, and Malaysia, totaling ten countries a year later. The TPP expansion became a major agenda for the Asia-Pacific Economic Cooperation (APEC) meeting held in Yokohama in November 2010. A framework agreement was reached in the Honolulu meeting and the final conclusion was postponed by one year. As discussed below, Prime Minister Abe announced participation in the expansion negotiations despite limited public support, strong sectoral opposition, and a rift within the LDP. The question is, what has caused this trade policy change and how has coordination been achieved between disagreeing groups of the governing coalition?

7.4.1 Emergence of a Quasi-trade Representative?

Despite weak public support and the LDP's internal division, the Abe Cabinet has shown strong determination to negotiate and conclude the TPP. It established the TPP Headquarters within the Cabinet Secretariat led by Economic Policy Minister Akira Amari, supported by the chief negotiator (MOFA deputy director-general) and the domestic inter-ministerial coordinator (assistant chief cabinet secretary) with approximately 100 staff. A headquarters in the Cabinet Secretariat is a powerful institution usually set up for national emergencies, such as international crises, large-scale natural disasters, nuclear accidents, and the like. With enhanced capabilities to coordinate relevant ministries, the TPP Headquarters is more effective than the four-ministry co-chair system in forging a *quid pro quo* or linkage deal with its foreign counterpart – it can offer a concession on one issue in exchange for the foreign government's concession on another. Without such an arrangement, individual ministries would spearhead international negotiations on their jurisdictional issues, hence leaving little room for intergovernmental compromise.

At the time of writing, a conclusion to the TPP had yet to be reached: only a preliminary agreement was struck in October 2015. It is therefore too early to analyze the performance of the TPP Headquarters as an instance of central command directly. Nonetheless, some evaluations can be extracted from the EPA with Australia (JAEPA), a TPP participating liberal state, agreed in June 2014. In the seventh year of the negotiations, the Abe Cabinet reached agreement with the Abbott Cabinet by overcoming the most tenacious obstacle, Japanese beef imports. Against stiff domestic opposition, the Abe Cabinet pledged to reduce the beef tariff rate from 38.5 percent to 19 percent, promising (1) safeguards to lessen a substantial injury to the domestic sector; (2) an export promotion program for Japanese beef; and (3) an income support program for farming families, as compensatory programs to obtain domestic consent. Minister Amari stated that, although his headquarters did not take part in the EPA negotiations with Australia, the TPP and the Japan–Australia EPA negotiations would produce a synergic effect in promoting the bilateral agreement because both took place concurrently and dealt with similar sensitive trade products such as beef.[13]

7.4.2 Distributive Problems and Coordination Strategies

Even if it were to function as a central command or trade representative, the TPP Headquarters would still need an effective coordination strategy to deal with distributive problems and secure domestic consent. To solve these problems, the Abe Cabinet has turned to the three coordination strategies discussed below that appear similar to those used for the Kishi-Ikeda initiative and the SII described earlier.

Compensation

The Abe Cabinet has expanded the income compensation (support) program on rice to other products, including wheat, soybeans, beef, and so on, totaling approximately 600 billion yen in volume. The LDP government has inherited the program from the preceding Democratic Party of Japan (DPJ) government. In 2010, the DPJ, which replaced the LDP as the primary governing party in the previous year, enacted a farming family income compensation program on rice as a measure to promote its FTA policy.[14] In general, income compensation is less trade distortionary than import control and is more consistent with the interests of consumers, including workers from whom the DPJ obtains considerable electoral support. While it was undoubtedly the DPJ's electoral strategy to strip farm votes from the LDP, the program was expected to replace high import tariff rates and reduce food prices to benefit consumers while keeping farming families' income at stable levels. Thus, the shift to the income compensation program will have a major effect in gaining consent from domestic producers and in promoting coordination between producers and consumers for lower import tariffs. A piece of analogous evidence comes from Switzerland, a country with inefficient agriculture that has reduced its agricultural protection ratio rapidly since the introduction of income compensation in 1989 (Figure 7.3).

The DPJ's policy is in sharp contrast to the LDP's traditional farm protection measures that relied on high import tariffs and subsidies for targeting specific producers at the expense of general consumers. The policy difference between the rival parties is clearly derived from the differences in their support structures. The Abe Cabinet's adoption of the DPJ's income compensation is a major turning point in the LDP's agricultural policy. Because the DPJ proved compatibility between agricultural protection and trade liberalization, the Abe Cabinet might find it politically unacceptable to return to the old practices of high tariffs and subsidies. Nonetheless, the new practice still differs from majoritarian consumerism in that it entails the compensation that costs consumers dearly via taxation. This point will be discussed in greater detail shortly.

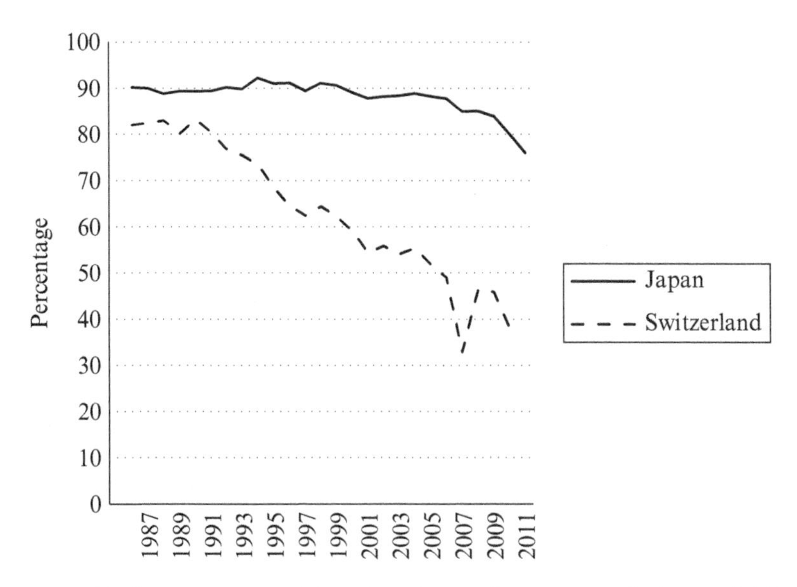

Sources: The figure is constructed from the estimates of support to agriculture in OECD StatExtracts. The tariff protection ratio is computed from the market price support estimates divided by the producer support estimates (PSEs) found in the OECD data.

Figure 7.3 Agricultural tariff protection ratio

Political attrition

The Japanese agricultural sector has been experiencing a gradual attrition of its political influence in conjunction with the shrinking farm population and the electoral change in the House of Representatives.[15] Moreover, the Abe Cabinet has begun to follow an unprecedented strategy to speed up the attrition. As discussed earlier, attrition is a coercive political strategy to weaken opposition and facilitate coordination for a new policy.[16] The Abe Cabinet extended the following reform proposal to the Japan Agricultural Cooperatives (JA), the dominant organization representing five million farmers and non-farmers and the core of liberalization resistance:[17]

1. *The securitization of JA's capital.* This will change the organization's existing one-farm household, one-vote system into a weighted vote system based on stockholdings, giving greater voice to large (efficient) farms at the expense of numerous small (inefficient) farms. JA's existing vote system favors the latter who oppose liberalization.[18] The shift to the weighted vote system will augment the influence of large efficient farms, thus reversing JA's policy position.

2. *The dissolution of JA's Central Union (Zenchu).* The Central Union conducts lobbying activities and auditing of local cooperatives, stifling their business innovation and efficiency improvements. This proposal will stop its protectionist lobbying and give local cooperatives autonomy and opportunities to innovate.[19]
3. *The abrogation of JA's antimonopoly exemption.* Because of the legal exemption, JA can engage in multiple business activities, including distribution, banking, insurance, real estate, and retailing. The proposal will specialize JA exclusively in agriculture.

The reform proposal generated uproar within the LDP and the MAFF. It overturned the LDP's conventional pro-JA position, assuming that JA is at the center of the inefficient regulatory regime on agriculture, supported by its own organizational interest, LDP members' electoral interests, and the MAFF's bureaucratic interest. Through bitter closed-door negotiations, JA agreed to transform its status from a cooperative to a non-profit association by abolishing the Central Union's auditing and oversight roles, while the cabinet conceded on antimonopoly exemption, enabling JA to provide a variety of services for agricultural households.[20] Yet still, the Abe Cabinet's strategy was unprecedentedly coercive based on the enhanced central command and security concerns discussed below.

Issue-dimensional politics

A final coordination strategy relies on the manipulation of issue dimensions with an emphasis on the issue of national security. Security concerns are specific to trade, unseen in other public policy domains discussed thus far in this book. From the viewpoint of political realism, security is of paramount importance to states (Waltz, 2010). States' security concerns greatly influence the flow of commercial transactions as well as the formation of the institutions that govern such transactions. Since trade affects the transfer of wealth, states are sensitive to gaps in trade gains that might strengthen their adversaries' economic and military power disproportionately, and thus seek to regulate the flow of trade (Gowa, 1993). If a state concludes a trade liberalization agreement or an FTA with its ally, gains from the agreement will be used to reinforce the ally's economic and military capability and then to contribute to the state's own security (positive security externality). By contrast, if the state concludes an FTA with a rival state, trade gains will be used to aggrandize the rival's capability and threaten the state's own security (negative security externality). Thus, realism predicts that a trade agreement will only be formed between allies, not between enemies (Mansfield and Bronson, 1997). Like any other international institution, a trade agreement is an effect rather than a cause of expectations of peace and cooperation. The negotiations for FTAs based on security concerns have to be led by political leadership with the highest constitutional authority. Furthermore, realism holds that trade as a security policy has to be located in the realm of high politics conducted by political leadership, while ordinary economic policy is located in the realm of low politics conducted by bureaucracies in close association with private groups (Hirschman, [1945] 1980).

As predicted by realist theory, when he announced Japan's participation in the TPP negotiations, Prime Minister Abe viewed the TPP as an agreement between states upholding the 'universal values of freedom, democracy, basic human rights, and the rule of law'. He stated that 'deepening economic interdependence with these countries in a common economic order will significantly contribute to the security of our country and also to the stability of the Asia-Pacific region'. The new economic order 'should serve as a basis for rule-making beyond the TPP, in Regional Comprehensive Economic Partnership (RCEP) and in the larger initiative of Free Trade Area of the Asia-Pacific (FTAAP)'.[21]

These security concerns are shared by the United States, Japan's major ally, which has begun to adopt the new policy of 'rebalancing' in the Asia-Pacific region. In November 2011, US Secretary of State Hillary Clinton (2011, p. 58) stated that the United States' ambition, as part of the rebalance, is to establish a 'framework for stability in the Asia-Pacific' similar to that which the United States helped to construct in Europe. 'Alliance building and the strengthening of regional institutions' is therefore absolutely fundamental to the rebalance, and, in Washington's eyes, the stability of the international order. As Clinton argues, the United States' 'challenge is to build a web of partnerships and institutions across the Pacific that is as durable and as consistent with US values as the web we have built across the Atlantic'.

The US overture for Japan's participation (to be explained shortly) was based on the expectations that it would improve the economic, diplomatic, and strategic benefits of an expanded TPP. The trade agreement would increase US access to the growing markets in Asia, help stimulate growth in US exports, generate export-related jobs, and foster an economic recovery, while enhancing the protection of US intellectual property rights and ensuring that US companies are competing in a fairer and more impartial regional market. Diplomatically, the TPP agreement would demonstrate US commitment and engagement in the region, as well as help promote deeper ties with other member nations. Strategically, the potential risks associated with the transport of goods and services in the Asia-Pacific region would conceivably be reduced, as the TPP members would share a common interest in maintaining a reliable and safe flow of cargo across the Indian and Pacific Oceans (Manyin et al., 2012).

On the Japanese side, because of the TPP's security implications, Prime Minister Abe has taken direct control of negotiations based on the TPP Headquarters. Through the security rhetoric, Prime Minister Abe has established central command, backed not just by the corporate members of the LDP coalition, but also by members of the conservative circles who are usually silent about trade policy. However, the TPP Headquarters runs the risk of weakening the ability to create meticulous institutional arrangements that are achievable by the four-ministry co-chair system with information and expertise.

In sum, the three coordination strategies used for the TPP by the Abe Cabinet resemble those used for the Kishi-Ikeda initiative and the SII discussed in Section 7.2.3. The former are adopted under the centralized post–1955 system with a majoritarian flavor, while the latter were adopted under the decentralized 1955 system with strong sectoral influences. This implies that the contemporary attempts at trade liberalization are faced with the same stiff domestic opposition that plagued previous attempts under the decentralized system: both require strong coordination strategies implementable by central political command. In the following subsection, I will explore the motive for and the path to adopting central political command with reference to the competing leadership models.

7.4.3 Causes of the FTA Policy Change

Public opinion

Among the leadership models, the presidential model postulates that a populist prime minister would seek to transform public opinion into public policy without recourse to the governing party and bureaucracies, as if he or she were chosen directly by the public. The model predicts that public opinion will lead public policy via the prime minister as a legitimate translator of public opinion. However, in the case of TPP, the public opinion survey conducted by Nippon Television (NTV), a major national TV broadcasting firm, contradicts this hypothesis by showing that the public seems to follow Prime Minister Abe's initiative, rather than form its own opinion independent of the leadership's policy action (Figure 7.4). Before the prime minister's announcement on the cabinet decision to participate in the TPP negotiations in March 2013, the public had been ambivalent about its merit, with the opponents and undecided respondents outnumbering the positive respondents. Yet the polls taken between 15 and 17 March, just after the announcement, indicated that approval rose, exceeding 50 percent and remaining at the level thereafter with the exception of the poll taken in October 2013 when the Abe Cabinet decided to raise the consumption tax rate. It seems that the prime minister's

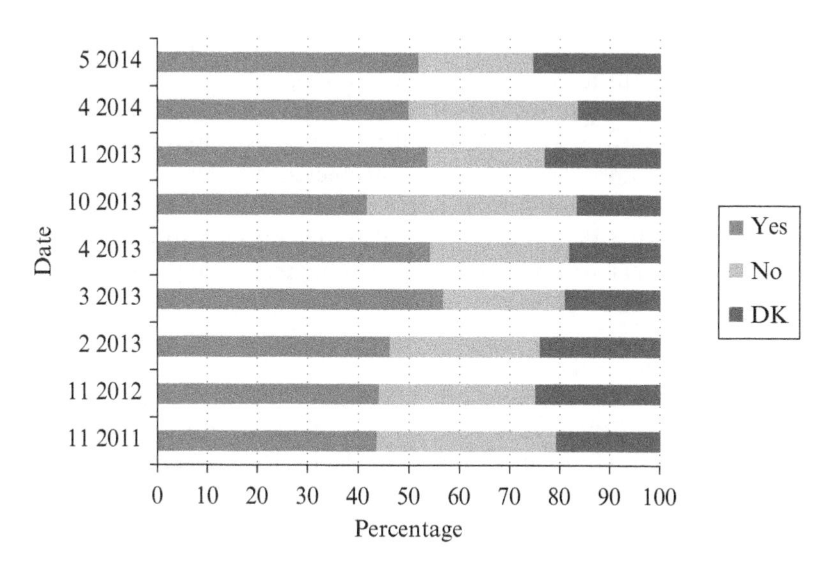

Note: From the Nippon Television (NTV) Public Opinion Survey Questionnaire: 'Do you have high hopes for Japan's participation in the TPP negotiations?' DK = don't know. In the original Japanese questionnaire, hopes were worded as *kitai*, which means the act of waiting for the realization of good outcomes. A survey is taken in the middle of a month.

Figure 7.4 Public opinion on TPP participation

announcement had a major positive effect on publicizing and legitimizing the TPP among the Japanese public.

Electoral change

According to the Westminster model, the electoral change for the House of Representatives in 1994 should have had a major transformative effect in centralizing policy-making institutions and promoting majoritarian consumerism through the Diet (including a vigorous FTA policy). The shift from the SNTV system to first-past-the-post (FPTP) votes should reduce the influence of sectoral votes and protectionist policies for producers. The problem with this argument is that the electoral change in the mid-1990s is too anteceded to be viewed as a direct cause of the change in the trade policy-making institution and the FTA policy in 2013. More importantly, the argument has not paid appropriate attention to the distribution of parliamentary seats between urban industrial and rural agricultural districts. The reapportionment of seats from rural to urban districts in accordance with population shifts has been taking place very slowly, as noted in Chapter 5. The Nikkei survey in February 2013 reported that 233 of the 337 LDP members belonged to an anti-TPP parliamentary group.[22] Furthermore, until June 2013, 44 out of the 47 prefectural assemblies had passed resolutions against the TPP, all of which were supported by LDP-led assembly groups.[23] The LDP members' activities as well as the opinion polls in Figure 7.4 indicate a weak consumerist median voter-majority–party-cabinet connection for the TPP under the constrained majoritarian system, suggesting that strong political leadership had to be evoked to defeat protectionist forces within the governing party and promote change in the FTA policy.

Changing regional security environments

While neither public opinion nor a majority party provided a strong impetus for the TPP, a remaining source of momentum is an external ancillary authority through alliance ties, like in earlier trade liberalization efforts discussed earlier in this chapter. The security motive stressed here corresponds to the coordination strategy of issue dimensions suggested in the previous section.

There is circumstantial evidence that links Japanese TPP participation to US overture or pressure in conjunction with the changing security environment in East Asia. Even before the explicit US request in fall 2011, the DPJ-led Kan Cabinet (2010–11) already had considered participating in the TPP negotiations in relation to the bilateral security treaty with the United States as early as November 2010, when the APEC meeting was held in Yokohama. Prime Minister Naoto Kan tried to mend the bilateral relations that had been strained over the problem of US military base relocation in Okinawa during the tenure of the preceding Hatoyama DPJ Cabinet (2009–10), by participating in the US-led TPP expansion. In contrast, the Obama Administration was initially unenthusiastic about Japanese participation because administration officials still believed that the Japanese government would take the usual protectionist attitude and prolong the negotiation well beyond the target completion date of November 2011.

However, the Obama Administration's attitude changed in the fall of 2011, in the wake of the initiation of the rebalancing policy in the Asia-Pacific region. When both leaders met in New York on 21 September, President Obama reportedly requested DPJ Prime Minister Noda to enter the TPP negotiations.[24] Prime Minister Noda refrained from an immediate answer but later announced his cabinet's decision to consult with the participating countries on entering the TPP negotiations at a news conference on 11 November, fixing the DPJ's previously indeterminate position.[25] The next day, Noda informed President Obama of the cabinet decision in Honolulu.[26] On 13 December, Prime Minister Noda set forth consultations for entering the TPP negotiations as a top priority for the

National Strategy Council (*Kokka Senryaku Kaigi*)[27] that was established at the Cabinet Secretariat with the chief mission to 'revitalize Japan' in the aftermath of the Great East Japan Earthquake. The council, chaired by the prime minister and attended by selected cabinet ministers and representatives of businesses and labor unions, was supposed to form a central command unit and lead the four-ministry co-chair system with respect to international negotiations, domestic coordination, and public relations.

Nonetheless, the DPJ soon lost to the LDP in the December 2012 snap election for the House of Representatives.[28] The LDP led by former Prime Minister Shinzo Abe won the election, reiterating the party's campaign pledge that it would 'oppose participation in the TPP negotiations as long as the prerequisite for participation compelled the Japanese government to make commitment to eliminate tariffs with no sanctuary' (*sei'iki*).[29] On 15 March 2013, as noted earlier, Prime Minister Abe announced Japan's participation in the TPP negotiations, claiming that he had obtained the sanctuary from President Obama on February 22 – he could use it to protect an inefficient farm sector and legitimize his decision before the agricultural LDP supporters. He stressed the TPP as an agreement between states sharing universal values, distinguishing them from states without such values (without naming China). On the contrary, Obama Administration officials stated that they never approved of the sanctuary[30] and did not intend to exclude states without the universal values from the TPP either, welcoming them instead.[31]

Undoubtedly, the two states share an interest in strengthening the liberal order in the Asia-Pacific region through the TPP, while differing on the issue of sanctuary and the scope of membership. Under the strategic ambivalence of double talk, the Obama Administration's initiation of rebalancing generated a major impetus for the decisions by the DPJ-led Noda Cabinet and the LDP-dominated Abe Cabinet to participate in the TPP negotiations and establish central command – the abortive National Strategy Council and the TPP Headquarters, respectively. The key to overcoming domestic opposition is the US authority, from which Prime Minister Abe allegedly obtained the 'sanctuary' for Japanese agriculture and with which Japan has deepened ties for growth and security.

7.5 CONCLUSION: TRADE LIBERALIZATION AND ISSUE-DIMENSIONAL POLITICS WITH EXTERNAL AUTHORITY

Even in the age of information and communication technology, trade has continued to be a major vehicle for economic growth and national well-being. In general, trade openness promotes growth but generates distributive effects on industrial sectors and the governing coalition members. The governing party and bureaucratic ministries, with intrinsic ties to industrial sectors and coalitional members, seek to constrain the state's trade policy on behalf of their client groups' particularistic interests. Under these constraints, strategic authority reallocation is the key to negotiating and concluding welfare-improving trade agreements with large economies. This chapter has shown how Japan has conducted trade policy by allocating policy authority under the constraints of the bureaucratic-cabinet system and the governing coalition. The following conclusions emerge from the analyses.

First, the bureaucratic delegation approach was palatable under the GATT regime of embedded liberalism that permitted incremental and sectoral liberalization in pursuit of growth and stability. More specifically, the approach helped postwar Japan maintain the governing coalition composed of efficient and inefficient sectors as well as the Japanese-style CME system based on long-term relational contracts, including patient capital, contingent corporate governance, and long-term employment. The bilateral trade negotiations with the United States were occasionally used to check bureau-pluralistic protectionist rents that might reduce industrial efficiency and general well-being. The use of external ancillary authority was combined with compensatory and rhetorical measures to secure domestic consent to trade liberalization.

Second, under the devolved global trade order with bilateral and regional FTAs in the early 2000s, the four-ministry co-chair system of bureaucratic delegation was used to achieve meticulous agreements with small trade partners through improved bureaucratic incentives and expertise. Equipped with investment promotion and intellectual property rights protection clauses, these FTAs have provided a partial adjustment of the Japanese economy to the emergent trade order.

Third, a drawback of bureaucratic delegation is the inability to negotiate welfare-improving FTAs with large economies because of major coordination problems that are resolvable only by central political command. In this sense, the four-ministry co-chair system can be viewed as an outcome of structural manipulation to create multiple veto gates and protect vested interests from international competition. The maintenance of the co-chair system under economic stagnation is explicable only by the fear that central command would undermine the governing party's electoral fortunes in the short run, even though it could promote competition, efficiency, and growth in the long run.

Fourth, negotiating an FTA with a large economy needs major coordination between ministries' policy tasks and between domestic sectoral interests. This requires central command to pursue strong coordination strategies, including compensation for import injuries, political attrition against recalcitrant protectionists, and issue-dimensional politics based on security imperatives. For a conservative prime minister such as Abe, issue-dimensional politics appear to be not just a rhetorical instrument for coordination but a major motive to enter a trade agreement with a powerful ally in pursuit of security in changing regional political environments. Prime Minister Abe's trade policy resembles the Kishi-Ikeda liberalization initiative that was promoted through alliance diplomacy under the intensifying Cold War environments in the early 1960s.

These recent Japanese experiences have confirmed the realist hypothesis that finds trade policy in the realm of high politics rather than low politics. Current Japanese FTA policy has increasingly been put under central command in concert with a neoliberal ally abroad, detached from parliamentary and party politics at home, while the general public signals its skepticism about enhanced security cooperation with the United States. Such trade politicking contradicts the Westminster model, favoring a core-executive type with a realist flavor.

NOTES

1. The pioneering work by Johnson (1982) emphasized the continuation of bureaucracy-led interwar economic planning with mercantilist strategies of import controls and export promotion through administrative guidance and the Fiscal Investment and Loan Program (FILP). The second generation of scholars (Okimoto, 1990; Calder, 1995) stressed the importance of government-led credit allocation and research and development to enhance industrial innovation. These analyses ignored the importance of economic institutions highlighted by the endogenous growth theory and comparative institutionalism.
2. Prime Minister Ikeda's general policy speech in the House of Councillors [sic] on 12 December 1960.
3. The loan program and the local ordinances have failed to prevent the contraction of family-owned small retail stores that suffered not only from newly opened large stores, but also from their own managerial and succession problems. The number of small retail stores reduced to 1.14 million in 2007 from 1.72 million in 1982, according to METI Trade Statistics [Shogyo Tokei-hyo].
4. Agenda-setting is analyzed extensively in the context of deliberative councils in Chapter 6. See Shepsle and Weingast (1987) for a general analysis of agenda-setting.
5. *The Final Report of the East Asian Study Group*, Phnom Penh, Cambodia, 4 November 2002, p. 43.
6. However, the anticipated FTA enlargement has stalled because of heightened security problems in East Asia, as discussed later in the chapter.
7. Article 107 of the Japan–Philippine Economic Partnership Agreement states that 'the disputing Party may, at its option or discretion, grant or deny its consent in respect of each particular investment dispute and that, in the absence of the express written consent of the disputing Party, an international conciliation or arbitration tribunal shall

have no jurisdiction over the investment dispute involved'. See http://www.mofa.go.jp/region/asia-paci/philippine/epa0609/main.pdf; accessed 27 September 2014.

8. From a statement by a Japanese official involved in the negotiations, quoted in the *Investment Treaty News* (ITN), 20 September 2006, http://www.iisd.org/investment/itn/news.asp; accessed 27 September 2014.
9. From a statement by an unnamed Filipino official quoted in the *Manila Bulletin*, 18 May 2006. It also cites the Philippines' ongoing dispute with a German firm, Fraport AG, over an investment in Manila's Ninoy Aquino airport as the reason for the reluctance to use international arbitration.
10. Article 106 of the Japan–Indonesia Economic Partnership Agreement, http://www.mofa.go.jp/region/asia-paci/indonesia/epa0708/agreement.pdf; accessed 29 September 2014.
11. The ratio of liberalization is calculated based on the ratio of reduced tariff items to the total number of items. These comparative figures are frequently cited by the METI and MOFA to inform the public of the relative backwardness of the Japanese FTA strategy.
12. Kazuomi Takahashi, Chief Analyst of International Affairs at the Marubeni Economic Institute, who was a member of the EPA office at the MOFA between 2003 and 2005, described treacherous inter-ministerial negotiations when he was involved in the EPA negotiations between Japan and Malaysia. 'Kuto no EPA Kosho' [EPA negotiations], *Nihon Boekikai Gepo* [*Monthly Report of the Japan Trade Association*] No. 632, December 2005, pp. 68–71.
13. Minister Amari's statement was mentioned in Deputy Director-General of the Cabinet Bureau Kazuhisa Shibuya's briefing on the TPP negotiations in Nagano, 28 March 2014.
14. During the APEC Summit Meeting held in Yokohama in November 2010, Prime Minister Kan stated that his cabinet would introduce an income compensation program as part of the basic agricultural policy to pursue comprehensive economic partnership agreements.
15. Seat reallocations in favor of populous urban districts have been made incrementally. As for the House of Councillors, eight seats were added to urban prefectures while eight seats were subtracted from rural prefectures in 1994, four seats were added and subtracted respectively in 2006, and four seats in 2012. As for the House of Representatives, urban districts gained eight seats and rural districts lost seven in 1986, with nine gains and ten losses in 1992, and five gains and five losses in 2002, respectively.
16. Alesina and Drazen (1991) show the effectiveness of attrition theoretically for macroeconomic stabilization.
17. The Regulatory Reform Council issued the second regulatory reform proposal on 13 June 2014, which included the ideas on the JA reform and was approved as the Implementation Plan on Regulatory Reform by the cabinet on 23 June 2014.
18. JA has historical roots in the wartime food control system (*nogyo-kai*). The Supreme Commander for the Allied Powers (SCAP) tried to transform it into a private agricultural cooperative, like those in Europe and North America, in conjunction with the agrarian reform for economic democratization. While endorsing the agrarian reform, the Japanese government opposed the privatization of JA and had kept it under government control as the main distribution mechanism of rice because of acute food shortage in the immediate postwar period. JA's organizational status has been kept intact since then. JA's monopolistic rice distribution was partially abolished to comply with the GATT Uruguay Round agreement.
19. The initial proposal was watered down significantly in the June 2014 meeting of the Regulatory Reform Council within the Cabinet Office. The council's recommendation stated that securitization was JA's decision, conditional upon antimonopoly exemption. JA has received legal exemption for its broad business activities. Without the exemption, JA would have to be broken up into separate firms.
20. 'JA-Zenchu accepts gov't's reform plan', *The Japan News*, 10 February 2014.

21. News conference by Prime Minister Abe Shinzo on 15 March 2013, http://japan.kantei.go.jp/96_abe/statement/201303/15kaiken_e.html; accessed 27 February 2015.
22. 'Abe must steer toward participation in TPP talks', *The Japan News*, 10 February 2013. On a related note, the group also changed its name, 'Association Seeking Immediate Revocation of Participation in the TPP Negotiations' (TPP sanka no sokuji tettai wo motomeru-kai), to 'Association Seeking the Immediate Withdrawal from Participation in the TPP' (TPP Kosho niokeru kokueki wo mamorinuku-kai) on 22 March 2013, after Prime Minister Abe's declaration.
23. Most of the prefectural assembly elections are conducted with the use of the SNTV system and are influenced by sectoral interests.
24. 'Noda chose words carefully – TPP language thought to be aimed at soothing opponents', *The Japan News*, 13 November 2011.
25. The DPJ was concerned that the TPP would liberalize investment and medicine, destabilizing labor relations and undermining the national medical insurance system.
26. The Obama Administration announced that the Japanese government would put all goods and services on the negotiation table. The Japanese Ministry of Foreign Affairs denied the statement and requested correction, but the administration rejected the request, arguing that the announcement was correct ('Japan, U.S. differ on TPP remarks', *The Japan News*, 15 November, 2011). However, for a time, other TPP participating states did not approve Japan's entry into the closed negotiations because they believed that the internally divided Japan would delay the already difficult negotiations even further.
27. The National Strategy Council was criticized for its ambiguous legal status – there was no Establishment Act for the council.
28. A snap election was called because Prime Minister Noda dissolved the House of Representatives over the controversial rate hike of the consumption tax and not the TPP.
29. See http://japan.kantei.go.jp/96_abe/diplomatic/201302/22_e.html; accessed 27 February 2015.
30. Obama Administration officials did not mention the sanctuary or exemption. In February 2013, Prime Minister Abe and President Obama merely confirmed the existence of sensitive items on both sides, including agricultural products for Japan and manufactured products for the United States. In late October 2013, US Trade Representative Michael Froman called Akira Amari, state minister in charge of the TPP, and asked that Japan eventually eliminate tariffs on all imports ('Lew's bid to hasten TPP talks gets mixed response in Tokyo', *The Japan News*, 14 November, 2013). Although the United States would allow a grace period of more than 20 years for certain items, Japan insisted that TPP exemptions be placed on products in the five most important categories of rice, barley and wheat, sugar crops, dairy products, and beef and pork.
31. On 21 November 2013, National Security Adviser Susan Rice said that China and other countries will be welcome to join the Trans-Pacific Partnership in the future, so long as they commit to meeting the high standards that will be laid out in the trade agreement. Rice outlined US plans to cooperate with the Asia-Pacific region on several fronts, including trade and economic issues, security, and promoting democratic values and human rights. See http://www.whitehouse.gov/the-press-office/2013/11/21/remarks-prepared-delivery-national-security-advisor-susan-e-rice; accessed 27 February 2015.

8. Crisis politics for banking regulation reform

8.1 ADAPTATION OF BANKING REGULATION

This chapter focuses on the financial core of the Japanese-style coordinated market economy (CME) – the main bank system and the related public policy domain of banking regulation. It has undergone adaptation to the neoliberal international financial order that emerged in the late 1980s. The order is based in part on the Basel Capital Adequacy Accord that emphasizes solid capital foundations for commercial banks and a rule-based supervisory regime. The accord was expected to improve the Japanese regulatory regime in pursuit of efficiency and trustworthiness of the Japanese banking system. Initially, it was widely anticipated that, using Basel as a learning step, Japan could adjust its non-liberal banking system to the neoliberal financial order through regulatory adaptation (Himino, 2005). The adjustment was needed for banks to be able to compete squarely with their US and European counterparts, without upsetting the existing financial core of the Japanese-style CME. In addition, the banks' new practice would generate the complementary effect of improving their client firms' management through the main bank system and the related oversight function.

However, in practice, the enforcement of the accord coincided with the problems of the asset price collapse and non-performing loans (NPLs) that had corrosive effects on Japanese banks' capital. In the wake of the asset bubble burst in 1991 and continuing stock price slides, banks' NPLs mushroomed, thus reducing their second-tier capital. Against the backdrop of their deteriorating balance sheets, bank officials were pressured to reduce lending sharply in attempts to meet the minimum capital requirements, thereby threatening the survival of small and medium-sized enterprises (SMEs) that relied exclusively on bank loans for capital formation and business operations.

The Japanese banking crisis between 1997 and 2001 cost its national economy a severe output loss equivalent to approximately 45 percent of real GDP. This was far more substantial than 17 percent in France, 19 percent in Germany, 24 percent in Britain, and 25 percent in the

United States during the 2008 global financial crisis (Laeven and Valencia, 2010). The greater losses in Japan imply that its policy reaction might have been more protracted and more timid than those in other countries. The severe banking crisis kept the Japanese government from adapting its banking system to the global financial order – the Japanese banking system has lagged behind the global competition with respect to trustworthiness, efficiency, and profitability. Why did regulatory adaptation and the NPL resolution cost so much time and money in Japan?

The standard interest-based political explanation put forward by Toya (2006) and Muramatsu and Okuno (2002) states that Japan's policy indecisiveness stemmed from an informal tripartite collusion among bank, Liberal Democratic Party (LDP), and Ministry of Finance (MOF) officials who sought to forgo appropriate government interventions, such as strict bank supervision and bailouts, until natural economic recovery diluted the NPL problem through asset price rebounds. They believed that bank bailouts would be extremely costly and undermine their political fortunes as well as the interests of their clients in banking, business, and bureaucracy.

The collusion hypothesis hinges on the general belief that the decentralized arrangement associated with the convoy system is prone to regulatory capture – regulatory agents are pressured for leniency to cater to the interests of the regulated private sector rather than the public (Stigler, 1971). The regulated private sector seeks leniency by providing regulators with post-agency employment and elected officials with votes and political contributions. Contradicting the globalist thesis, the collusion hypothesis suggests that bureau-pluralistic practices worsened the NPL problem, constrained regulatory adaptation to the global financial order, and complicated crisis resolution.

A corollary of this hypothesis is that if it had been politically independent, the regulatory agency could have improved its expertise, consistency, and efficiency in bank supervision and even prevented the NPL problem from mushrooming. From this perspective, political interference is the primary cause of moral hazard and even a crisis. Indeed, the international movement toward regulatory independence has been facilitated by the preceding financial crises, including the Latin-American sovereign debt crisis in the 1980s and the Asian currency crisis in the 1990s, which were believed to be caused by highly politicized monetary and regulatory policies. Since then, the International Monetary Fund (IMF) has urged contracting states to establish political independence in their regulatory regimes (Quintyn and Taylor, 2002).

I have no qualms about the usefulness of the collusion hypothesis for explaining the delays in regulatory adaptation and crisis resolution with regard to the lack of political independence in the regulatory regime and individual actors' aversions to bank bailouts. I would suggest though that the hypothesis could not explain the eventual crisis resolution through strict supervision and major public funds injections.

A crisis is often a promoter of policy change. Japan is no exception to the rule: having experienced the non-bank crisis in the early 1990s, it created the Financial Supervisory Agency (FSUPA) to conduct banking supervision that had been one of the tasks of the Banking Bureau of the MOF (the acronym, FSUPA, is not formal but is used in this book to distinguish it from the Financial Services Agency mentioned below). Even after the functional separation, the bureau retained the task of stabilization. The 1998–99 financial crisis led to the abolition of the Banking Bureau and the creation of the Financial Services Agency (FSA) within the Cabinet Office with the combined tasks of supervision and stabilization, paving the way for Basel compliance and change in the Japanese banking system toward the neoliberal financial order.

In this chapter, I will analyze the politics of reallocation of authority over the banking policy, focusing on the problems of Basel compliance, crisis resolution, and post-crisis policy change. Before that, I revisit the pre-crisis bureaucracy-led banking policy and the significance of the Basel Accord for the Japanese financial system and then discuss problems with regulatory adaptation under bureaucratic delegation.

8.2 THE POLITICS OF GLOBAL REGULATORY REFORM

8.2.1 Pre-Basel Banking System

Commercial banks have been central to the Japanese-style market economy. They have provided relational or 'patient' capital enabling both independent and affiliated firms connected with the banks through industrial networks (*keiretsu*) to make long-term business plans. Japanese firms solved intra- and inter-firm coordination problems with suppliers, clients, shareholders, workers, and governments by treating them as stakeholders and catering to their joint interests through long-term relational contracts. They coordinated bargaining over wages with labor unions for long-term contracts. Through firms' programs, Japanese workers developed competencies and asset-specific job skills. Workers stayed loyal to their companies because of their non-transferable skills and sluggish labor markets, while businesses provided them with stable employment in return for firm-specific human capital.

Companies' high dependence on stocks was believed to be a source of managerial instability, exposing them to the risks of speculation and takeover. In contrast, bank credits with long maturity could provide firms with stability, predictability, and protection from these risks. Typically, a Japanese firm designates its main bank that provides a variety of services, referred to as relational banking or relational-contingent banking. Relational banking means that main banks supply funds to client firms and conduct ex ante, interim, and ex post monitoring to discipline top management. At interim, banks supply new additional money to fund well-performing projects and terminate underperforming ones, while mitigating asymmetric information between lenders and borrowers through financial oversight. Main banks do not intervene in the management of well-performing borrowers, but dispatch representatives to oversee troubled clients, and even take over their boards to assume the initiative in restructuring efforts, if necessary. The disciplinary mechanism differed from that of the Anglo-American system, which has relied on the market-based mechanism of takeover and bankruptcy (Arikawa and Miyajima, 2008, p. 51). In theory, the efficacy of relational banking hinges on the credibility of a threat to terminate a loan that is directly related to the bank's financial health. Because of a credible threat, the main bank system can support the Japanese-style market economy, resulting in improved economic efficiency and dynamic capability (Aoki, 2000, pp. 70–79). If the threat lacks credibility, relational banking will be reduced to either short-termism (underinvestment) or a soft-budget constraint (overinvestment).

To reduce credit risks and provide patient capital, Japanese banks needed low interest rate environments and regulatory protection from excessive competition. The MOF provided such environments via (1) market segmentation dividing the banking sector into nationwide retail, regional retail, trust, debenture-based long-term investment, foreign exchange, and so on; (2) marketing regulations controlling financial products and retail locations; and (3) implicit insolvency protection. A set of these measures constituted the 'convoy system' that provided the regulatory environment to help banks fulfill their main bank functions. For instance, suppose that the Banking Bureau detected an insolvent bank through its supervisory mechanism. The bureau would consult with the Budget Bureau and request a healthy bank to acquire the ailing one with implicit government credit guarantees in the form of central bank loans or, occasionally, public funds. The convoy system had a fine track record of no serious banking crisis in the postwar era for half a century, thus creating a popular myth that major Japanese banks would never collapse under the MOF's aegis. This made a formal large-scale deposit insurance system unnecessary.[1]

Finally, political leadership or the governing party delegated regulatory authority over the banking sector to the MOF's Banking Bureau, both because the system required expertise and close public–private partnership, and because it shared interests with the MOF in the development of the national economy through a bank-centric financial system that was controllable by government. For these reasons, the convoy system was self-enforcing: no major players – bankers, client firms, bureaucrats, and politicians – had rational incentives to defect from it.

However, the system increasingly became inefficient and unenforceable in the wake of financial liberalization in the advanced industrial world. Gradually losing its competitiveness, the Japanese economy was pressured to adjust to the more liberal international financial order. In the late 1980s, the government liberalized interest rates, foreign exchange rates, and corporate bond markets in attempts to modernize the Japanese financial system. These initiatives dramatically increased capital mobility and changed the relationship between commercial banks and business firms. Large companies increasingly gained the ability to raise capital by issuing corporate bonds at lower rates than bank loans, whereas SMEs sought continued bank lending. In contrast, banks were still confined to their conventional relational lending, but replaced lending to *keiretsu* firms with lending to SMEs, taking land as collateral, while also expanding into even riskier real estate lending in the wake of an unprecedented asset price boom. This shift in the lending portfolio exposed banks to asset price risks that did not become apparent until the bubble burst in 1991. As a result, Japanese commercial banks faced difficulties in operating profitably in the newly deregulated environment in which the MOF no longer provided regulatory rents. With reduced profits, the system itself became difficult to maintain (Aoki, 2000, pp. 128–30).

8.2.2 Basel I Negotiations

The Basel Accord was expected to help modernize the Japanese financial system and its regulatory regime. Minimum capital requirements on banks are a central element of the Basel Accord's regulatory construction, which aims to contain systemic risks in the banking sector. Capital requirements are commonly seen as a complement to deposit insurance in preventing bank runs. They can curb banks' risk-taking incentives by enforcing a minimum level of solvency for banks. Basel I refers to the Basel Capital Accord of 1988 adopted by the Basel Committee on Banking Supervision (BCBS) in 1988, under which international banks faced a flat 8 percent minimum capital requirement against any assets in their corporate loan portfolio.

The 1982 Latin-American sovereign debt crisis had ushered in an era of severe financial difficulties for major US banks. In 1982, US bank loans to Mexico, Brazil, and Argentina amounted to more than 140 percent of the capital of the nation's nine largest banks. A debt crisis threatened the solvency of several major US banks and the stability of the US financial system as a whole. The regulatory response was to implement stricter capital standards to prevent future crises. However, it became clear that unilateral adoption of such standards would jeopardize the competitiveness of US banks in international markets. Starting in the mid-1980s, the United States used G10 as a forum to negotiate uniform international capital standards that would allow it to raise its own capital standards while preserving a 'level playing field' in international banking (Verdier, 2009, pp. 135–6).

Several countries resisted the proposal, including Japan and Germany – two major financial powers with CME traditions. Japanese and German banks had been much less involved in lending to less developed countries (LDCs) than their counterparts in the United States and the United Kingdom. As explained earlier, for Japanese banks, lower capital levels were needed to provide relational lending and to increase their competitiveness. While German and other European regulators supported capital regulation in principle, they argued that their unique banking structure – including substantial corporate equity holdings by banks – made uniform rules inappropriate.

A breakthrough occurred in January 1987, when the United States and the United Kingdom announced a bilateral accord on minimum capital requirements. The two countries then multilateralized talks with Japan and Germany, backed by the implicit threat that they would restrict access to their markets by banks from countries that did not implement the new requirements. The resulting negotiations led to the adoption of Basel I in 1988. In essence, Basel I included a definition of regulatory capital and a risk-weighting formula designed to determine how much capital a bank must maintain given the size and riskiness of its investments. The global capital standards advocated by the United States and the United Kingdom were clearly perceived as producing unequal gains for potential participants.[2] In particular, Japan and Germany resisted the bilateral accord's definition of capital that did not include holdings of corporate equities, traditionally an important class of Japanese and German bank assets. Japanese banks also had large unrealized gains on securities and real estate that their government negotiated to be included as Tier 2 capital (however, the gains and Tier 2 capital for Japanese banks eroded because of asset price falls, as discussed earlier).

8.2.3 Transgovernmental Regulatory Agreement and Continuous Bureaucratic Delegation

The final Basel Accord resolved differences on capital by adopting a two-tiered mutual recognition framework.[3] Allowable capital was bifurcated into two tiers that allowed national regulators to fit their extant regulatory practices into the international code. Banks were required to maintain 4 percent of the value of their assets in Tier 1 capital and 8 percent in total (Tier 1 + Tier 2) capital. Banks were required to multiply their assets (e.g., loans extended to clients) by a pre-established multiplier whose value corresponded to the ex ante determination of a client's default risk (Quillin, 2008). Like the definition of capital, some latitude was provided for these required ratios and risk weightings.

The capital minima are important for the theme of this book on the following three accounts. First, the requirements are of vital importance for the prevention of banks' excessive exposure to risk assets that will worsen their solvency positions and destabilize the states' financial systems. Under intense international business competition without such requirements, banks would expand lending (or banks' assets) excessively in proportion to their capital, while the states' political and bureaucratic authorities would promote rather than restrain the banks' lending in pursuit of short-term economic growth by relaxing supervision over banks. In order to reduce the problem of lenient regulation, uniform rules on minimum capital requirements need to be established and enforced across states, independent of political and bureaucratic pressure. Such rules constitute an institutional foundation for an efficient liberal market economy.

Second, the BCBS is an important example of a 'transgovernmental' regulatory network that exercises vast powers, seemingly without any form of democratic accountability (Kahler and Lake, 2009, pp. 272–3).[4] The BCBS entails transnational networks and coordination arrangements, which are characterized by the absence of a binding formal decision-making structure and the dominance of informal cooperation among state regulators. This horizontal form of administration can, but need not, take place in a treaty framework.[5] Central banks and related monetary authorities have similar preferences for coordinating their monetary policies and pursuing financial stability. Private markets reinforce the upward pressure – major banks wish to be seen as regulated by market participants to secure international credibility. Given the relative autonomy already granted to central banks and other monetary authorities by national governments, a network of homogeneous financial actors could be created to exclude other, larger groups that suffer from collective action problems and are already prevented by politically independent domestic institutions from being veto players in the issue areas. No higher authority is necessary for implementation.

Third, the Basel Accord is an informal, soft-law agreement created through forums attended by members of domestic regulatory agencies, industrial associations, and non-governmental organizations (NGOs) with technical expertise and information. Even in the absence of formal compliance mechanisms, such a soft-law agreement still generates regulatory norms and network effects through which compliance is secured, while permitting the contracting governments to interpret the texts of the agreement for the way that best suits their domestic conditions. 'Soft law generally presumes consent to basic standards and norms of state practice, but without the *opinio juris* necessary to form binding obligations under customary international law' (Alexander, 2000, p. 2). 'Soft' is used to refer to those forms of domestic or interstate law or simply norms that are non-binding or are not enforced using some form of punishment mechanism, and used as a precursor to hard law or as a supplement for a hard law instrument. Soft law allows treaty parties to authoritatively resolve ambiguities in the text or fill in gaps. The BCBS does not possess any legal enforcement authority, and states comply with the accord at their own discretion. The accord establishes a minimum harmonization or baseline of rules that states must adopt, yet provides a high degree of national discretion for interpreting these rules depending on national banking regulations and codes (Quillin, 2008, p. 24). The accord is useful in the sense of enabling states with very different policies to accept a single, unifying standard. More specifically, national regulators develop conformity procedures and other forms of regulatory coordination. Thus, a balance is struck between the harmonization and persistent competition of rules. Contrastingly, legal formalism is both ineffective and inflexible in meeting rapidly shifting regulatory environments and states' heterogeneous domestic conditions, whereas informalism is not.

The reputational factor is viewed as a major facilitator for conducting rigorous banking supervision based on the international capital standard. Basel-consistent supervision is market-rational and self-enforcing. If international banks fail to meet the minimum capital standards, they will lose access to lucrative financial markets in Great Britain and the United States (Kahler and Lake, 2009, p. 271). Weighing the sanction costs and the defection benefits, rational agents determine whether they seek compliance or defection. Once the standards become dominant, defection is costly and irrational – regulators and regulated private actors have few incentives to defect from the dominant standard. Thus, because banks' compliance is driven by markets, the role of regulators is to inform market players of banks' true capital positions through supervision and disclosure.

With the agreement flexibility noted above and the newly acquired capital gains, Japanese banks were expected to comply easily with the Basel Accord and gain an international reputation for being trustworthy financial intermediaries. Likewise, the Japanese regulatory authority was expected to undergo smooth adaptation to a rule-based regime without upsetting banks' relational lending practices. The Bank of Japan (BOJ) and the MOF had been deeply involved in the BCBS and other related transgovernmental networks. These agencies shared the view that the Basel rules, if implemented in Japan, could provide a necessary institutional arrangement for the 'modernization' of its banking industry. As the Japanese government liberalized interest rates and foreign exchange rates in the late 1980s, Japanese banks began to expand lending at home and abroad. The international capital requirements would be a good preventive measure against excessive risks. The soft-law nature of Basel I would permit Japanese regulators and bank officials to adapt gradually to a market-based regulatory regime without undermining their unique bank-centric financial system characterized as the main bank system.

This was an archetypal case of bureaucratic delegation in pursuit of enforcing a highly technical international regulatory agreement through enhanced bureaucratic incentives and initiatives. In other words, as predicted by globalists, the adaptation of the Japanese banking system to the neoliberal global order would be facilitated efficiently through transgovernmental and bureaucratic processes in the absence of central political command. However, the initial optimistic scenario was subject to revision. Enforcement turned out to be more complicated than expected. The 'flat-rate' capital requirements posed a problem for Japanese banks. As the cost of holding capital was incorporated into loan prices, the flat-rate requirement effectively meant that low-risk customers would cross-subsidize high-risk borrowers. This increased the attractiveness of high-risk loans and thus raised the average credit risk in a bank's loan portfolio. The procyclical effect of Basel I was large particularly in the Japanese-style market economy in which many business firms relied on relational banking. By definition, long-term relational lending is multi-period investment with options that is susceptible to expansion at the time of economic boom.

Before the 1980s, cross-country differences in capital adequacy policy had been justifiable given the international financial order amenable to states' unique financial histories and markets. Banking had remained a mostly domestically oriented business. However, as explained earlier, the internationalization of the banking business has compelled previously benign differences in capital policies to become a new source of competitive advantage or disadvantage. This created the need for a multilateral capital adequacy standard based on the idea that the only way to solve this market failure was through collective regulatory action and soft law through international collaboration. Rules must be sufficiently stringent to induce prudential behavior from regulated banks and yet sufficiently lax to prevent domestic banks from losing international competitiveness. However, such regulatory subtlety had to be secured within a decentralized system of delegation and was susceptible to regulatory capture.

8.3 THE POLITICS OF REGULATORY ADAPTATION IN JAPAN

8.3.1 Burst of the Bubble

When the Basel Accord was incorporated into the Japanese Banking Law in 1992, it was expected that the Banking Bureau would be able to lead regulatory adaptation in pursuit of transparency, efficiency, and competition without sacrificing its traditional policy goals of growth and stability. In theory, stricter supervision through the adoption of the Basel Accord had to be met with regulatory improvement. In Japan, this re-harmonization process was ill timed with the burst of the asset bubble and the subsequent banking crisis.

The continuous drop in asset prices eroded large parts of banks' capital (Tier 2 capital) rapidly, raising concerns among Japanese and international regulatory authorities. From 1991 to 1992, the revaluation reserves were halved, resulting in a significant erosion of banks' capital. Furthermore, the stock market's slide led to soaring unrealized losses on banks' balance sheets, which had to be deducted fully from Tier 1 capital, while making it virtually impossible for banks to issue new stocks classified as Tier 1 capital. Since the flat-rate capital requirements augmented risk assets in their portfolios, Japanese banks needed to reduce relational lending in the economic downturn because additional long-term assets would contain risks that needed to be avoided to comply with the capital requirements. The reduction pressure was strong for SMEs because of their intrinsic financial fragility, in comparison with large and medium-large firms. In spite of the initial optimism, many Japanese banks were now faced with the difficult choice between compliance with Basel I and the reduction of lending to client firms.

The MOF's Banking Bureau was both a regulator and protector of Japanese banks, but it could hardly be an impartial enforcer of the Basel Accord. In order to allow continuous lending under the minimum capital requirements, the Banking Bureau chose to show that Japanese banks were compliant with the requirements by taking advantage of the soft-law nature of Basel I with regard to three points. First, the bureau defined the types of financial institutions obligated to follow the minimum capital requirements. Internationally operating banks would have to meet a capital to weighted assets ratio of 8 percent by the end of 1992. In Japan, the bureau interpreted this date as the end of fiscal 1992 (i.e., the end of March 1993), and that it would be applied to internationally operating banks only. For domestic banks, that is, banks with no international offices, the 8 percent requirement was lowered to only 4 percent.

Second, the revised Banking Law neither made compliance a legal obligation, nor mandated the MOF to take administrative action against non-compliant banks (Himino, 2005, p. 58). With this non-obligatory status of the minimum capital requirements, the Banking Bureau relied on banks' financial statements for information on their risk assets. In March 1993, all banks began to disclose their overall risk assets that totaled 12.7 trillion yen, without revealing the specifics. In March 1996, major banks disclosed slightly more precise information on (1) loans to borrowers with solvency problems; (2) repayment-ceased loans; and (3) restructured loans. Although it was widely speculated that Japanese banks held much greater NPLs than they reported, the bureau did not undertake independent assessments of banks' risk assets.

8.3.2 NPLs and Soft Supervision

Having attributed the supervisory constraint to the intertwined fiscal and financial authorities within the MOF, the Hashimoto Cabinet pursued functional separation in conjunction with its wholesale administrative reform project that presumably strengthened political leadership.[6] It established the FSUPA as an external organ of the Prime Minister's Office (currently the Cabinet Office) to perform the task of supervising commercial banks.[7] Cabinet Assistant Secretary Mitsuyoshi Shirasu stated that the functional separation and organizational independence were meant to improve regulatory transparency and impartiality.[8] However, the MOF still retained the tasks of rule-making and stabilization within the newly created Planning Bureau. The FSUPA headed by a minister of state (always an elected official of the governing party) was hardly immune to the domestic political pressure for supervisory leniency even after the 1998 revision to the Banking Law that mandated the FSUPA to take swift action in cases of non-compliance.[9] In the fall of 1998, by taking advantage of the soft-law nature of the Basel Accord noted above, the FSUPA approved three accounting changes that allowed banks to make their financial statements look better than was truly warranted (Tamura, 2005).

A first new rule enabled banks to choose to use either market or book values for their holdings of stocks in other firms and for their real-estate holdings. According to the Antimonopoly Law, Japanese banks could hold up to 5 percent of the equity of a single firm. Virtually all of banks' assets were on their books at the historical acquisition prices (typically decades old); even though asset prices were well below peak values, a switch to market values instantly raised the value of the banks' assets. By 1998, banks had about 24 trillion yen of stockholdings on their books. Typically, banks would quickly buy back the stocks to retain relationships with their clients after selling the shares to collect the capital gains. The market price for many stocks that had been sold and repurchased was below the book value. Given the rise in share prices during the so-called 'bubble' period, these cross-stockholdings embodied substantial revaluation reserves, and consequently the unrealized gains on these securities holdings were included in Tier 2 capital. Under Japanese law, up to 45 percent of banks' latent gains on securities holdings were allowed to be counted as Tier 2 capital. With these capital gains, Japanese banks were viewed as compliant with the Basel Accord.

A second change was to incorporate subordinated debts into Tier 2 capital; that is, corporate debts whose maturity exceeds five years and that are junior to deposits and other credits. Japanese banks reacted by issuing substantial amounts of subordinated debts that counted as Tier 2 capital, and that were largely absorbed by Japanese insurance companies and could be counted as capital under the MOF interpretation (Hanazaki and Horiuchi, 2003). The new rule was used by many Japanese banks to issue subordinate debts in order to compensate for the apparent capital shortages derived from fallen stock values (Ito and Sasaki, 2002).

A third change was to regard deferred tax payments as a bank's capital. In Japan, loan loss reserves are not tax deductible. Even if a bank establishes a large loan loss reserve out of its profits to prepare for future loan losses, the bank has to pay a corporate tax on the profits reserve. If a loss really accrues, the tax payment will be returned to the bank. This accounting change ensued when large loan losses were likely and permitted banks to use deferred tax assets (DTAs)[10] as capital. These three unconventional accounting procedures helped banks overvalue stated capital levels. In addition, the existence of various types of long-term relationships in the Japanese economic system, such as the main bank system and the industrial networks (*keiretsu*), helped the country's banks to transfer their NPLs to various affiliated companies.

These accounting changes provided a tentative solution to the problem of the substitutive relationship between compliance and lending, enabling banks to continue to lend. However, they made it difficult to evaluate banks' true solvency positions accurately, thus calling into question the efficacy of functional separation that embodied the establishment of the FSUPA.[11] The functional separation worsened the coordination problem, providing FSUPA regulators and MOF officials with veto authorities. Parenthetically, the change could be viewed as a bureau-pluralistic practice by FSUPA regulators and MOF officials to avoid large-scale bank bailouts that would be detrimental to their organizational interests.

As seen in the next section, despite its CME properties, Japan had initially used the market approach preferred by LME states, rejecting the bailout approach that would be costly and disliked by holders of vested interests. However, because the crisis was too immense for the market approach, leadership had to resort to major bailouts that required the functional integration of strict supervision and stabilization based on central political command.

8.4 CRISIS POLITICS FOR POLITICAL CONTROL

8.4.1 Crisis Stage 1

In 1998, the Japanese economic climate worsened substantially because of the currency crises in East Asia and Russia as well as the rate increase in the Japanese consumption tax. A sharp business downturn expanded NPLs held by Japanese banks. International bankers and investors became suspicious of the creditworthiness of Japanese banks riddled with NPLs and inadequate capital positions. In October 1997, their suspicion led to the imposition of the 'Japan premium' (Figure 8.1), a premium on rates of interbank loans that US and European banks charged their Japanese counterparts. Equally important, the premium was directed toward the Japanese government for its indeterminism in stabilizing the financial system. The premium was small but was enough to inform Japanese political leaders of the severity of the NPL problem and compel them to act quickly (Whitehead, 2005).

The most vocal reformist official, Fiscal and Economic Policy Minister Heizo Takenaka, argued that given the emergence of the Japan premium public fund injection was inevitable for reducing a systemic risk and stabilizing the nation's financial system in the short run, even at the cost of raising moral hazard in the long run (Takenaka, 2008). In contrast, LDP officials disliked spending taxpayers' money to rescue banks and client firms that were involved in irrational lending and borrowing. The LDP's loss in the 1998 upper house election made them more averse to large-scale bailouts. For a slightly different reason, FSUPA Minister Yanagisawa and Finance Minister Miyazawa, both former MOF officials, were opposed

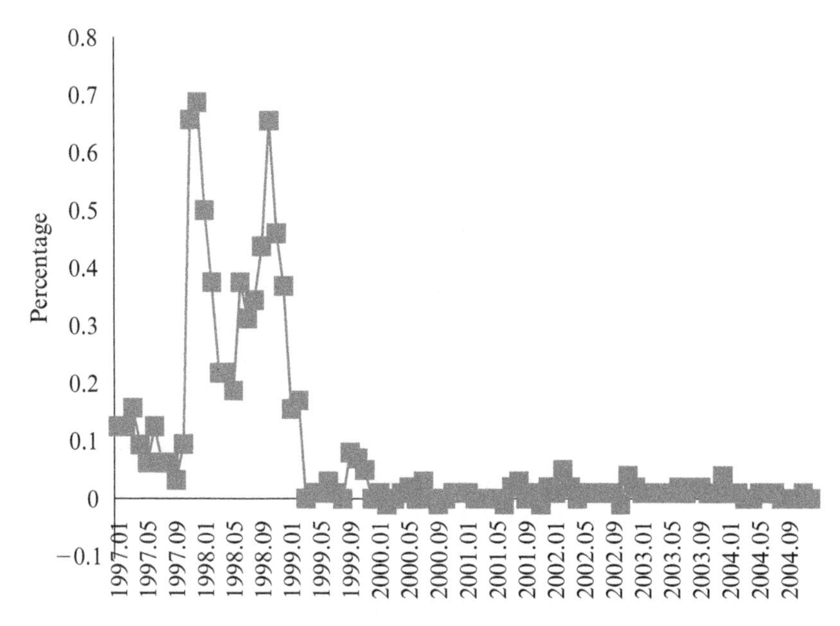

Source: The data are derived from the website of the Bank of Japan.

Figure 8.1 Japan premium (three-month rate)

to bailouts and advocated for the traditional Japanese-style resolution based on mergers and private banks' contributions (*hokacho hoshiki*) to deal with failed banks.[12] However, because there were not enough healthy banks anymore, it became necessary to create separate asset management corporations to buy up NPLs from ailing banks and inject small amounts of public funds to facilitate asset transfers.

Asset management

On 18 February 1998, the Obuchi Cabinet enacted the Financial Function Stabilization Act (Kinyu Kino Anteika Ho). The act had two roles: one was to create the Resolution and Collection Bank (RCB)[13] that would acquire assets from failed banks, while another was to provide blanket public funds injections to 21 major banks that totaled 1.8 trillion yen, a mere fraction of the NPLs. Both measures were ill conceived. The RCB, a basically private entity with limited capital, could not purchase sufficient amounts of assets, which were quickly becoming worthless.

Blanket public funds injections

As for public funds injections, undercapitalized banks had no incentives to disclose the correct amount of their NPLs for fear of being labeled risky. Despite their varying capital positions, major banks applied for almost identical amounts of public funds because their applications could not be evaluated critically without rigorous asset inspection requirements. Each of the nine city banks received 100 billion yen in the form of subordinated debt, preferred stocks, or loans, although the interest rates were differentiated in accordance with their perceived financial health. The amount of 100 billion yen was determined based on the financial condition of the healthiest bank, Bank of Tokyo Mitsubishi. For other banks, the amount was utterly short of what they really needed to restore adequate capital positions. In total, only 1.8 trillion yen was injected into 21 banks in the spring of 1998. This round of public funds injections mandated by the Japanese Financial Function Stabilization Act was neutral to banks' risk assets and was equivalent to the 'blanket capital injections' of the Troubled Asset Relief Program (TARP) instituted by the Emergency Economic Stabilization Act of 2008 in the United States.[14]

In effect, the Stabilization Act could not achieve its fundamental goal of stabilizing the banking system because of the difficulties coordinating supervision and stabilization under the separate functional arrangements. FSUPA Director Masaharu Hino stated that, under the law, his agency could not compel private banks to disclose their asset evaluations categorizing their risk assets into four groups based on the individual banks' private rules, and thus disclosure would merely generate confusion and even chaos among debtors, investors, and depositors who might wrongly compare the results across banks.[15] His belief was apparently inherited from the defunct convoy system within which the MOF had sought to protect all banks unconditionally through discretionary procedures. This 'paternalistic' belief also underpinned the blanket capital injections that provided banks with equivalent public funds, thus failing to reduce NPLs of almost all banks with the exception of a few of the healthiest ones.

Public funds injections

On 4 September 1998, the Democratic Party of Japan (DPJ), the second largest party in both the lower and upper house of the Diet, proposed bills to reduce banks' NPLs through functional unification and central command. The bills would mandate differentiated treatments based on banks' distinct solvency positions that would be evaluated using uniform standards. One bill (later enacted as the Financial Function Revitalization Act) would establish a 'bridge bank' to take over assets of an insolvent bank, while another bill (enacted as the Early Rehabilitation Act) would inject public funds into solvent but undercapitalized banks. DPJ Secretary-General Yukio Edano argued that the differentiated treatments would accord with the market principle and could prevent moral hazard that might have occurred if undifferentiated measures had been taken.[16]

Furthermore, DPJ Vice-President Yoshito Sengoku argued that the Japan premium indicated the international financial community's fundamental skepticism toward the stability of the Japanese banking system and the lack of disclosure of NPLs.[17] Sengoku claimed that the LDP's failure was to be attributed to the system of fragmentary functions; that is, supervision by the FSUPA, crisis resolution by the MOF, and deposit protection by the Deposit Insurance Corporation of Japan (DICJ).[18] The DPJ's proposal was meant to solve the functional fragmentation by creating a central political command organ, a Financial Reconstruction Commission (FRC) within the Prime Minister's Office (later the Cabinet Office). The FRC, headed by a cabinet minister, encompassed the Financial Services Agency (FSA, renamed from FSUPA in 2000) and could direct the FSA to inspect banks' assets rigorously based on uniform standards and determine the amounts of public funds needed to fill the shortage of reserves for estimated NPLs.[19]

Having exhausted all measures and failing to resolve the NPL problem, the LDP-led Obuchi minority Cabinet had no choice but to accept the DPJ's bills for swift resolution of the crisis. In the spring of 1999, shortly after the enactment of the DPJ's bills with minor amendments, recapitalization took place under the auspices of the FRC. All the major banks except for Bank of Tokyo Mitsubishi applied. Based on the FRC's assessments, the government injected 7.5 trillion yen into 15 banks in the form of preferred stocks and subordinated debts with variable terms and conversion options into common stocks. During the period of optional conversion from subordinate debts to common stocks, the threat of nationalization could keep bankers honest and earnest in their recapitalization efforts. At the same time, the deposit insurance scheme was set to ensure deposits of banks whose capital fell below 4 percent. The earlier round of public funds injections in 1998 was effective primarily in helping major city banks to clear the 8 percent capital adequacy ratio required under the Basel Accord. The second round of injections was even more effective, boosting capital adequacy ratios for regional as well as city banks, and encouraging other policy objectives such as increased lending to SMEs. In effect, the two rounds of public funds injections virtually eliminated the Japan premium by the summer of 1999 (see Figure 8.1).

The central command to execute the twin tasks of supervision and stabilization was the ultimate solution to the substitutive relationship between compliance with the minimum capital requirements and continuous lending to firms for economic recovery. Nonetheless, the two rounds of public funds injections were still insufficient to eradicate the NPLs that continued to mushroom in the stagnant economy. The remaining task was relegated to the Koizumi Cabinet that employed a similar central-command approach with a bit more rigorous inspection.

8.4.2 Crisis Stage 2

2002–03 crisis and public funds injections with stress test

In April 2001, Prime Minister Koizumi proclaimed his strong commitment to renovating the ailing Japanese economy using three measures: (1) implementing across-the-board structural reforms; (2) ending the deflationary spiral that plagued the Japanese economy for almost a decade; and (3) resolving the NPL problem within two to three years. In October 2001, the Koizumi Cabinet endorsed an early reform program as part of the comprehensive 'Structural Reform of the Economic Society', calling for special inspections or 'stress tests' of questionable banks and borrowers. The NPL problem needed an urgent resolution since unlimited deposit protection was scheduled to end in April 2002, possibly prompting depositors to choose trustworthy banks and thus forcing undercapitalized banks into trouble. After initial refusal, FSA Minister Yanagisawa, under strong pressure from Prime Minister Koizumi, decided to conduct special inspections of 13 banks (with loan assets of 12.9 trillion yen) and 149 borrowers. This intrusive inspection marked a major change in the FSA's conventional practice of relying on banks' financial statements.

Fiscal and Economic Policy Minister Takenaka was aware of interdependence between lenders' NPLs and borrowers' managerial problems. Timed with the cabinet reshuffling of September 2002, Takenaka, who was an academic with no electoral ambition,[20] was appointed by the prime minister as minister for the FSA as well as chairman of the cabinet-level committee on economic and fiscal policy. With the supervisory and fiscal authorities, Takenaka acquired the commanding position to implement both recapitalization and strict bank supervision.

In October 2002, Minister Takenaka announced a comprehensive Financial Revitalization Program (FRP) (led by a special taskforce team within the FSA) that attempted to halve the NPL ratios of major banks within two years by (1) tightening supervision through proper valuation of DTA used to inflate banks' capital; (2) strengthening corporate governance with the use of the discounted cash flow (DCF) method for rigorous evaluation of firms' assets; and (3) ensuring the injection of public funds into undercapitalized banks through the formal deposit insurance scheme.[21] Furthermore, the program established the Industrial

Revitalization Corporation (IRC, effective from April 2003 to April 2007) to reconstruct insolvent firms through debt–equity swaps and to enforce managerial overhauls.

Several top LDP officials, including Upper House Leader Mikio Aoki, Secretary General Taku Yamazaki as well as the heads of LDP coalition partners, opposed the FRP, arguing that it would reduce banks' capital below the minimum requirements and compress their lending even further to worsen the deflationary spiral.[22] Japan Bank Association President Masashi Teranishi opposed it, claiming that the sudden rule change would upset financial markets and banking business.[23] Furthermore, opinion polls showed that the public overwhelmingly opposed a bank bailout plan with a three to one margin.[24] Despite strong intra-party and public opposition, Prime Minister Koizumi instructed Minister Takenaka to execute the plan.

The Financial Revitalization Program had a real effect when it was reported that capital positions of a major regional bank, Resona Bank, had fallen below 4 percent. Rejecting the allegation that Resona was already insolvent, Minister Takenaka decided to inject public funds (1.96 trillion yen) into the bank from the DICJ, based on Article 102(1) of the Deposit Insurance Law. Because the government did not inquire into managerial liability in the Resona case, relieved managers of other banks quickly declared their undercapitalization problems and solicited public funds injections. The government's denial of insolvencies and managerial liability was criticized by media as corrupt but could be described as a necessary evil to elicit bankers' admission of undercapitalization and restore the financial system.

The stress tests helped reveal the magnitude of banks' NPLs and firms' managerial problems more accurately. The disclosed NPLs held by city banks and regional banks showed rapid increases in 2002 in the wake of the improved banking supervision by the FSA (Figures 8.2 and 8.3). The unambiguous, if not unbiased, information led to massive risk-based public capital injections. The DICJ injected a total of 37 trillion yen into 32 banks between March 2002 and March 2006, while IRC acquired 434 billion yen worth of corporate assets. By the fall of 2004, the FRP achieved its goal of halving the NPL ratios of major banks from approximately 8 percent to 4 percent.

Moreover, the Financial Revitalization Program strengthened commercial banks' lending capabilities by solving the undercapitalization problems through public funds injection. As shown in Figure 8.4, the lending attitude indices (diffusion index [DI]) for large enterprises and large-medium enterprises improved with the first major public funds injection in 1999, and enhanced even further with the second one in 2003. The improvement

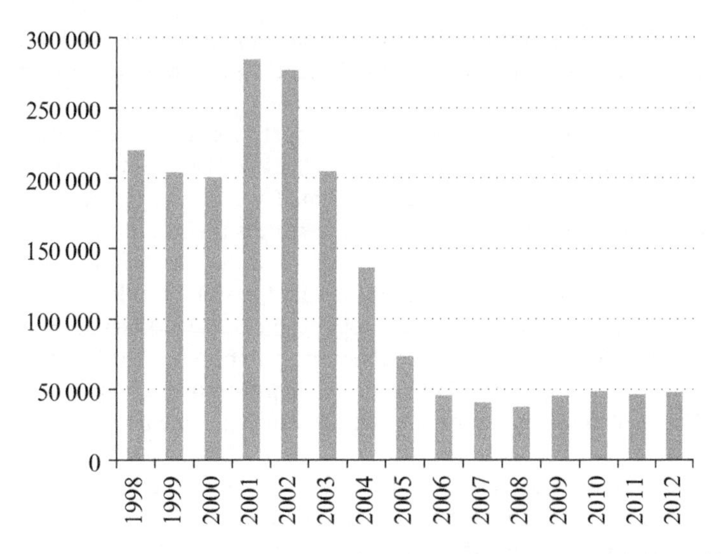

Source: The figure is constructed from the Financial Services Agency's statistical archive, http://www.fsa.go.jp/en/regulated/statistics/index.html; accessed 26 June 2015.

Figure 8.2 Non-performing loans held by city, trust and long-term credit banks (100 million yen)

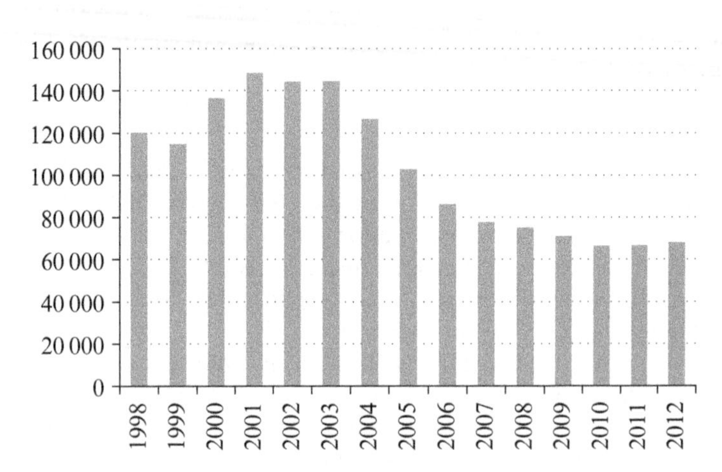

Source: The figure is constructed from the Financial Services Agency's statistical archive, http://www.fsa.go.jp/en/regulated/statistics/index.html; accessed 26 June 2015.

Figure 8.3 Non-performing loans held by regional banks (100 million yen)

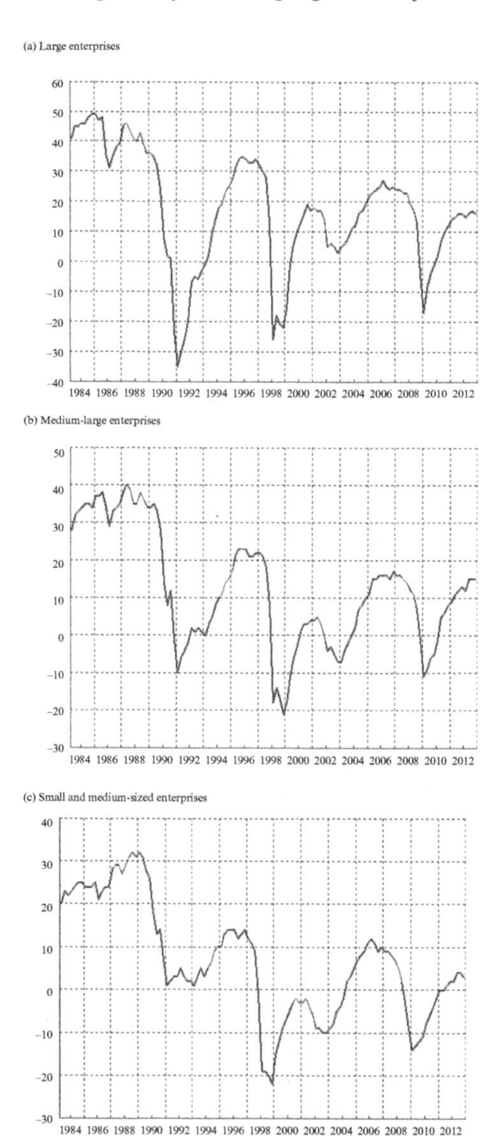

Note: The DIs are calculated by the Bank of Japan based on its TANKAN survey, a survey conducted on the cash positions of business firms and the lending attitudes of banks as seen from the perspective of firms.

Source: The figure is constructed from the statistical archive of the Bank of Japan, www.boj.or.jp/en/statistics/pub/boj_st/; accessed 26 October 2015.

Figure 8.4 Commercial banks' lending attitude: DIs

for SMEs was less sanguine but still discernible. The idea behind the public funds injection program was that the NPL-ridden banks had to reduce lending under the minimum capital requirements,[25] worsening the client firms' solvency positions and the macroeconomic climate, which in turn increased banks' NPLs and reduced their lending even further. The program was aimed at breaking this vicious circle by relieving banks' capital constraints and revitalizing their lending for business investment and economic recovery.

8.4.3 Authority Reallocation and Crisis Resolution

In sum, the functional integration of supervision with stabilization was made possible by central command and could solve the problem of coordination efficiently, uncovering the actual magnitude of the NPL problem and providing fiscal power to inject public funds. Both external and internal agents, who were unconnected with the failed old policy, acted out of self-interest to facilitate the crisis resolution. Foreign banks simply sought to maximize their expected profits by charging their Japanese counterparts with low creditworthiness a high interest rate premium. As an opposition party in pursuit of power, the DPJ wanted to convince the electorate that it had superior policy finesse relative to the incumbent LDP by announcing a policy proposal to serve the public interest. The crisis politics paved the way for the reallocation of policy authorities to dilute the bureau-pluralistic influence lingering even after the electoral and administrative reforms and implement strict banking supervision as well as major bailouts.

8.4.4 International Comparison

Gadinis (2013) shows that post-crisis reform for political control is not limited to Japan, but is widespread among countries that suffered from the 2008 global financial crisis. In these countries, politicians were granted the power to not only intervene in failing institutions at times of crisis but also make critical decisions for banks during regular times, before any clouds of trouble arise on the horizon. Gadinis provides a breakdown of politicians' increased powers in banking regulation across the following issue areas: prudential authority (e.g., granting banking licenses and reviewing capital adequacy), resolution (e.g., determining whether to intervene, take over, or liquidate a failing bank), supervisory authority (e.g., day-to-day monitoring of accounting records and practices), and deposit insurance (e.g., guaranteeing payouts to depositors). In 2007, seven of the 14 countries included in the survey allowed politicians direct authority in prudential supervision. By 2010, 11 of the 14 countries gave politicians these powers. As described above, Japan was no exception to the trend.

8.5 EFFECTS ON THE POST-CRISIS JAPANESE ECONOMY

8.5.1 Basel II

The crisis resolution has had mixed effects on the Japanese CME system. On the one hand, it has had a positive effect on the continuation of the commercial bank-centric financial system on two counts. First, the bank bailouts convinced the public of the relative safety of bank deposits over stock investments. Even though the banking crisis reduced the confidence in commercial banks, the bailouts reconfirmed the credibility of government protection. Second, the bank bailouts inspired a series of bank mergers that created megabanks with improved capital that are capable of complying with the Basel standards and expanding profits. The new megabanks cut across the *keiretsu* lines and thus were better positioned to reduce non-performing relational loans than the pre-merger ones linked intrinsically to *keiretsu* firms. In addition, they have improved managerial efficiency by adopting the holding company technique and using the temporary work programs (see Chapter 6). The mergers contributed to increasing banks' capitalization levels from 8 to 12 percent on average. In general, a corporate merger is purely an outcome of a rational business calculus to improve firms' profitability or reduce their default risks. However, none of the two outcomes was observed in the cases of bank mergers, suggesting that the mergers seem to be politically motivated. Having compared Japanese banks' pre- and post-merger performance, Harada and Ito (2011) have found that mergers did not generate significant improvements in terms of earnings and the distance to default. They instead reached the conclusion that the mergers were initiated based on the expectations that the government would rescue large (systemically important) banks in order to prevent a systemic financial crisis. The expectations were based on the 'too-big-to-fail' principle that had been employed on a de facto basis to guide the public funds injections programs described earlier. Furthermore, the mergers were concluded to exploit the provision of Basel II that allowed large banks to use small risk weights on their 'safe' assets and expand their lending portfolios.

On the other hand, the crisis resolution has yielded a negative effect on the main bank function. To comply with the Basel minimum capital ratios, commercial banks had to reduce their holdings of business firms' stocks and thus curtail managerial oversight of these client firms. This effect is clearly observed in reduced bank loans that constituted businesses' capital stocks (see Figure 8.4). The contraction of the main bank function in turn pressures companies to create their own oversight mechanisms, such as a committee system with external board membership. Firms rely less on banks' traditional functions of long-term loans for capital formation, personal exchanges, and managerial oversight than they did in the 1980s and 1990s. They instead rely more on commercial banks for the underwriting of corporate bonds and the acquisition of syndicated loans for the time when companies' credit ratings decline (RIETI corporate survey in Hirota, 2009). The financial reform has had a downsizing effect on the main bank function and a positive effect on corporate governance reform, which is still in its infancy (see Chapter 6).

Finally, the bank rescue package had a negative effect in that it preserved inefficient firms through the weakening of soft-budget constraints – the banks that were bailed out are able to keep lending to these corporations, dubbed 'zombies' by Caballero et al. (2008).[26] The central command mechanism has to be a temporary institution and thus has to be abolished to relegate the supervisory authority to an independent agency in order to avoid moral hazard and implement the highly technical task. Indeed, the FRC was abolished and the FSA has taken direct charge of supervision. However, it appears that the FSA has been pressured for another round of lenient supervision during the next business upturn by banks for extra profits, and during the downturn by elected officials for continuous lending to firms.[27] The apparent reversion implies that no optimal authority allocation scheme capable of responding to both regulatory adaptation and functional coordination needs has emerged yet.

8.6 CONCLUSION: CRISIS POLITICS AND NEOLIBERAL ADJUSTMENT

In this chapter, I have focused on the public policy domain of commercial banks and analyzed the transformation of the convoy system embedded deeply within the Japanese-style CME into a market-based regulatory regime. My analysis centered on political forces and strategies behind the policy change and obtained three conclusions.

First, the policy change transpired through coordination based on political control, rather than through regulatory adaptation based on bureaucratic delegation. The change required the functional integration of supervision with stabilization based on central command to solve the major distributive problem associated with the financial crisis. This has two interrelated implications. For one, the transformation of the convoy system into a market-based regulatory regime was politically contentious because it had a major distributive effect on the governing coalition, which needed to be resolved through political control. For another, this contradicts the globalist expectation of regulatory adaptation based on bureaucratic delegation. Ironically, the soft-law and transgovernmental nature of the Basel Accord permitted the system of bureaucratic delegation to persist with a seed of regulatory capture and eventual crisis, as predicted by the collusion hypothesis.

Second, to establish central command, authority reallocation was facilitated during a crisis by actors outside the governing party, including transgovernmental networks and an opposition party. The incumbent party, which was responsible for the past flawed policy and the resulting crisis, could not initiate a major policy change because it still believed that the bureaucracy-led convoy system was effective for resolving the NPL crisis or because it had vested interests within the system. The deepening of the crisis ultimately undermined the efficacy of the convoy system and justified policy change. In retrospect, the ancillary authorities were an integral part of crisis politics of bold decisions.

Third, improved supervision led to Basel compliance and lending contraction that facilitated the adjustment of the main banking system and corporate governance to the neoliberal order. The policy change cannot be assessed appropriately from the perspective of majoritarian democracy, because it is difficult to evaluate whether the policy change is driven by median voter preference. It is even harder for voters to determine optimal policy for a highly technical financial question. Stabilization was deeply unpopular because it would impose high costs on taxpayers in the short run, even though it was the only way to exit the financial mess and improve economic conditions in the long run. Thus, it is rather sensible to view the policy change as a result of elite-level contestations about what the appropriate policy should be and how policy authority should be allocated.

NOTES

1. There was a small-scale deposit insurance system for credit and saving unions created in 1971 by a consortium between the government, the Bank of Japan (BOJ), and private banks. For a major bank failure, the MOF's discretionary bailout package was used.
2. Oatley and Nabors (1998) argued that the United States leveraged upon its large financial markets to impose the accord on G10 states. It designed the Basel I accord to improve US banks' competitiveness with regard to their foreign rivals.
3. Tier 1 includes common stocks, preferred stocks, disclosed reserves, retained profits, and minority interests. Tier 2 includes undisclosed reserves, revaluation reserves, general provisions, and subordinated debt.

4. Kingsbury and his associates (2005) identify five main types of globalized administrative regulation: (1) administration by formal international organizations; (2) administration based on collective action by transnational networks of cooperative arrangements between national regulatory officials; (3) distributed administration conducted by national regulators under treaty, network, or other cooperative regimes; (4) administration by hybrid intergovernmental private arrangements; and (5) administration by private institutions with regulatory functions.
5. Slaughter (2004, p. 3) points out the *sine qua non* of transgovernmental networks, including 'common ties, personal relationships, camaraderie, shared professional and social beliefs, and regulatory norms'.
6. The reformist officials of the ruling LDP (Shiozaki and Mizuno) and the MOF (Sakakibara) had been aware of the inefficiency of the convoy system. These officials strategically used special committees and pilot teams separate from ordinary policy channels (deliberative councils within bureaucracies and Policy Affairs Research Committees [PARCs], within the ruling LDP) to form basic reform proposals. They avoided the normal channels in which vested interests were influential and could veto reform proposals unfavorable to their goals. In addition, the reform proposals were concentrated on the MOF's jurisdiction. The ministry lost policy credibility and the ability to dislodge unfavorable proposals because of the banking crisis and its officials' scandals (Toya, 2006). With the MOF's acquiescence, the reformist officials formed a proposal and then turned to the normal channels with take-it-or-leave-it offers to obtain consent from financial communities. Because the proposal had both favorable and unfavorable elements, representatives of special interests could not raise effective opposition. Specifically, for brokerage firms, cross-entry was unfavorable, while mutual fund retailing at bank counters was favorable for increasing their sales. For banks, the reduction of segmentation barriers was unfavorable, while the legalization of holding companies was favorable for mixing various financial technologies for greater efficiency and profitability.
7. The Financial Supervisory Agency was created as an external organ of the Prime Minister's Office through Article 3 of the National Government Organization Act that ensures political independence. However, the reality was different, as indicated in the text.
8. Cabinet Assistance Secretary Mitsuyoshi Shirasu statement before the Special Committee on Administrative Reform in the House of Representatives, 28 May 1997, Committee Minutes No. 11, p. 28.
9. The LDP's defeat in the 1998 upper house election turned the LDP-led coalition government into a minority one. Furthermore, the government was divided, despite the political and administrative reforms that were believed to unify political parties and strengthen political leadership with regard to the bureaucracies. The 'twisted' parliament weakened Prime Minister Obuchi's leadership and emboldened rank-and-file party members. This fragmentary condition had continued until October 1999 when the Komeito joined the coalition to help regain majority control in the upper house.
10. DTAs are credits against taxes on future taxable income. They help in reducing the company's future tax liability. They are only recognized when the difference between the loss value and depreciation of the asset is expected to offset future profit. When first recognized in fiscal year 1998, net DTAs at the major Japanese banks totaled 6.6 trillion yen, or about 29 percent of shareholders' equity – all of the major Japanese banks would have fallen below minimum capital levels without this accounting change (Skinner, 2008, p. 219).
11. The three major banks that collapsed at the height of the Japanese banking crisis – Hokkaido-Takushoku Bank, Long-Term Credit Bank of Japan (LTCB), and Nippon Credit Bank – had published capital ratios well above 8 percent just prior to their collapse. Even when the banks' assets started to lose market value and became non-performing, the assets' values looked unchanged on the banks' books because of the accounting methods noted in the text (Hanazaki and Horiuchi, 2003).

12. Even prior to its announcement of capital shortage, government officials knew about the Long-Term Credit Bank's (LTCB) serious financial trouble. Finance Minister Miyazawa, an ex-MOF career official, sought to pre-empt the bank's collapse by merging it with the healthier Sumitomo Trust Bank with MOF credit guarantees, the conventional strategy of the convoy system to avert a bank failure. Yet Sumitomo Trust Bank refused to take Miyazawa's offer. This instance suggested that the conventional strategy was no longer appropriate.
13. The RCB was based on two preceding asset management corporations: one was the Tokyo Kyodo Bank, set up in January 1995 to acquire the assets held by failed credit unions, and another was the Housing Loan and Administration Corporation (HLAC) established in 1996 to absorb loans of troubled housing loan companies (*jusen*). The RCB and the HLAC were merged to create the Resolution and Collection Corporation (RCC) in 1999 that was allowed to buy NPLs from solvent banks (though they were not compelled to sell any). From 1999 to June 2005 (when the RCC stopped buying assets), the RCC spent a mere 353 billion yen to purchase loans with a face value of 4 trillion yen from solvent banks. In total, the RCC restructured 6.2 trillion yen worth of debt for 577 borrowers (see the RCC website at http://www.kaisyukikou.co.jp; accessed 28 September 2014).
14. Business magnate George Soros told the US Conference of Mayors that the 700 billion dollar financial bailout known as the TARP had been carried out in a 'haphazard and capricious way' and 'without proper planning'. Soros said the United States needed 'radical and unorthodox policy measures' to prevent a repeat of the Great Depression of the early twentieth century, which include recapitalizing banks ('U.S. stimulus not enough, TARP bailout misused', *Reuters*, 19 January 2009, accessed 28 September 2014 at http://www.reuters.com/article/2009/01/19/us-usa-economy-stimulus-soros-idUSTRE50I4XZ20090119). Soros was right about the magnitude of the US financial crisis. Likewise, the Japanese Financial Function Stabilization Act was too small to avert the country's own crisis.
15. FSUPA Director Masahara Hino's statement before the Special Committee on Financial Stabilization, the House of Representatives, 1 September 1998, Committee Minutes No. 6. He elaborated further that banks could choose their own inspection rules, the MOF rule, or the Certified Public Accountant (CPA) rule, implying the absence of uniform rules.
16. MP Edano's statement in the Special Committee on Financial Stabilization, House of Representatives, 7 September 1998, Committee Minutes No. 10.
17. MP Sengoku's statement during his question to the Bank of Japan President Yu Hayami in the Special Committee on Financial Stabilization, House of Representatives, 16 September 1998, Committee Minutes No. 16.
18. MP Sengoku's statement in the Special Committee on Financial Stabilization, House of Representatives, 2 October 1998, Committee Minutes No. 18.
19. This inspection was known as ordinary inspection, implemented based on Articles 3 and 4 of the Law of Establishment of the Financial Reconstruction Commission. Ordinary inspection was less rigorous than special on-site inspection or a 'stress test' that was applied by the Koizumi Cabinet in 2002–03.
20. Takenaka held an upper house seat between 2004 and 2006 just to head the Ministry of General Affairs in order to enact a bill for postal service privatization.
21. The collapse of regional banks Kizu Credit Union and Hyogo Mutual Bank in August 1995 led to the establishment of the Deposit Insurance Corporation of Japan (DICJ) that has guaranteed up to 10 million yen per person per bank. In order to contain depositors' fears, the deposit payoff arrangement had been suspended until the end of the banking crisis. The difference was made up by formal government credit guarantees through the Financial Function Stabilization Act (Kinyu Kino Anteika Ho).
22. Ono (2005, pp. 62–3); Namikawa (2003, pp. 72–5); 'Aoki's words put pressure on Koizumi', *The Japan News*, 24 October 2002.
23. 'Bankers rap Takenaka over bad-loan stance', *The Japan News*, 24 October 2002.

24. *Asahi Shimbun* public opinion survey in April 2002; FNN TV survey in October 2002; *Yomiuri Shimbun* survey in June 2003.
25. There were other suspected reasons for lending retrenchment, including high monitoring costs and competition with other sources of funding. However, Arikawa and Miyajima (2008, p. 65) argue that the Basel minimum capital requirements were the most important reason for the reduction of bank loans.
26. This pro-cyclical regulatory deregulation has been observed across countries (Engel and McCoy, 2011). Basel III seeks to reduce pro-cyclicality in financial institutions' capital foundations, not in regulatory supervision, by mandating capital buffers. It was too early to observe its effect at the time of writing, but McCoy (2015) argues that counter-cyclicality is difficult to establish for a variety of reasons.
27. According to Hoshi (2011), regulatory leniency was observed in the FSA's inspection manual and the Financial Facilitation Act in the aftermath of the 2008 global financial crisis that did not originate in the Japanese economy.

9. Political leadership under the global neoliberal order

9.1 GLOBALIZATION, AUTHORITY ALLOCATION, AND INSTITUTIONAL REFORM

Like many other states, contemporary Japan is faced with a globalizing economy – that is, an increasing density of global networks based on market-consistent practices. Globalization ensues under a neoliberal order that facilitates unrestricted cross-border economic transactions. Under these circumstances, states' roles are converging to the improvement of market efficiency and economic competitiveness through the adoption of global rules and standards.

As noted in the Introduction, globalization has generated two interrelated controversies. One controversy hinges on political command and bureaucratic delegation. The political command hypothesis believes that globalization necessitates coordinated political responses to powerful market forces, while the bureaucratic delegation hypothesis stresses the importance of bureaucratic expertise in adapting to global rules and standards. Another controversy involves globalists and comparative institutionalists. The globalists embrace a trickle-down effect of neoliberal reform on social well-being that is defined as majoritarian-consumerist interest. In contrast, comparative institutionalists stress a distributive effect of reform and incremental institutional reform derived from policy inertia and contentious consensus formation among domestic sectoral interests.

In order to keep up with changes in the international order and stay competitive, states are pressured to pursue appropriate policy reform and undertake authority allocation, depending on the relative importance of adaptation (informational) to coordination (distributive) problems. In theory, central political command is needed to solve distributive problems and achieve coordination via compensation, rhetoric, or coercion. In contrast, bureaucratic delegation facilitates information and expertise – the key to solving informational problems and facilitating adaptation. Politicians and bureaucrats possess distinct personal qualities and career goals, keeping their prescribed action incentive compatible. The authority allocation schemes of command and delegation amplify their performance.

In this book, I have incorporated into the controversies the empirical models of government structure with different schemes of authority allocation. I have analyzed how historical and contemporary Japan sought to adjust to changes in the international order by vacillating between political command and bureaucratic delegation under the constraints of structural dilemmas and manipulation. Major empirical findings are summarized below.

9.1.1 Cases of Bureaucratic Delegation

One of the most remarkable adaptive bureaucratic governments in Japanese political history was the bureaucratic-cabinet system for the post–World War II period, as discussed extensively in Chapter 4. The ruling Liberal Democratic Party (LDP) delegated policy authority to bureaucracies that adapted the public policy domains to changes in the international order of embedded liberalism through sector-specific liberalization and protection. Through their administrative and regulatory finesse, bureaucracy-controlled public policy domains nurtured and protected the Japanese-style market economy, or coordinated market economy (CME), composed of the main bank system, manager-centric contingent corporate governance, long-term employment, and integrated industrial networks. The LDP's cross-sectoral governing coalition remained conspicuously unchanged with coalitional members' interests being deeply entrenched within the bureaucracy-controlled policy domains. In effect, both the bureaucratic-cabinet system and the CME constituted stable equilibrium institutions under the international order of embedded liberalism, thus producing long-term economic growth.

Even within the order, strong liberalizing pressures occasionally arose with acute coordination problems. Because the decentralized government was structurally inept at solving the problems, the bureaucratic-cabinet system responded by resorting to temporary authority reallocation in conjunction with external pressure. However, unable to coordinate between sectoral interests of the governing coalition for the emergent neoliberal order, the bureaucratic-cabinet system became increasingly bureau-pluralistic, resulting in the 'lost decades' of economic stagnation.

Another example of a decentralized government's abortive adjustment is represented by the Taisho party governments under the interwar liberal order, as discussed in Chapter 3. Despite the embryonic state of parliamentary democracy at home, party governments failed to adjust to the liberal order abroad through Cooperative Diplomacy. The fragmentary government structure and rigid bureaucracy-controlled policy domains set forth by the Meiji Imperial Constitution hindered domestic coordination for open trade, gold standards, and disarmament, instead permitting the expansion of mercantilism and militarism that had been strategic complements under the preceding competitive order.

9.1.2 Cases of Political Command

Despite Japanese political history being replete with decentralized governments, central command was evoked intermittently for rapid and comprehensive adjustment. Most notably, the Meiji oligarchic government transformed the feudal state into a modern industrial one under the forced non-autonomous tariff regime, developing embryonic capitalism with active stock markets, holding companies, flexible labor contracts, and performance-based remunerations. In addition, the SCAP and the succeeding Japanese government transformed the war command economy into a market economy that thrived in the subsequent four decades.

Establishing central command necessitates authority reallocation from the prior system. The vested interests that feel threatened by forthcoming policy and institutional reform attempt to prevent the reallocation efforts. The historical instances of central command were inspired by major crises, such as the colonial threat and war defeat, which undermined the legitimacy of the old systems and policies. These cases are consistent with the Schumpeterian thesis of creative destruction (Schumpeter [1912] 1934), postulating that a major institutional reform is derived not from benign policy reform, but from an external shock, disequilibrium, and contentious internal politics of authority reallocation. A question for the contemporary era hinges on which authority allocation has been used to pursue policy adjustment to the emergent global neoliberal order.

9.2 NEOLIBERAL ORDER AND CENTRALIZATION PROBLEMS

For several analysts (Berger, 2007; Rosenbluth and Thies, 2010), contemporary Japan, through electoral and administrative reforms that have had centralizing effects on the political system and facilitated policy adjustment to the neoliberal order, has become an adaptive-liberal or quasi-neoliberal state. The electoral reform of the House of Representatives replaced the LDP-led predominant party system with a two-party system within which centripetal competition would make elected officials sensitive to a majoritarian-consumerist or median voter preference. Moreover, administrative reforms have improved political leadership's policy coordination capability with regard to bureaucratic ministries to help pursue policies embraced by leadership. In short, the hypothesis of a quasi-neoliberal state entails globalism and political command, predicting sweeping policy adjustments in a majoritarian-centrist fashion or the co-evolution of majoritarian democracy and liberal market economy. However, the majoritarian hypothesis suffers from the following shortcomings.

First, the Japanese mixed electoral system for the House of Representatives, central to the majoritarian hypothesis, has not produced a coherent two-party system with centripetal competition: it contains the PR portion and the resurrection rule that nullify rational third-party withdrawal and incentivize elected officials to represent sectoral interests (see Chapter 5). Second, under the imperfect two-party, even multi-party, system, coalition governments ensue in the bicameral Diet and seldom set forth the electoral median as their policy guide because of their power asymmetry (e.g., LDP–Komeito coalition for the years 1999–2009 and 2012–present). Third, the neoliberal order still needs a system of bureaucratic delegation because the order has to operate with enhanced regulatory environments – regulatory agencies can be manipulated to protect vested interests, as found in the trade and banking policies (see Chapters 7 and 8).

Given these constraints, a core-executive system has been created for selected policy domains to promote adjustment to the neoliberal order. In theory, a core-executive model is suited to addressing the problems of adaptation and coordination because it combines political leadership with bureaucratic expertise at the cabinet level. Neither the Westminster nor the presidential model can provide such a mix – both models stress the virtue of robust political leadership at the expense of bureaucratic expertise and are susceptible to agency slack or sabotage.[1]

However, it is unclear as to whether the core-executive system would seek a majoritarian-consumerist preference because it has neither strong voter-majority–party-cabinet connections nor public–populist connections that are central to the Westminster and the presidential model, respectively. What is clear is that the core-executive system (headed by an LDP prime minister) cannot satisfy the sectoral preferences enshrined within the bureaucratic-cabinet system or the 1955 system any longer, because of the reduced party-bureaucratic processes. Although leaders claim that they pursue the 'public interest', there are no informational and institutional foundations left that can lead them to do so. The core executive with the repeated use of fiat may become coercive or susceptible to particularistic interests or both. These points have been demonstrated by the empirical analyses in Part II, showing that the shifts to new market-based arrangements were derived from manipulative agenda-setting, issue-dimensional politics, and crisis politics. It is superficial to think that policy change in accordance with the neoliberal global order will ultimately benefit the general public, as the trickledown theory of neoliberalism assumes. The core-executive system relies exclusively on the leadership's policy benevolence and finesse, but runs short of rigorous procedures for defining public interest critically.

Furthermore, the policy changes analyzed in Part II have not generated economic institutions that are sufficiently stable and consistent with the global order. As for banks, the financial reform has had a diminishing effect on the main bank function. Firms rely less on banks' traditional functions of long-term loans for capital formation, personal exchanges, and managerial oversight than they did in the 1980s and 1990s. Instead, they rely more on commercial banks for the underwriting of corporate bonds and the acquisition of syndicated loans for the time when their credit ratings decline (RIETI corporate survey in Hirota, 2009). Without bank oversight, firms are experimenting with alternative oversight mechanisms based on multilayered law. Many Japanese companies are creating hybrid governance systems, such as variants of market-based financing with flexible employment or long-term employment (Jackson and Miyajima, 2008; Aoki, 2010). Because of the asymmetric labor law, work places are increasingly segmented between regular employees and temporary workers, leading to differentiated treatments and the feeling of unfairness.

The economic institutions characterized above are still transitory and have not yet achieved the appropriate levels of institutional complementarity and incentive compatibility. The historical analyses in Part I indicate that robust institutions do not evolve spontaneously and require proper government interventions. Thus, future governments will continue to be responsible for adapting the institutions still in flux to the global order through further policy change. The core-executive system that is supposed to lead policy change has not yet established transparency, political accountability, or policy control. Thus, it is uncertain that a benign co-evolution of majoritarian democracy and liberal market economy will emerge in the foreseeable future.

9.3 GLOBALIZING STATE AS AN OPEN CORE-EXECUTIVE STATE

The empirical analyses also provide some clues of how to keep political leadership in check under reduced policy procedures.

9.3.1 Internal Ancillary Authority

First, as democratic theory suggests, opposition parties are viable scrutinizers to political leadership. Under a competitive party system, they are tempted to publicize innovative policy information and correct unfair government policy practices because they have their own rational incentives to convince the electorate that they can run an effective government and because they represent the social interests that are excluded from the governing coalition. As shown in Part II, the Democratic Party of Japan (DPJ) and other smaller opposition parties condemned the LDP government for prioritizing corporate interests and labor market efficiency single-mindedly at the expense of stability and fairness, demanding the implementation of the equal treatment principle for temporary workers. As for trade, the income compensation program for agriculture proposed by the DPJ and inherited by the LDP is relatively efficient in protecting domestic farmers without injuring consumerist interests too much – the LDP had maintained subsidies and import protection even after the adoption of the mixed electoral system that would presumably enhance consumerist interests. As for banking regulation, the DPJ criticized the LDP government for permitting lenient bank supervision of continuous lending to illiquid firms and neglecting the broader national economic health, urging stricter supervision and bailouts to regain financial efficiency and stability.

9.3.2 External Ancillary Authority

Second, in contradistinction to fairness, external actors can provide policy information or rules for efficiency, discouraging political leadership from catering to particularistic interests. Even if it tries to initiate a new policy program for efficiency, political leadership may amend part of the program to protect its clients under reduced domestic scrutiny. To break the rent-seeking practice at the leadership level, it is useful to take advantage of intergovernmental or transgovernmental networks as external oversight.

The empirical analyses in Part II showed that, with regard to corporate governance, the LDP-led coalition government has reduced main bank oversight and strengthened internal oversight through directorial independence. However, the Abe Cabinet enacted the comply-or-explain clause to permit legally non-binding directorial independence, while approving a mandatory but still lenient corporate governance code for firms listed on the Tokyo Stock Exchange. In effect, the multilayered corporate governance system has given greater discretion to company managers. As for banking, although knowing that the minimum capital requirements were useful for enhancing financial prudence, the LDP leadership was averse to the strict enforcement of the requirements and left lenient bank supervision intact for continuous lending that prolonged the non-performing loan crisis. These rent-seeking practices at the leadership level can be attributed to the politics of the core executive within which corporate and financial interests are increasingly overrepresented. In the realms of corporate governance and banking supervision, there are some instances in which international investors and financial institutions punished the practices by suing corporate managers for their poor governance[2] and by increasing interest rates against highly leveraged Japanese banks, respectively.

9.3.3 Open Core Executive

In general, multilateral institutions assist states' political institutions in controlling the power of special interests and increasing capacities to achieve important public purposes (Keohane et al., 2009). Opposition parties are also indispensable for democratic governance, innovative public policy, and public welfare enhancement by representing non-members of the governing coalition (Dahl, 1977). The Japanese experiences provide evidence for these general claims. In a globalizing setting, facilitators for policy change are diverse. The use of internal and external ancillary authorities embodies a flexible governance scheme appropriate for the age of globalization. From this perspective, the regular authority allocation scheme associated with parliamentary democracy is too rigid and ineffective.

The prewar experiences suggest that excessive government centralization could pave the way for political monopoly and coercion and generate a catastrophic consequence when central command was cut off from the flow of information and communication. Under the postwar democratic constitution, the decentralized bureaucratic-cabinet system kept leadership in check, not so much through the Supreme Court,[3] but through the governing party and bureaucracies.[4] Electoral and administrative reforms have weakened the procedural constraints, reincarnating the fear of monopolistic leadership. This fear is felt acutely by non-members of the governing coalition who anticipate that they will suffer from neoliberal policies without adequate compensation or countermeasure to reduce their losses.[5] In contrast, the policies are supported strongly by members of efficient sectors who are endowed with competitive assets and will profit directly from reforms, and marginally supported by members of the governing coalition who may not benefit from it but may be compensated for their losses. To help facilitate neoliberal policy reform, efficient sectors transfer portions of the profits as political contributions to the incumbent politicians, enabling them to maintain their seats in the mixed electoral system by securing less than 50 percent of district votes. Thus, short of appropriate domestic scrutiny, neoliberal policy will continue unabated with a distributive bias insofar as it supplies substantial profits to a small segment of society.[6]

Despite its attractive features noted in the initial section of this chapter, the core-executive system is not a panacea and has to incorporate ancillary authorities for both pragmatic and normative reasons, as argued thus far. Pragmatically, internal or external ancillary authorities are useful for reducing structural dilemmas and facilitating policy reform, whereas, normatively, they are valuable for improving transparency and accountability under weakened procedural constraints on political leadership. In contradistinction, reliance on the ancillary authorities raises another concern, namely that the diffusion of concentrated power will undermine the intrinsic virtue of the core executive in policy initiation and coordination. What this means is that subtle authority reallocation is essential for keeping political leadership non-dictatorial and robust in the age of globalization.

NOTES

1. Such bureaucratic sabotage was a major cause of policy failures caused by the Democratic Party of Japan (DPJ)–led coalition government. Having won the 2009 general election, the DPJ formed a non-LDP coalition government with an electoral mandate for the first time in more than half a century. Emboldened with a parliamentary majority, the DPJ government sought to establish political control over the gigantic bureaucratic system and force its policy proposals upon existing bureaucratic policies without consultation. The analysis in Chapter 7 cited one instance in which the DPJ's proposal on corporate governance reform deadlocked because of business and bureaucratic objections within the key deliberative council. Similar conclusions are reached by several studies (Ito and Miyamoto, 2014; Yamaguchi and Nakakita, 2014) that have assessed the DPJ's failures in many other policy domains.
2. See endnote 27 in Chapter 6.
3. The Japanese Supreme Court has maintained judicial restraint based on the principle of popular sovereignty.
4. The arrangements that constrained political leadership were prior consultation with the governing party and policy delegation to the bureaucratic system (see Chapter 4 for details).
5. The Social Stratification and Social Mobility (SSM) survey in 2005 shows divided public preferences on socioeconomic equality and economic freedom. On average, economic freedom is prioritized by individuals in high-income brackets (typically those in efficient sectors and urban areas with high levels of education), while those in low-income brackets (typically those in inefficient sectors and rural areas with low levels of education) had little faith in economic freedom. Saito (2010) attributes this divided picture of individual preferences to increasing income inequality between the rich and the poor that is caused in part by competitive economic policy. This is in sharp contrast to the conventional wisdom that there is a consensus among the Japanese public on economic equality and social harmony.
6. The thesis of neoliberal collusion has been put forward by a number of Japanese authors, including Shibayama (2012) and Nakano (2013).

Bibliography

Abbott, K. and D. Snidal (2000), 'Hard and soft law in international governance', *International Organization*, **54**(3), 421–56.
Abbott, K. and D. Snidal (2009), 'The governance triangle: regulatory standards institutions and the shadow of the state', in W. Mattli and N. Woods (eds), *The Politics of Global Regulation*, Princeton, NJ: Princeton University Press, pp. 44–88.
Alesina, A. and A. Drazen (1991), 'Why are stabilizations delayed?', *The American Economic Review*, **81**(5), 1170–88.
Alesina, A. and G. Tabellini (2007), 'Bureaucrats or politicians? Part I: a single policy task', *The American Economic Review*, **97**(1), 169–79.
Alexander, K. (2000), 'The role of soft law in the legalization of international banking supervision', *Working Paper No. 168*, ESRC Centre for Business Research, University of Cambridge.
Alt, J.E. (1985), 'Political parties, world demand, and unemployment: domestic and international sources of economic activity', *American Political Science Review*, **79**(4), 1016–40.
Alvarez, J.E. (2001), 'Do liberal states behave better? A critique of Slaughter's liberal theory', *European Journal of International Law*, **12**(2), 183–246.
Amyx, J.A. (2006), *Japan's Financial Crisis: Institutional Rigidity and Reluctant Change*, Princeton, NJ: Princeton University Press.
Anderson, K. (2005), 'Squaring the circle? Reconciling sovereignty and global governance through global government networks', *Harvard Law Review*, **118**(4), 1255–321.
Aoki, M. (1983), *The Economic Analysis of the Japanese Firm (Contributions to Economic Analysis)*, Amsterdam: Elsevier Science Ltd.
Aoki, M. (1998), 'The evolution of organizational conventions and gains from diversity', *Industrial and Corporate Change*, **7**(3), 399–431.
Aoki, M. (2000), *Information, Corporate Governance and Institutional Diversity: Competitiveness in Japan, the USA, and the Transitional Economies*, Oxford, UK: Oxford University Press.
Aoki, M. (2001), *Toward a Comparative Institutional Analysis*, Cambridge, MA: MIT Press.
Aoki, M. (2010), *Corporations in Evolving Diversity: Cognition, Governance, and Institutions*, Oxford, UK: Oxford University Press.

Aoki, M. and R.P. Dore (eds) (1994), *The Japanese Firm: The Sources of Competitive Strength*, Oxford, UK: Oxford University Press.

Aoki, M. and M. Okuno (1996), *Keizai Shisutemu no Hikaku Seido Bunseki* [A Comparative Institutional Analysis of Economic System], Tokyo: Tokyo Daigaku Shuppankai.

Aoki, M. and H.T. Patrick (eds) (1995), *The Japanese Main Bank System: Its Relevance for Developing and Transforming Economies*, Oxford, UK: Oxford University Press.

Aoki, M., G. Jackson, and H. Miyajima (eds) (2008), *Corporate Governance in Japan: Institutional Change and Organizational Diversity*, Oxford, UK: Oxford University Press.

Aoyagi, C. and G. Ganelli (2014), 'Unstash the cash!: corporate governance reform in Japan', *IMF Working Paper No. 14/140*, Washington, DC: International Monetary Fund.

Arikawa, Y. and H. Miyajima (2008), 'Relational banking in post-bubble Japan: co-existence of soft- and hard-budget constraints', in M. Aoki, G. Jackson, and H. Miyajima (eds), *Corporate Governance in Japan: Institutional Change and Organizational Diversity*, Oxford, UK: Oxford University Press, pp. 51–78.

Bank of Japan (1966), *Hundred Year Statistics of the Japanese Economy*, Tokyo: Statistics Department, The Bank of Japan.

Banno, J. (2014), *Japan's Modern History, 1857–1937: A New Political Narrative*, London: Routledge.

Barr, M.S. and G.P. Miller (2006), 'Global administrative law: the view from Basel', *European Journal of International Law*, **17**(1), 15–46.

Beasley, W.G. (1993), *Japanese Imperialism, 1894–1945*, Oxford, UK: Oxford University Press.

Bebchuk, L.A. and M.J. Roe (1999), 'A theory of path dependence in corporate ownership and governance', *Stanford Law Review*, **52**(1), 127–70.

Berger, T.U. (2007), 'The pragmatic liberalism of an adaptive state', in T.U. Berger, M. Mochizuki, and J. Tsuchiyama (eds), *Japan in International Politics: The Foreign Policies of an Adaptive State*, Boulder, CO: Lynne Rienner Publishers, pp. 259–300.

Caballero, R.J., T. Hoshi, and A.K. Kashyap (2008), 'Zombie lending and depressed restructuring in Japan', *The American Economic Review*, **98**(5), 1943–77.

Cabinet Office (2001), *Dai Hyaku Goju Ikkai Kokkai niokeru Koizumi Shusho no Shoshin Hyoumei Enzetsu* [Prime Minister's General Policy Address to the 151st Diet Session], Tokyo: Cabinet Office.

Cabinet Office (2006), *Kisei Kaikaku Hyouka Hokokusho No. 6: Kin'nen no Kisei Kaikaku no Sinchoku to Seisansei no Kankei* [Sixth Evaluation

Report on Regulatory Reform: Relationship between Recent Regulatory Reform and Productive Efficiency], Tokyo: Cabinet Office.

Cabinet Office (2008), *Nenji Keizai Zaisei Hokukusho* [The Annual Economic and Fiscal Report], Tokyo: Cabinet Office.

Cabinet Office (2009), *Nenji Keizai Zaisei Hokukusho* [The Annual Economic and Fiscal Report], Tokyo: Cabinet Office.

Calder, K.E. (1988a), *Crisis and Compensation: Public Policy and Political Stability in Japan, 1949–1986*, Princeton, NJ: Princeton University Press.

Calder, K.E. (1988b), 'Japanese foreign economic policy formation: explaining the reactive state', *World Politics*, **40**(4), 517–41.

Calder, K.E. (1995), *Strategic Capitalism: Private Business and Public Purpose in Japanese Industrial Finance*, Princeton, NJ: Princeton University Press.

Carlson, M. (2008), 'Japan's postal privatization battle: the continuing reverberations for the Liberal Democratic Party of rebels-assassins conflicts', *Asian Survey*, **48**(4), 603–25.

Clinton, H. (2011), 'America's Pacific century', *Foreign Policy*, **189**(1), 56–63.

Coase, R.H. (1960), 'Problem of social cost', *Journal of Law and Economics*, 3, 1–44.

Cox, G.W. (1997), *Making Votes Count: Strategic Coordination in the World's Electoral Systems*, Cambridge, UK: Cambridge University Press.

Cox, G.W. and M.D. McCubbins (2005), *Setting the Agenda: Responsible Party Government in the U.S. House of Representatives*, Cambridge, UK: Cambridge University Press.

Cox, G.W., M. Masuyama, and M.D. McCubbins (2000), 'Agenda power in the Japanese House of Representatives', *Japanese Journal of Political Science*, **1**(1), 1–21.

Cox, G.W., F.M. Rosenbluth, and M.F. Thies (1999), 'Electoral reform and the fate of factions: the case of Japan's Liberal Democratic Party', *British Journal of Political Science*, **29**(1), 33–56.

Crawford, V.P. and J. Sobel (1982), 'Strategic information transmission', *Econometrica: Journal of the Econometric Society*, **50**(6), 1431–51.

Crowley, J.B. (1966), *Japan's Quest for Autonomy: National Security and Foreign Policy, 1930–1938*, Princeton, NJ: Princeton University Press.

Cusack, T.R., T. Iversen, and D. Soskice (2007), 'Economic interests and the origins of electoral systems', *American Political Science Review*, **101**(3), 373–91.

Dahl, R. (1977), *Polyarchy: Participation and Opposition*, New Haven, CT: Yale University Press.

Dahl, R.A. (2006), *A Preface to Economic Democracy*, expanded edition, Berkeley, CA: University of California Press.

De Nicolò, G.L. Laeven, and K. Ueda (2008), 'Corporate governance quality: trends and real effects', *Journal of Financial Intermediation*, **17**(2), 198–228.

Dore, R. (2000), *Stock Market Capitalism: Welfare Capitalism: Japan and Germany Versus the Anglo-Saxons*, Oxford, UK: Oxford University Press.

Dower, J.W. (2000), *Embracing Defeat: Japan in the Wake of World War II*, New York: W.W. Norton.

Downs, G.W., D.M. Rocke, and P.N. Barsoom (1996), 'Is the good news about compliance good news about cooperation?', *International Organization*, **50**(3), 379–406.

Drezner, D.W. (2007), *All Politics is Global: Explaining International Regulatory Regimes*, Princeton, NJ: Princeton University Press.

Drucker, P.F. (1998), 'In defense of Japanese bureaucracy', *Foreign Affairs*, **77**(5), 68–80.

Dunleavy, P. and R.A.W. Rhodes (1990), 'Core executive studies in Britain', *Public Administration*, **68**(1), 3–28.

Dyer, J.H. (1996), 'Specialized supplier networks as a source of competitive advantage: evidence from the auto industry', *Strategic Management Journal*, **17**(4), 271–91.

Economic Planning Agency (1979), *Kokumin Seikatsu Hakusho* [White Paper on National Life], Tokyo: Economic Planning Agency.

Economic Planning Agency (2000), *Annual Economic Report*, Tokyo: Economic Planning Agency.

Engel, K.C. and P. McCoy (2011), *The Subprime Virus: Reckless Credit, Regulatory Failure, and Next Steps*, Oxford, UK: Oxford University Press.

Estévez-Abe, M. (2006), 'Japan's shift toward a Westminster system: a structural analysis of the 2005 lower house election and its aftermath', *Asian Survey*, **46**(4), 632–51.

Estévez-Abe, M. (2008), *Welfare and Capitalism in Postwar Japan: Party, Bureaucracy, and Business*, Cambridge, UK: Cambridge University Press.

Evans, P. (1995), *Embedded Autonomy: States and Industrial Transformation*, Princeton, NJ: Princeton University Press.

Freeman, R.B. and L.F. Katz (eds) (1995), *Differences and Changes in Wage Structures*, Chicago, IL: University of Chicago Press and NBER.

Fukao, K. (2012), *'Ushinawareta 20-nen' to Nihon Keizai: Kozo-teki Gen'in to Saisei e no Gendoryoku no Kaimei* [The 'Lost Two Decades' in the Japanese Economy: An Analysis of Structural Causes and

Driving Forces for Reconstruction], Tokyo: Nihon Keizai Shimbun Shuppansha.

Fukao, K. and T. Miyagawa (eds) (2008), *Seisansei to Nihon no Keizaiseicho: JIP Database niyoru Sangyo/Kigyo Reberu no Jissho Kenkyu* [Productivity and Economic Growth in Japan: Industry- and Firm-level Analysis Based on JIP Database], Tokyo: Tokyo Daigaku Shuppankai.

Fukao, M. (2004), 'Japan's lost decade and its financial system', in G.R. Saxonhouse and R.M. Stern (eds), *Japan's Lost Decade: Origins, Consequences and Prospects for Recovery*, Oxford, UK: Blackwell.

Furukawa, S. (2011), *Kasumigaseki Hanseiki: Gonin no Sori wo Sasaete* [Half a Century in Kasumigaseki: Serving for Five Prime Ministers], Saga: Saga Shimbunsha.

Gadinis, S. (2013), 'From independence to politics in financial regulation', *California Law Review*, **101**(2), 327–406.

Garrett, G. (1998), *Partisan Politics in the Global Economy*, Cambridge, UK: Cambridge University Press.

Gerschenkron, A. (1962), *Economic Backwardness in Historical Perspective: A Book of Essays*, Cambridge, UK: Belknap Press of Harvard University Press.

Gilpin, R. (2001), *Global Political Economy*, Princeton, NJ: Princeton University Press.

Gilson, R.J. (2001), 'Globalizing corporate governance: convergence of form or function', *The American Journal of Comparative Law*, **49**(2), 329–57.

Gilson, R.J. and C.J. Milhaupt (2005), 'Choice as regulatory reform: the case of Japanese corporate governance', *American Journal of Comparative Law*, **53**(2), 343–77.

Gordon, A. (1988), *The Evolution of Labor Relations in Japan: Heavy Industry, 1853–1955*, Cambridge, MA: Harvard University, Council on East Asian Studies of Harvard University.

Gourevitch, P. (1978), 'The second image reversed: the international sources of domestic politics', *International Organization*, **32**(4), 881–912.

Gourevitch, P. and J. Shinn (2007), *Political Power and Corporate Control: The New Global Politics of Corporate Governance*, Princeton, NJ: Princeton University Press.

Gowa, J.S. (1993), *Allies, Adversaries, and International Trade*, Princeton, NJ: Princeton University Press.

Green, M. (2003), *Japan's Reluctant Realism: Foreign Policy Challenges in an Era of Uncertain Power*, New York: Palgrave.

Greif, A. (2006), *Institutions and the Path to the Modern Economy: Lessons from Medieval Trade*, Cambridge, UK: Cambridge University Press.

Grofman, B., A. Blais, and S. Bowler (eds) (2009), *Duverger's Law of Plurality Voting: The Logic of Party Competition in Canada, India, the United Kingdom and the United States*, Berlin: Springer.

Grossman, E. and C. Woll (2014), 'Saving the banks: the political economy of bailouts', *Comparative Political Studies*, **47**(4), 574–600.

Grossman, G.M. and E. Helpman (2002), *Interest Groups and Trade Policy*, Princeton, NJ: Princeton University Press.

Hall, P.A. and D. Soskice (eds) (2001), *Varieties of Capitalism: The Institutional Foundations of Comparative Advantage*, Oxford, UK: Oxford University Press.

Hanazaki, M. and A. Horiuchi (2003), 'A review of Japan's bank crisis from the governance perspective', *Pacific-Basin Finance Journal*, **11**(3), 305–25.

Hansmann, H. and R. Kraakman (2001), 'The end of history for corporate law', *Georgetown Law Journal*, **89**(2), 439–68.

Harada, K. and T. Ito (2011), 'Did mergers help Japanese mega-banks avoid failure? Analysis of the distance to default of banks', *Journal of the Japanese and International Economies*, **25**(1), 1–22.

Hayek, F.A. (1945), 'The use of knowledge in society', *The American Economic Review*, **35**(4), 519–30.

Heginbotham, E. and R.J. Samuels (1998), 'Mercantile realism and Japanese foreign policy', *International Security*, **22**(4), 171–203.

Himino, R. (2005), *BIS Kisei to Nippon* [The Basel Regulations and Japan], Tokyo: Kinyu Zaisei Jijo Kenkyukai.

Hino, A. (2009), 'Senkein Kotai ha Ichinichi nishite Narazu' [The change of government wasn't built in one day], in A. Tanaka, M. Kono, A. Hino, and K. Iida (eds), *Naze Seikenkotai Dattanoka* [Why Change of Government?], Tokyo: Keiso Shobo.

Hirota, S. (2009), *Nihon no Mein Banku Kankei: Monitaringu kara Risukuhejji e* [Japan's Main Bank Relationships: From Monitoring to Risk Hedging], Tokyo: Research Institute of Economy, Trade and Industry.

Hirschman, A. ([1945] 1980), *National Power and the Structure of Foreign Trade*, Berkeley, CA: University of California Press.

Hirst, P. and G. Thompson ([1996] 2009), *Globalization in Question: The International Economy and the Possibilities of Governance*, Cambridge, UK: Polity Press.

Hiscox, M.J. (2002), *International Trade and Political Conflict: Commerce, Coalitions, and Mobility*, Princeton, NJ: Princeton University Press.

Holliday, I. and T. Shinoda (2002), 'Governing from the centre: core executive capacity in Britain and Japan', *Japanese Journal of Political Science*, **3**(1), 91–111.

Hood, C., O. James, B.G. Peters, and C. Scott (2004), *Controlling Modern Government: Variety, Commonality and Change*, Cheltenham, UK and Northampton, MA, USA: Edward Elgar Publishing.

Horiuchi, A. (1999), 'Nihon niokeru Kinyu Kozo no Kiso' [Foundation of the Japanese financial structure], *Fainansharu Rebyu*, **50**, 1–32.

Hoshi, T. (2011), 'Nihon no Kinyu Sisutemu ni Kakusareta Risuku' [Hidden risks under the Japanese financial system], *NIRA Opinion Paper No. 4*.

Hoshi, T. and A.K. Kashyap (2010), 'Will the U.S. bank recapitalization succeed? Eight lessons from Japan', *Journal of Financial Economics*, **97**(3), 398–417.

Hoshi, T., A. Kashyap, and G. Loveman (1994), 'Lessons from the Japanese main bank system for financial system reform in Poland', in M. Aoki and H. Patrick (eds), *The Japanese Main Bank System: Its Relevancy for Developing and Transforming Economies*, Oxford, UK: Oxford University Press, pp. 592–633.

Huber, J.D. and C.R. Shipan (2008), 'Politics, delegation, and bureaucracy', in B.R. Weingast and D. Wittman (eds), *The Oxford Handbook of Political Economy*, Oxford, UK: Oxford University Press, pp. 256–72.

Iida, K. (2009), 'Shitsubo to Kitai ga Umu Seikenkotai' [Change of government through expectations and disappointments], in A. Tanaka, M. Kono, A. Hino and K. Iida (eds), *Naze Seikenkotai Dattanoka* [Why Change of Government?], Tokyo: Keiso Shobo, pp. 131–52.

Iio, J. (2007), *Nihon no Tochi Kozo* [The Governing Structure of Japan], Tokyo: Chuo Koron.

Ikai, T. (2005), 'Meiji Ishin to Yushi Seido no Seiritsu' [Meiji Restoration and the formation of oligarchic rule], *Machikaneyama Ronso*, **39**, 1–30.

Imamura, T. (2006), *Kancho Sekushonarizumu* [Bureaucratic Sectionalism], Tokyo: Tokyo Daigaku Shuppan-kai.

Industrial Policy Bureau of the Ministry of International Trade and Industry (MITI) (1994), *21 Seiki no Sangyo Kozo* [Industrial Structure in the Twenty-first Century], Tokyo: MITI.

Inoguchi, T. (1993), *Japan's Foreign Policy in an Era of Global Change*, London: Pinter.

Inoguchi, T. and T. Iwai (1987), *Zoku Gi'in no Kenkyo* [A Study of Zoku Parliamentarians], Tokyo: Nihon Keizai Shimbunsha.

Inoue, T. (2011), *Senzen Nihon no 'Gurobarizumu': Ichi Kyu San Rei-nendai no Kyokun* ['Globalism' in Prewar Japan: Lessons from the 1930s], Tokyo: Shinchosha.

Irwin, D.A. (1993), 'Multilateral and bilateral trade liberalization in the world trading system: an historical perspective', in J. De Melo and A. Panagariya (eds), *New Dimensions in Regional Integration*, Cambridge, UK: Cambridge University Press, pp. 90–119.

Ishikawa, M. (1999), *Bunpai no Keizaigaku* [The Economics of Distribution], Tokyo: Tokyo Daigaku Shuppankai.

Ito, K. (2001), 'Kokkai Shingi Kasseika-Ho no Seiji Katei' [The political process of the law for activating dietary deliberations], *Hokudai Hogaku Ronshu*, **51**(6), 89–127.

Ito, M. (2007), 'Kantei Shudo Gata Seisaku Kettei Shisutemu niokeru Seikan Kankei: Joho Hitaisho-sei Shukugen no Seiji' [The ministerial bureaucracy and the centralization of the core executive under the Koizumi Cabinet], *Nenpo Gyosei Kenkyu*, **42**, 32–59.

Ito, M. and T. Miyamoto (2014), *Minshuto Seiken no Chosen to Zasetsu: Sono Keiken kara Nani o Manabu ka* [Challenges and Setbacks of the DPJ Government: What Do We Learn from the Experiences?], Tokyo: Nihon Keizai Hyoron-sha.

Ito, T. (2004), 'Restropective on the bubble period and its relationship to development in the 1990s', in G.R. Saxonhouse and R.M. Stern (eds), *Japan's Lost Decade: Origins, Consequences and Prospects for Recovery*, Malden, MA: Blackwell, pp. 17–34.

Ito, T. and Y. Sasaki (2002), 'Impacts of the Basel Capital Standard on Japanese banks' behavior', *Journal of the Japanese and International Economies*, **16**(3), 372–97.

Ito, Y. (2007), *Genro Saionji Kinmochi* [Prince Kinmochi Saionji], Tokyo: Bungei Shunju.

Iversen, T. (2009), 'Democracy and capitalism', in R.E. Goodin (ed.), *Handbook of Political Science*, Oxford, UK: Oxford University Press, pp. 826–48.

Iversen, T. and D. Soskice (2006), 'Electoral institutions and the politics of coalitions: why some democracies redistribute more than others', *American Political Science Review*, **100**(2), 165–81.

Jackson, G. and H. Miyajima (2008), 'Introduction: the diversity and change of corporate governance in Japan', in M. Aoki, G. Jackson and H. Miyajima (eds), *Corporate Governance in Japan: Institutional Change and Organizational Diversity*, Oxford, UK: Oxford University Press, pp. 1–49.

Japan Defense Agency (1976), *Boei Hakusho: Nihon no Boei* [Whitepaper on Defense: Defense of Japan], Tokyo: Japan Defense Agency.

Jessop, R.D. (2002), *The Future of the Capitalist State*, Cambridge, UK: Polity Press.

Johnson, C. (1982), *MITI and the Japanese Miracle: The Growth of Industrial Policy: 1925–1975*, Stanford, CA: Stanford University Press.

Kahler, M. and D.A. Lake (2009), 'Economic integration and global governance: why so little supranationalism?', in N. Woods and W. Mattli (eds), *The Politics of Global Regulation*, Princeton, NJ: Princeton University.

Katase, K. and K. Seiyama (eds) (1998), *Seiji Ishiki no Genzai* [Political Cognition in Contemporary Japan], Tokyo: 1995-Nen SSM Chosa Shirizu.

Katz, R. (1998), *Japan: The System that Soured: The Rise and Fall of the Japanese Economic Miracle*, Armonk, NY: ME Sharpe.

Kawato, S. (1992), *Nihon no Seito Seiji 1890–1937-nen: Gikai Bunseki to Senkyo no Suryo Bunseki* [Party Politics in Japan 1890–1937: A Quantitative Analysis of the Diet and Elections], Tokyo: Tokyo Daigaku Shuppankai.

Keidanren (2008), *2008 Nen Kisei Kaikaku Yobo* [Recommendations for Regulatory Reform in 2008], accessed 8 October 2014 at http://www.keidanren.or.jp/japanese/policy/2008/041.html.

Keohane, R.O. and J.S. Nye (1977), *Power and Interdependence: World Politics in Transition*, Boston, MA: Little Brown.

Keohane, R.O., S. Macedo, and A. Moravcsik (2009), 'Democracy-enhancing multilateralism', *International Organization*, **63**(1), 1–31.

Kettl, D.F. (2000), 'The transformation of governance: globalization, devolution, and the role of government', *Public Administration Review*, **60**(6), 488–97.

King, D.C. (1997), *Turf Wars: How Congressional Committees Claim Jurisdiction*, Chicago, IL: The University of Chicago Press.

Kingsbury, B, N. Krisch, and R.B. Stewart (2005), 'The emergence of global administrative law', *Law and Contemporary Problems*, **68**(3), 15–61.

Kitaoka, S. (1978), *Nippon Rikugun to Tairiku Seisaku: 1906–1918 Nen* [The Japanese Imperial Army and the Continental Policy: 1906–1918], Tokyo: Tokyo Daigaku Shuppan-kai.

Kitaoka, S. (2008), *Jiminto: Seiken Seito no 38 nen* [LDP: 38 Years of Government], Tokyo: Chuo Koron-sha.

Kitaoka, S. (2012), *Kanryo-sei to shite no Nippon Rikugun* [The Japanese Imperial Army as a Bureaucratic Organization], Tokyo: Chikuma Shobo

Kojo, Y. (2010), 'Kokusai Seiji to Nihon no Kisei Kanwa, Kozo Kaikaku: Kokusai Seiji no Henka to Gaiatsu' [International politics and Japanese deregulation, structural reform: change in international politics and external pressure'], in J. Teranishi (ed.), *Kozo Mondai to Kiseikanwa* [Structural Problems and Deregulation], Tokyo: Keio Daigaku Shuppankai, pp. 45–76.

Krasner, S.D. (1991), 'Global communications and national power: life on the Pareto frontier', *World Politics*, **43**(3), 336–66.

Krauss, E.S. and B. Nyblade (2005), '"Presidentialization" in Japan? The prime minister, media and elections in Japan', *British Journal of Political Science*, **35**(2), 357–68.

Krauss, E.S. and R.J. Pekkanen (2010), *The Rise and Fall of Japan's LDP: Political Party Organizations as Historical Institutions*, New York: Cornell University Press.

Krugman, P.R. (ed.) (1986), *Strategic Trade Policy and the New International Economics*, Cambridge, MA: MIT Press.

Krugman, P.R. (1999), 'What happened to Asia', in R. Sato, R.V. Ramachandran and K. Mino (eds), *Global Competition and Integration*, Boston, MA: Kluwer Academic Publishers.

Kusano, A. (1995), 'Tettei Kensho: Shingikai wa Kakuremino dearu' [Investigation: deliberative councils as disguise], *Shokun*, **27**(7), 98–10.

La Porta, R., F. Lopez-de-Silanes, and A. Shleifer (2000), 'Investor protection and corporate governance', *Journal of Financial Economics*, **58**(1), 3–27.

Laeven, L. and F. Valencia (2010), 'Resolution of banking crises: the good, the bad, and the ugly', *Working Paper No. WP/10/146*, Washington, DC: International Monetary Fund.

Leaman, J. (2009), *The Political Economy of Germany Under Chancellors Kohl and Schröder: Decline of the German Model?*, New York: Berghahn Books.

Lijphart, A. (1994), *Electoral Systems and Party Systems: A Study of Twenty-seven Democracies, 1945–1990*, Oxford, UK: Oxford University Press.

Lindblom, C.E. (1979), 'Still muddling, not yet through', *Public Administration Review*, **39**(6), 517–26.

Lucas, R.E. (1988), 'On the mechanics of economic development', *Journal of Monetary Economics*, **22**(1), 3–42.

Machidori, S. (2012), *Shusho Seiji no Seido Bunseki: Gendai Nihon Seiji no Kenryoku Kiban Keisei* [An Institutional Analysis of Premier Politics: The Formation of Political Power in Contemporary Japan], Tokyo: Chikura Shobo.

Makihara, I. (2009), *Gyosei Kaikaku to Chosei no Shisutemu* [Administrative Reform and the System of Coordination], Tokyo: Tokyo Daigaku Shuppan-kai.

Mansfield, E.D. and R. Bronson (1997), 'Alliances, preferential trading arrangements, and international trade', *American Political Science Review*, **91**(1), 94–107.

Mansfield, E.D., H.V. Milner, and B.P. Rosendorff (2000), 'Free to trade: democracies, autocracies, and international trade', *American Political Science Review*, **94**(2), 305–22.

Manyin, M.E., S. Daggett, B. Dolven, and S.V. Lawrence (2012), *Pivot to the Pacific? The Obama Administration's 'Rebalancing' Toward Asia*, CRS Report to Congress No. R42448, Washington, DC: Congressional Research Service.

Martin, C.J. (2013), 'Neoliberalism and the working class hero', in V. Schmidt and M. Thatcher (eds), *Resilient Liberalism in Europe's Political Economy*, Oxford, UK: Oxford University Press, pp. 226–56.

Martin, L.L. and B.A. Simmons (1998), 'Theories and empirical studies of international institutions', *International Organization*, **52**(4), 729–57.

Mattli, W. and N. Woods (2009a), 'In whose benefit? Explaining regulatory change in global politics', in W. Mattli and N. Woods (eds), *The Politics of Global Regulation*, Princeton, NJ: Princeton University Press, pp. 1–43.

Mattli, W, and N. Woods (eds) (2009b), *The Politics of Global Regulation*, Princeton, NJ: Princeton University Press.

McCoy, P. (2015), 'Countercyclical regulation and its challenges', Faculty Paper, Boston, MA: Boston College Law School.

McCubbins, M.D., R. Noll, and B. Weingast (1989), 'Structure and process, politics and policy: administrative arrangements and the political control of agencies', *Virginia Law Review*, **75**(2), 431–82.

McLean, I. (2001), *Rational Choice and British Politics: An Analysis of Rhetoric and Manipulation from Peel to Blair*, Oxford, UK: Oxford University Press.

Miller, G.J. (1992), *Managerial Dilemmas: The Political Economy of Hierarchy*, Cambridge, UK: Cambridge University Press.

Mitani, T. (2010), *Kindai Nihon no Senso to Seiji* [War and Politics in Modern Japan], Tokyo: Iwanami Shoten.

Mittelman, J.H. (2002), 'Globalization: an ascendant paradigm?', *International Studies Perspectives*, **3**(1), 1–14.

Miyajima, H. (2008), 'The performance effects and determinants of corporate governance reform in Japan', in M. Aoki, G. Jackson, and H. Miyajima (eds), *Corporate Governance in Japan: Institutional Change and Organizational Diversity*, Oxford, UK: Oxford University Press, pp. 330–69.

Miyajima, H. (ed.) (2011), *Nihon no Kigyo Tochi: Sono Saisekkei to Kyosoryoku no Kaifuku ni Mukete* [Japanese Corporate Governance: Toward the Reassessment and Restoration of Competitiveness], Tokyo: Toyo Keizai Shinposha.

Miyano, M. (1998), 'Shokugyo to Seito Siji 1955–1995 nen' [Occupation and party support 1955–1995], in K. Katase (ed.), *Seiji Ishiki no Genzai* [Political Perception], Tokyo: SSM Kenkyukai, pp. 45–63.

Moe, T.M. (2005), 'Power and political institutions', *Perspectives on Politics*, **3**(2), 215–33.

Montgomery, H. and S. Shimizutani (2009), 'The effectiveness of bank recapitalization policies in Japan', *Japan and the World Economy*, **21**(1), 1–25.

Moravcsik, A. (1997), 'Taking preferences seriously: a liberal theory of international politics', *International Organization*, **51**(4), 513–53.

Moravcsik, A. (1998), *The Choice for Europe: Social Purpose and State Power from Messina to Maastricht*, Ithaca, NY: Cornell University Press.

Morikawa, M. (2012), 'Nihon Kigyo no Kozo Henka: Keiei Senryaku, Naibu Soshiki, Kigyo Kodo' [Structural changes in the Japanese companies: management strategies, internal organization, corporate behavior], *RIETI Discussion Paper Series 12-J-0117*, Tokyo: Research Institute of Economy, Trade and Industry.

Mosley, L. (2003), *Global Capital and National Governments*, Cambridge, UK: Cambridge University Press.

Muramatsu, M. (2010), *Sukuramu Gata Ridashippu no Hokai* [The Collapse of Political-Bureaucratic Leadership], Tokyo: Toyo Keizai Shinpo-sha.

Muramatsu, M. and E. Krauss (1984), 'Bureaucrats and politicians in policymaking: the case of Japan', *American Political Science Review*, **78**(1), 126–46.

Muramatsu, M. and E. Krauss (1990), 'The dominant party and social coalitions in Japan', in T.J. Pempel (ed.), *Uncommon Democracies: The One-party Dominant Regimes*, Ithaca, NY: Cornell University Press, pp. 282–305.

Muramatsu, M. and M. Okuno (2002), *Heisei Baburu no Kenkyu* [Research on the Heisei Bubble], Tokyo: Toyo Keizai Shinposha.

Musashi, T. (2008), 'Seiji no Daitoryo-Seika to Rippokatei eno Eikyo' [Presidentialization and its impact on legislative processes], *Kokusai Kokyo Seisaku Kenkyu*, **13**(1), 273–90.

Naikaku-Seido Hyakunen-Shi Hensan Iinkai (1985), *Naikaku-Seido Hyakunen-Shi* [The One-Hundred Year History of the Cabinet System], Tokyo: MOF Shuppan-Kyoku.

Nakakita, K. (2001), 'Sen Kyuhyaku GoJu Go-nen Taisei no Seiritsu' [The establishment of the 1955 system], *Journal of Law and Politics of Osaka City University*, **47**(4), 761–826.

Nakamura, T. (2012), *Showa-Shi* [The History of Showa], Tokyo: Keizai Shinposha.

Nakano, T. (2013), *Han Jiyu Boeki-ron* [Anti-Free Trade Theory], Tokyo: Shincho-sha.

Nakatani, I. (2008), *Naze Shihonshugi wa Jikaisita no ka* [Why Capitalism Self-Destructed?], Tokyo: Shueisha.

Namikawa, O. (2003), *Kin'yu Jikai: Rekishi wa Kurikaesunoka* [Financial Self-destruction: Does History Repeat Itself?], Tokyo: Toyo Keizai Shinposha.

Nonaka, N. (2008), *Jiminto Seiji no Shuen* [The End of LDP Politics], Tokyo: Chikuma.

North, D.C. (1990), *Institutions, Institutional Change and Economic Performance*, Cambridge, UK: Cambridge University Press.

Nye, J.S. and J.D. Donahue (2000), *Governance in a Globalizing World*, Washington, DC: Brookings Institution Press.

Oatley, T. and R. Nabors (1998), 'Redistributive cooperation: market failure, wealth transfers, and the Basle Accord', *International Organization*, **52**(1), 35–54.

OECD (2008), *Growing Unequal? Income Distribution and Poverty in OECD Countries*, Paris: OECD.

Ogawa, H. (1997), 'Yami ni Tozasareta Shingikai' [Deliberative councils hidden in the shadows], *Horitsu Jiho*, **69**(1), 54–5.

Ohkawa, K. and H. Rosovsky (1973), *Japanese Economic Growth: Trend Acceleration in the Twentieth Century*, Stanford, CA: Stanford University Press.

Ohmae, K. (1999), *The Borderless World, Power and Strategy in the Interlinked Economy*, revised edition, New York: Harper Business.

Ohtake, H. (2003), *Nihon gata Popurizumu: Seiji eno Kitai to Genmetsu* [Populism in Japanese Politics: Expectation and Disillusionment], Tokyo: Chuokoron-sha.

Ohyama, R. (2003), *Hikaku Gikai Seiji Ron* [Comparative Parliamentary Politics], Tokyo: Iwanami Shoten.

Okazaki, T. (1994), 'Nihon niokeru Koporeto Gabanansu' [The Development of Japanese corporate governance], *Kinyu Kenkyu*, **13**, 59–95.

Okazaki, T. (2004), 'Seiji Shisutemu to Zaisei Pafomansu: Nihon no rekishi-teki Keiken' [Political system and fiscal performance: historical experience of Japan], Tokyo: Research Institute of Economy, Trade and Industry.

Okazaki, T. and M. Okuno-Fujiwara (eds) (1999), *The Japanese Economic System and Its Historical Origins*, Oxford, UK: Oxford University Press.

Okimoto, D.I. (1990), *Between MITI and the Market: Japanese Industrial Policy for High Technology*, Stanford, CA: Stanford University Press.

Oku, K. (1990), 'Meiji Koki no Nihon no Kanzei Seisaku' [Japanese tariff policy in the late Meiji era], *Yamaguchi Keizaigaku Zasshi*, **39**(3/4), 145–65.

Olson, M. (1960), *The Logic of Collective Action: Public Goods and the Theory of Groups*, Cambridge, MA: Harvard University Press.

Ono, N. (2005), *Takenaka Heizo no Senso: Kin'yu Saisei ni Idonda 730-nichi* [Heizo Takenaka's War: Financial Reconstruction in 730 Days], Tokyo: PHP Kenkyujo.

Otake, F. (2005), *Nihon no Fubyodo* [Inequality in Japan], Tokyo: Nihon Keizai Shimbunsha.

Overbeek, H., B. van Apeldoorn, and A. Noelke (eds) (2007), *The Transnational Politics of Corporate Governance Regulation*, London: Routledge.

Ozawa, I. (1994), *Blueprint for a New Japan*, Tokyo: Kodansha International.

Patrick, H.T. and H. Rosovsky (eds) (1976), *Asia's New Giant: How the Japanese Economy Works*, Washington, DC: Brookings Institution.

Pempel, T.J. (1998), *Regime Shift: Comparative Dynamics of the Japanese Political Economy*, Ithaca, NY: Cornell University Press.

Persson, T. and G. Tabellini (2004), *The Economic Effects of Constitutions*, Cambridge, MA: MIT Press.

Persson, T., G. Roland, and G. Tabellini (2004), 'How do electoral rules shape party structures, government coalitions, and economic policies?', *NBER Working Paper No. 10176*, Cambridge, MA: National Bureau of Economic Research.

Peters, B.G. (2001), *The Future of Governing*, Lawrence, KS: University Press of Kansas.

Peters, B.G., R.A.W. Rhodes, and V. Wright (eds) (2000), *Administering the Summit: Administration of the Core Executive in Developed Countries*, Basingstoke, UK: Palgrave Macmillan.

Poguntke, T. and P. Webb (eds) (2007), *The Presidentialization of Politics: A Comparative Study of Modern Democracies*, Oxford, UK: Oxford University Press.

Putnam, R.D. (1988), 'Diplomacy and domestic politics: the logic of two-level games', *International Organization*, **42**(3), 427–60.

Pyle, K.B. (2008), *Japan Rising: Power and Purpose*, Cambridge, MA: Public Affairs.

Quillin, B. (2008), *International Financial Co-Operation: Political Economics of Compliance with the 1988 Basel Accord*, London: Routledge.

Quintyn, M. and M. Taylor (2002), 'Regulatory and supervisory independence and financial stability', *CESifo Economic Studies*, **49**(2), 259–94.

Rajan, R.G. and L. Zingales (2003), 'The great reversals: the politics of financial development in the twentieth century', *Journal of Financial Economics*, **69**(1), 5–50.

Ramseyer, J.M. and F.M. Rosenbluth (1997), *Japan's Political Marketplace*, Cambridge, MA: Harvard University Press.

Raustiala, K. (2002), 'The architecture of international cooperation:

transgovernmental networks and the future of international law', *Virginia Journal of International Law*, **43**(1), 1–92.

Rebelo, S. (1991), 'Long-run policy analysis and long-run growth', *Journal of Political Economy*, **99**(3), 500–521.

Rhodes, R.A.W. (2007), 'Understanding governance: ten years on', *Organization Studies*, **28**(8), 1243–64.

Rhodes, R.A.W. and P. Dunleavy (eds) (1995), *Prime Minister, Cabinet and Core Executive*, London: Macmillan.

RIETI (Research Institute of Economy, Trade and Industry) (2013a), *Tsusho Sangyo Seisaku-Shi 2: Tsusho Boeki Seisaku* [The History of Trade and Industrial Policy 2: Trade Policy], Tokyo: RIETI.

RIETI (Research Institute of Economy, Trade and Industry) (2013b), *Tsusho Sangyo Seisaku-Shi 3: Sangyo Seisaku* [History of Trade and Industrial Policy 3: Industrial Policy], Tokyo: RIETI.

Riker, W.H. (1986), *The Art of Political Manipulation*, New Haven, CT: Yale University Press.

Riker, W.H. (1988), *Liberalism Against Populism: A Confrontation Between the Theory of Democracy and the Theory of Social Choice*, Prospect Heights, IL: Waveland.

Rodrik, D. (1997), *Has Globalization Gone Too Far?*, Washington, DC: Institute for International Economics.

Rogowski, R. (1989), *Commerce and Coalitions: How Trade Effects Domestic Political Arrangements*, Princeton, NJ: Princeton University Press.

Rogowski, R. and M.A. Kayser (2002), 'Majoritarian electoral systems and consumer power: price-level evidence from the OECD countries', *American Journal of Political Science*, **46**(3), 526–39.

Romer, P.M. (1986), 'Increasing returns and long-run growth', *Journal of Political Economy*, **94**(5), 1002–37.

Rönnmar, M. (2011), 'Flexicurity, labour law and the notion of equal treatment', in M. Rönnmar (ed.), *Labour Law, Fundamental Rights and Social Europe*, Bloomsbury Publishing.

Rosenbluth, F.M. and M.F. Thies (2010), *Japan Transformed: Political Change and Economic Restructuring*, Princeton, NJ: Princeton University Press.

Ruggie, J.G. (1982), 'International regimes, transactions, and change: embedded liberalism in the postwar economic order', *International Organization*, **36**(2), 379–415.

Saito, J. (2010), *Jiminto Choki Seiken no Seiji Keizai-gaku: Rieki Yudo Seiji no Jiko Mujun* [The Political Economy of the LDP Regime], Tokyo: Keiso Shobo.

Saito, T. (2011), 'Nihon Kigyo ni yoru Shagai Torishimariyaku no Donyu no Kettei Yoin to sono Koka' [Determinants and effects of the introduction of outside directors in Japanese companies], in H. Miyajima (ed.), *Nihon no Kigyo Tochi - sono Saisekkei to Kyoso-ryoku no Kaifuku ni Mukete* [Japanese Corporate Governance: Toward the Reassessment and Restoration of Competitiveness], Tokyo: Toyo Keizai Shinposha, pp. 181–213.

Sakai, T. (2007), *Kindainihon no Kokusai Chitsujo-ron* [The Political Discourse of International Order in Modern Japan], Tokyo: Iwanami Shoten.

Samuels, R.J. (2005), *Machiavelli's Children: Leaders and Their Legacies in Italy and Japan*, Ithaca, NY: Cornell University Press.

Samuels, R. (2007), *Securing Japan: Tokyo's Grand Strategy and the Future of East Asia*, Ithaca, NY: Cornell University Press.

Sartori, G. (1976), *Parties and Party Systems: A Framework for Analysis*, Cambridge, UK: Cambridge University Press.

Sato, S. and T. Matsuzaki (1982), *Jiminto Seiken* [LDP Governments], Tokyo: Chuo Koron-sha.

Schelling, T.C. (1960), *The Strategy of Conflict*, Cambridge, MA: Harvard University Press.

Schmidt, V.A. and M. Thatcher (eds) (2013), *Resilient Liberalism in Europe's Political Economy*, Cambridge, UK: Cambridge University Press.

Scholte, J.A. (2005), *Globalization: A Critical Introduction*, 2nd edition, New York: Palgrave.

Schoppa, L.J. (1997), *Bargaining with Japan: What American Pressure Can and Cannot Do*, New York: Columbia University Press.

Schumpeter, J.A. ([1912] 1934), *The Theory of Economic Development*, Cambridge, MA: Harvard University Press.

Schumpeter, J.A. (1976), *Capitalism, Socialism and Democracy*, London: Allen and Unwin.

Shepsle, K.A. and B.R. Weingast (1987), 'The institutional foundations of committee power', *American Political Science Review*, **81**(1), 85–104.

Shibayama, K. (2012), *Shizuka-naru Daikyoko* [Silent Great Depression], Tokyo: Shuei-sha.

Shimizu, Y. (2013), *Kindai Nihon no Kanryo: Ishin Kanryo kara Gakureki Erito e* [The Bureaucracy of Modern Japan: from Meiji-Restoration Bureaucrats to Educated Elites], Tokyo: Chuo Koron Shinsha.

Shiroyama, H. (2013), *Kokusai Gyosei-ron* [Theory of International Administration], Tokyo: Yuhikaku.

Shishido, Z. (2000), 'Japanese corporate governance: the hidden problems of the corporate law and their solutions', *Delaware Journal of Corporate Law*, **25**(2), 189–233.

Shishido, Z. (2008), 'The turnaround of 1997: changes in Japanese corporate law and governance', in M. Aoki, G. Jackson, and H. Miyajima (eds), *Corporate Governance in Japan: Institutional Change and Organizational Diversity*, Oxford, UK: Oxford University Press, pp. 310–29.

Shonfield, A. (1965), *Modern Capitalism: The Changing Balance of Public and Private Power*, Oxford, UK: Oxford University Press.

Simmons, B.A. (2000), 'International law and state behavior: commitment and compliance in international monetary affairs', *American Political Science Review*, **94**(04), 819–35.

Simmons, B.A. and Z. Elkins (2004), 'The globalization of liberalization: policy diffusion in the international political economy', *American Political Science Review*, **98**(1), 171–89.

Skinner, D.J. (2008), 'The rise of deferred tax assets in Japan: the role of deferred tax accounting in the Japanese banking crisis', *Journal of Accounting and Economics*, **46**(2–3), 218–39.

Slaughter, A.-M. (2004), *A New World Order*, Princeton, NJ: Princeton University Press.

Smith, M.J. (1999), *The Core Executive in Britain*, London: Macmillan.

Steiner, K., E.S. Krauss, and S.C. Flanagan (eds) (1980), *Political Opposition and Local Politics in Japan*, Princeton, NJ: Princeton University Press.

Stigler, G. (1971), 'The theory of economic regulation', *Bell Journal of Economics*, **2**(1), 3–21.

Strange, S. (1996), *The Retreat of the State: The Diffusion of Power in the World Economy*, Cambridge, UK: Cambridge University Press.

Streeck, W. (2001), 'Introduction: explorations into the origins of nonliberal capitalism in Germany and Japan', in W. Streeck and K. Yamamura (eds), *The Origins of Nonliberal Capitalism: Germany and Japan in Comparison*, Ithaca, NY: Cornell University Press.

Streeck, W. and K. Thelen (eds) (2005), *Beyond Continuity: Institutional Change in Advanced Political Economies*, Oxford, UK: Oxford University Press.

Streeck, W. and K. Yamamura (2001), *The Origins of Nonliberal Capitalism: Germany and Japan in Comparison*, Ithaca, NY: Cornell University Press, pp. 1–38.

Streeck, W. and K. Yamamura (2003), 'Introduction: convergence or diversity? Stability and change in German and Japanese capitalism', in *The End of Diversity? Prospects for German and Japanese Capitalism*, Ithaca, NY: Cornell University Press, pp. 1–50.

Suzuki, M. (2005), 'Determinants of multiparty competition under Japan's parallel electoral system', *Kyoto Journal of Law and Political Science*, **2**(2), 1–19.

Suzuki, M. (2010), 'The politics of coordination and miscoordination in the United States–Japan Alliance', *International Relations of the Asia-Pacific*, **10**(3), 491–51.

Tachibanaki, T. (2005), *Confronting Income Inequality in Japan: A Comparative Analysis of Causes, Consequences, and Reform*, Cambridge, MA: MIT Press.

Takahashi, K. (2006), *Gendai Rikkenshugi no Seido Koso* [An Institutional Foundation of Contemporary Constitutionalism], Tokyo: Yuhikaku.

Takami, K. (2008), *Nihon no Gikaisei to Kenpo* [Parliamentary Politics and the Constitution in Contemporary Japan], Tokyo: Iwanami Shoten.

Takenaka, Harukata (2006), *Shusho Shihai: Nihon Seiji no Henbo* [The Prime Minister's Government: Change in Japanese Politics], Tokyo: Chuo Koron Shinsha.

Takenaka, Heizo (2006), *Kozo Kaikaku no Shinjitsu: Takenaka Heizo Daijin Nisshi* [The Truths of Structural Reforms: The Diary of Minister Heizo Takenaka], Tokyo: Nihon Keizai Shimbunsha.

Takenaka, Heizo (2008), *The Structural Reforms of the Koizumi Cabinet: An Insider's Account of the Economic Revival of Japan*, Tokyo: Nikkei Publishing.

Tamura, K. (2005), 'Challenges to Japanese compliance with the Basel Capital Accord: domestic politics and international banking standards', *Japanese Economy*, **33**(1), 23–49.

Tanabe, S. (2011), 'Seito Shiji no Jidai Hensen' [Temporal change in party support], in Y. Saito and K. Misumi (eds), *Gendai no Kaiso Shakai 3: Ryudoka no Nakano Shakai Ishiki* [Contemporary Social Structure: Fluid Social Perceptions], Tokyo: Tokyo Daigaku Shuppankai, pp. 47–62.

Teranishi, J. (2005), *Evolution of the Economic System in Japan*, Cheltenham, UK and Northampton, MA, USA: Edward Elgar Publishing.

Teranishi, J. (2006), 'Senzen Nihon no Kin'yu Shisutemu wa Ginko Chushindeatta ka' [Was the financial system of pre-war Japan centered on banks?], *Kinyu Kenkyu*, **25**(1), 13–40.

Tiberghien, Y. (2007), *Entrepreneurial States: Reforming Corporate Governance in France, Japan, and Korea*, Ithaca, NY: Cornell University Press.

Toya, T. (2006), *The Political Economy of the Japanese Financial Big Bang: Institutional Change in Finance and Public Policymaking*, Oxford, UK: Oxford University Press.

Tsuji, K. (1995), *Nihon Kanryosei no Kenkyu* [A Study of the Japanese Bureaucracy], Tokyo: Tokyo Daigaku Shuppankai.

Tsunekawa, K. (2010), 'Kisei Kanwa no Seiji Katei: Nani ga Kawatta no ka' [The political process of deregulation: what has changed], in J. Teranishi (ed.), *Kozo Mondai to Kiseikanwa* [Structural Problems and Deregulation], Tokyo: Keio Daigaku Shuppankai, pp. 77–147.

Tsuneki, A. and M. Matsunaga (2008), 'Labor relations and labor law in Japan', *Discussion Paper No. 724*, Institute of Social and Economic Research, Osaka University.

Tsunoda, J. (1967), *Manshu Mondai to Kokubo Hoshin* [The Manchurian Problem and National Defense Policy], Tokyo: Hara Shobo.

Tsutsui, K. (2009), *Konoe Fumimaro: Kyoyo Shugi-teki Popyurisuto no Higeki* [Konoe Fumimaro: The Tragedy of a Populist Intellectual], Tokyo: Iwanami Shoten.

Uzawa, H. (1965), 'Optimum technical change in an aggregative model of economic growth', *International Economic Review*, **6**(1), 18–31.

Verdier, P.-H. (2009), 'Transnational regulatory networks and their limits', *Yale Journal of International Law*, **34**(1), 113–72.

Vitols, S. (2013), 'European corporate governance: is there an alternative to neo-liberalism?', in V.A. Schmidt and M. Thatcher (eds), *Resilient Liberalism in Europe's Political Economy*, Cambridge, UK: Cambridge University Press.

Vogel, S. (2003), 'The re-organization of organized capitalism: how German and Japanese models are shaping their own transformations', in W. Streek and K. Yamamura (2003), *The End of Diversity? Prospects for German and Japanese Capitalism*, Ithaca, NY: Cornell University Press, pp. 306–33.

Vogel, S. (2006), *Japan Remodeled: How Government and Industry are Reforming Japanese Capitalism*, Ithaca, NY: Cornell University Press.

Waltz, K.N. (2010), *Theory of International Politics*, Long Grove, IL: Waveland Press.

Weber, B. and S.W. Schmitz (2011), 'Varieties of helping capitalism: politico-economic determinants of bank rescue packages in the EU during the recent crisis', *Socio-Economic Review*, **9**(4), 639–69.

Weber, M. (2009), *From Max Weber: Essays in Sociology*, London: Routledge.

Weingast, B.R. and D. Wittman (eds) (2008), *The Oxford Handbook of Political Economy*, Oxford, UK: Oxford University Press.

Weiss, L. (1998), *The Myth of the Powerless State: Governing the Economy in a Global Era*, Cambridge, UK: Polity Press.

Whitehead, C.K. (2005), 'What's your sign? International norms, signals, and compliance', *Michigan Journal of International Law*, **27**, 695–741.

Whittaker, D.H. and S. Deakin (eds) (2009), *Corporate Governance and Managerial Reform in Japan*, Oxford, UK: Oxford University Press.

Williamson, O.E. (1985), *The Economic Institutions of Capitalism: Firms, Markets, Relational Contracting*, New York: Free Press.

Williamson, O.E. (1998), 'Transaction cost economics and organization theory', in G. Dosi, D. Teece, and J. Chytry (eds), *Technology,*

Organization, and Competitiveness, Oxford, UK: Oxford University Press, pp. 17–66.

Wilson, J.Q. (ed.) (1980), 'The politics of regulation', in *The Politics of Regulation*, New York: Basic Books.

Wilson, J.Q. (1989), *Bureaucracy: What Government Agencies Do and Why They Do It*, New York: Basic Books.

Yamaguchi, J. (2008), 'Kakusa Shakai no Genjo to Min'i [The status of the unequal society and public opinion], *Globalization and Governance Project Working Paper Series J-02*, Hokkaido University.

Yamaguchi, J. and K. Nakakita (eds) (2014), *Minshuto Seiken to wa Nanidatta no ka: Kipason-tachi no Shogen* [The Democratic Party of Japan in Government: Testimonies of Key Persons], Tokyo: Iwanami Shoten.

Yamazawa, I. (1984), *Nihon no Keizai Hatten to Kokusai Bungyo* [Japanese Economic Development and the International Division of Labor], Tokyo: Toyo Keizai Shinposha.

Yanagisawa, A. (2002), 'Shinryaku no Shakaikeizai Kiban' [Socioeconomic foundations of aggression], in K. Ishii, H. Akira, and T. Haruhito (eds), *Nihon Keizaishi 3: Ryo-taisen Senkanki* [Japanese Economic History Vol. 3: Interwar Period], Tokyo: Tokyo Daigaku Shuppankai, pp. 367–78.

Yoshimatsu, H. (1998), 'Japan's Keidanren and political influence on market liberalization', *Asian Survey*, **38**(3), 328–45.

Yoshimatsu, H. (2005), 'Japan's Keidanren and free trade agreements: societal interests and trade policy', *Asian Survey*, **45**(2), 258–78.

Index